D1564925

An Integrated Theory of Autosegmental Processes

SUNY Series in Linguistics
Mark R. Aronoff, Editor

AN INTEGRATED THEORY OF AUTOSEGMENTAL PROCESSES

Rochelle Lieber

State University of New York Press

Published by
State University of New York Press, Albany

For information, address State University of New York
Press, State University Plaza, Albany, N.Y., 12246

Library of Congress Cataloging-in-Publication Data

Lieber, Rochelle, 1954-
     An integrated theory of autosegmental processes.

     (SUNY series in linguistics)
     Bibliography: p.
     Includes index.
     1. Autosegmental theory (Linguistics) I. Title.
II. Series.
P217.7.L54   1987   414   86-30049
ISBN 0-88706-509-0
ISBN 0-88706-510-4 (pbk.)

10   9   8   7   6   5   4   3   2   1

CONTENTS

ACKNOWLEDGEMENTS

I am grateful to the Graduate School and the School of Liberal Arts at the University of New Hampshire for summer fellowships in the summers of 1983 and 1986, which allowed me to begin and end my work on this book. I also wish to thank Andrew Carstairs, Mary Clark, Larry Hyman, and Alec Marantz for generously providing comments on an earlier draft, and the reference and interlibrary loan staff at Dimond Library, University of New Hampshire—in particular, Debbie Watson—for tracking down many articles and books. Finally, for help and encouragement of all sorts, I wish to thank my colleagues in the English Department of the University of New Hampshire, especially Mary Clark and Carl Dawson, and on the home front, Cliff Wirth.

INTRODUCTION

The autosegmental theory of phonology was originally developed to account for the phenomenon of tone. In work as early as Firth (1957), Arnott (1964), and Edmondson and Bendor-Samuel (1966), it had been noted that in tone languages tone often acted independently of segmental information; for example, there might be rules which affected the segmental string without affecting the tonal melody or vice versa. Still, it was not until the mid-1970s, that such pioneering theorists as Leben (1973) and Goldsmith (1976) sought to account for such observations within the generativist school. On the basis of tone phenomena, they proposed the first autosegmental (or suprasegmental, for Leben) representations in which tones were afforded a status independent of segments, but were somehow synchronized with those segments.

While the autosegmental analysis of tonal systems has progressed steadily in the work of Goldsmith (1981, 1982), Leben (1978), Clements (1980b, 1984), Clements and Ford (1979), Halle and Vergnaud (1982, mss), Pulleyblank (1983), Clark (in preparation) and many others, it is only in the last seven years or so that a true explosion has taken place in autosegmental theory. Both Leben and Goldsmith noted early on that systems of nasal harmony seemed to have properties which were amenable to autosegmental treatment; a harmonizing feature like [nasal] could have a representation independent of, but synchronized with, ordinary segments. Multitiered representations have been extended beyond tone phenomena to other basically phonological processes as well—not

1

only to vowel and consonant harmony (see also Clements 1980a, Halle and Vergnaud 1981, Clements and Sezer 1982, van der Hulst and Smith 1985), but also to gemination and compensatory lengthening (Clements 1982, Steriade 1982) and to assimilation processes (Halle and Vergnaud 1981, Clements 1985). Starting with McCarthy's important work on Semitic, the autosegmental framework has also been extended to morphology. Autosegmental theory has yielded insights into such phenomena as root and pattern word formation (McCarthy 1979, 1981, 1984, forthcoming; Archangeli 1984), ideophones (McCarthy forthcoming), reduplication (Marantz 1982, Levin 1982, Broselow 1983), and consonant mutation (Lieber 1983b, 1984a, McCarthy 1983; Cowper and Rice 1986).

All past autosegmental analyses, whether phonological or morphological, have shared a number of assumptions:

> —that phonological and morphological representations may consist of more than one level or **tier**—perhaps a tone tier and a segmental tier, or a **skeleton** tier giving the arrangement of segments into consonants and vowels and a **melody** tier providing all other phonetic content to each segment,
> —that autosegmental tiers may be associated or synchronized with one another by some set of well-formedness conventions or linking rules,
> —and that some autosegmental tiers can have the status of morphemes.

But while all autosegmental analyses share some form of these assumptions, they have differed greatly, both in their individual realizations of the assumptions and in the degree to which they work them out explicitly. Certain areas of the theory have proven especially controversial, among them the nature of the skeleton tier (Levin 1982, Yip 1983, Clements and Keyser 1983, Hyman 1985), the extent to which rules or conventions of association and spreading are universal (Williams 1976, Goldsmith 1976, Clements and Ford 1979, Halle and Vergnaud 1982, Pulleyblank 1983), and the fate of autosegments which remain unlinked at the end of the derivation (Pulleyblank 1983). It is not my purpose here to give an exhaustive review of these controversies, or indeed of the history of autosegmental theory over the last ten years,[1] although I will touch upon most of these controversial issues in the chapters that follow. Rather, I intend to raise a problem which has remained surprisingly **uncontroversial** over this period, even though it involves the basic nature of autosegmental representations, to propose a solution to this problem, and to show how this solution leads to a generally more consistent and coherent autosegmental theory.

Autosegmental theory is based upon the notion that distinctive feature bundles can be partitioned and distributed onto a number of different tiers; autosegmental representations are therefore configurations of distinctive feature bundles. What has rarely been made explicit in autosegmental theory, however, is exactly how the distinctive features may be partitioned onto different tiers.[2] In fact, I will show in chapter 1 that some versions of autosegmental theory allow the same distinctive feature to be projected simultaneously on more than one tier, whereas other versions assume that a single distinctive feature can appear on one and only one tier. (1a) illustrates the sort of representation that might be allowed in the former theory (although not necessarily required), and (1b) the only sort of representation that is sanctioned by the latter type of theory:

(1) a.

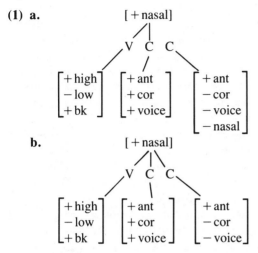

b.

Obviously we must make one choice or the other for our theory; either the duplication of features on different tiers is permitted or not. If autosegmental theory is to be a general theory of phonological and morphological representations, distinctive features must be distributed onto tiers in some principled fashion. Once the theory has been made consistent in this respect, however, it must then be shown that it works equally well for all sorts of processes that have been analyzed autosegmentally. This is the major goal of this book.

In chapter 1, I will therefore go back to the foundations of autosegmental theory, to the partitioning and reassembling of distinctive feature bundles, and show in some detail how the inconsistency in the distribution of distinctive features has arisen. In the course of this chapter I will show how this inconsistency can be resolved (my solution will be to allow duplication of features on more than one tier, but subject to severe restrictions), and how it can lead to a general theory of the precedence of duplicated features (that is, when the same feature is projected on more than one tier, which of the features will win out). In working out a theory of the precedence of duplicated features, I will also substantially revise the rules of association and spreading that are needed within autosegmental theory and will work out some explicit ground rules for their operation.

These general revisions to the theory will turn out to have wide empirical ramifications, as I will show in chapters 2, 3, and 4. Chapter 2 will be a detailed examination of consonant and vowel mutation, and chapter 3 of consonant and vowel harmony; chapter 4 will cover selected topics in tone systems. In these chapters I will try to show that the theoretical revisions proposed in chapter 1 reveal underlying similarities in seemingly disparate phenomena and also lead to substantial simplifications in particular analyses. It will turn out, for example, that infixes, neutral vowels, quirky (phonetically irregular) mutations, and depressor consonants in the southern Bantu languages can be analyzed as surface manifestations of the same sort of configuration of features. In chapter 2, I will argue that all mutations, regardless of how phonetically irregular they seem to be, can be analyzed as autosegmental, and in chapter 3 I will argue that all harmonies, even those which were previously treated as metrical, can be analyzed autosegmentally as well. In chapter 4, I will argue that the theory proposed here will also allow us to dispense with costly association and metathesis rules that have been proposed for tone systems. The result will be an overall simplification in the grammar. In addition, in chapters 2, 3, and 4 I will examine a number of interesting predictions made by the theory developed in chapter 1, and show that they prove to be correct.

The major purpose of this work will thus be to show that an integrated autosegmental theory—one that is both explicit and internally coherent—can result in simple and consistent analyses of many different phenomena, including tone, harmony, mutation, length, gemination, and root and pattern word formation. I also have a secondary purpose in focusing on the issue of duplication of features. The autosegmental frameworks that in the past have not permitted duplication of a single feature on different tiers have generally been concerned with problems of autosegmental phonology—that is, with tone and harmony systems where autosegmental tiers generally do not have the status of morphemes. In contrast, the frameworks that do allow duplication of the same feature on different tiers are usually concerned with problems of morphology—root and pattern word formation, reduplication or consonant mutation. If this were a necessary state of affairs, it would suggest that autosegmental phonology and autosegmental morphology might be entirely separate theories. If so, it would be odd, but it would also be an important result from the point of view of morphology.

Consider for a moment the recent history of the field of morphology. In the last decade there has been an enormous growth of interest in morphology, and although much of the literature on morphology (Chomsky 1970, Halle 1973, Aronoff 1976, Allen 1978, Lieber 1980, Selkirk 1982, Kiparsky 1982) has undertaken to prove that the phenomena of word formation are important in their own right, surprisingly few distinctly morphological rules or principles have been uncovered.

With regard to concatenative morphology (affixation and compounding) in languages like English, it appears more and more that virtually no independent morphological principles are needed. It is generally agreed that there is a lexicon in which morphemes are listed along with all of their phonological, semantic, and subcategorizational idiosyncrasies.[3] However, the principles which put together morphemes into words and which rule out overgeneration appear to be more general syntactic and semantic principles. For example, some form of the Projection Principle (Chomsky 1981) operating in the lexicon might ensure that the subcategorizations of morphemes are maintained at all levels of word derivation. Some form of Theta Theory or argument linking can be used to rule out impossible compounds (Lieber 1983a). And the existence of so-called bracketing paradoxes like the word *unhappier*[4] have given rise to several proposals that words have two levels of representation which are mediated by some sort of movement rule or mapping operation—either a form of May's (1977) Quantifier Rule (see Pesetsky 1985), or a mapping operation like that proposed for syntax by Marantz (1984) (see Sproat 1985). Other proposals for explaining sub-word-level phenomena by means of general principles of grammar can be found in Lieber (1984b) and Sproat (1985).

In short, on the basis of the familiar data of affixation and compounding, the search for a component of grammar containing purely morphological principles —an autonomous morphology—has come up relatively empty. This is why the claim that autosegmental phonology and morphology might be different theories would be an important result; it would provide some evidence for the existence of distinct morphological principles and perhaps for the existence of a distinct morphological component.

Another goal of this book, however, will be to show that this major formal and theoretical difference between autosegmental phonology and autosegmental morphology—that is, the difference in the treatment of duplicated features— is not a necessary one, and that autosegmental phonology and morphology are not distinct theories. In chapter 1, I will argue that in principle there can only be a single unified theory of autosegmental representations and a single autosegmental formalism. In chapters 2 and 3, I will show that such labels as *harmony* and *mutation* do not imply distinct sorts of rules, the former phonological and the latter morphological. Instead, both will turn out to be surface manifestations of a few simple and general autosegmental processes, including projection of features onto tiers, association, spreading, prespecification, and delinking.

In short, two threads will run through this work, one having to do with possible and impossible configurations of distinctive features in autosegmental theory, and the other having to do with the relationship between phonology and morphology. At times one thread will be more prominent than the other, but generally we will see that the two threads are closely intertwined.

NOTES: INTRODUCTION

1. For an excellent overview of autosegmental theory, see van der Hulst and Smith (1984).

2. Recent exceptions are Clements (1985) and Halle (1986), although neither considers the full range of data at issue here.

3. See, however, the works of Anderson (1982, 1984) and his students (Thomas-Flinders 1982) for another view.

4. The paradox is as follows. It is well known that the comparative morpheme *-er* attaches to most monosyllabic adjectives (*nice~nicer*), and to many disyllabic adjectives with weak second syllables (e.g., *grumpy~grumpier*, but *direct~*directer*). *-er* attaches to no trisyllabic adjectives (*eloquenter*). This fact suggests that the internal structure of *unhappier* is [un[[happy]er]], where *-er* attaches to the disyllabic *happy*. But this bracketing incorrectly represents the semantic structure of the word; *unhappier* means 'more unhappy' rather than 'not more happy', as the initial bracketing suggests. For semantic reasons, the following bracketing seems more appropriate: [[un[happy]]er]. In other words, one bracketing is preferable on phonological grounds, the other on semantic grounds.

Chapter *1*

AN INTEGRATED APPROACH TO AUTOSEGMENTAL THEORY

Autosegmental theory is primarily a theory of distinctive feature representations. Roughly speaking, each distinctive feature represents a distinct articulatory gesture: [nasal] the position of the velum; [anterior], [coronal], [high], [low], and [back] the position of the tongue; [voice] and tone features (all represented as configurations of [stiff vocal cords], [spread glottis], and [constricted glottis], according to Halle and Stevens [1971], the gestures of the laryngeal mechanism, and so on. Autosegmental theory tells us how these features (= gestures) can work independently of one another and how they can be synchronized with one another so as to form phonetically interpretable wholes. For example, a single gesture "velum down" (= [+ nasal]) can be spread over several segments, each involving a number of independent gestures. Those articulatory gestures that behave independently of other gestures in a language—like the [nasal] example above—are afforded their own tiers in autosegmental representations and are mapped onto or synchronized with other tiers composed of other features, as illustrated in (1):

(1)

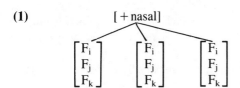

Autosegmental theory is thus, in some sense, a theory of phonological representations, that is, a theory of possible and impossible configurations of distinctive features (see also van der Hulst and Smith 1984).

If this view of autosegmental theory is correct, then autosegmental phonology and autosegmental morphology could not in principle be two entirely distinct theories. They could not, for example, sanction entirely different sets of representations or entirely different configurations of distinctive features, since the ultimate criterion of "pronounceability" would apply equally to all configurations of features. In other words, distinctive feature representations should be either possible or impossible, either pronounceable or unpronounceable according to autosegmental theory.

In fact, no theorist that I know of has explicitly advocated the view that autosegmental phonology and autosegmental morphology are entirely independent theories. Still, as I mentioned in the introduction, for all the assumptions which autosegmental phonology and morphology have in common, there is one crucial area in which they have come—perhaps more by accident than by design—to differ. I will first review what is held in common in all versions of autosegmental theory. Much of the remainder of this chapter, however, will be devoted to a point on which autosegmental phonology and morphology have, however subtly, diverged. I will show that by resolving this difference, by making autosegmental theory explicit in ways it has not been made explicit before, we can produce a theory which is not only internally consistent, but one which is also restrictive and which makes interesting predictions about interactions of possible morphological and phonological processes.

1.1 COMMON GROUND

There are three general areas in which autosegmental phonology and morphology appear to be in agreement: (i) the distinctive feature bundle may be partitioned into some number of tiers, (ii) tiers must be associated or synchronized in some way, and (iii) some tiers may be morphemes.

1.1.1 Tiers

At the very basis of all autosegmental theory, whether phonological or morphological, is the assumption that portions of the distinctive feature bundle can act independently of other portions. We may add or delete whole segments without at all affecting the autosegmental feature, or conversely, may add or delete an autosegment without affecting the rest of the phonological representation. Or the autosegmental feature may bear an independent meaning. Each feature or group of features which is independent in one or more of these ways is said to constitute a separate tier.

Some of the tiers that have been referred to repeatedly in the literature have received specific names. For example, the tier that gives the basic organization of segments into consonants and vowels has been called the "skeleton." That tier which contains the majority of features (including most place and manner of articulation features) is called the "melody"—sometimes the "phonemic melody" (see especially Steriade 1982, Clements 1985, Halle 1986). Melody and skeleton together have been referred to as the "phonological core" (Halle and Vergnaud mss). Other tiers are simply named for the feature or features of which they are constituted (for example, [nasal], [back], tone).

1.1.2 Synchronization

Partitioning the distinctive feature bundles into tiers gives us representations like the one roughly schematized in (2) (I am deliberately using the symbols F_i, F_j, etc., here rather than real features to abstract away from a number of issues which will be discussed below—for example, which tier attaches to which, how to state association rules which link a particular autosegmentalized feature only to certain segments, and so on):

(2) $\qquad [+F_i] \qquad [-F_i] \qquad [+F_i]$

$$\begin{bmatrix} +F_j \\ -F_k \end{bmatrix} \quad \begin{bmatrix} -F_j \\ +F_k \end{bmatrix} \quad \begin{bmatrix} +F_j \\ -F_k \end{bmatrix} \quad \begin{bmatrix} -F_j \\ +F_k \end{bmatrix}$$

$\qquad\quad [+F_l] \qquad\qquad\qquad [-F_l]$

If each of F_i–F_l constitutes an articulatory gesture, these gestures must somehow be put together, coordinated, or synchronized so that each segment can be pronounced. (We might assume that in order for a segment to be "pronounceable" it must contain a + or − value for each distinctive feature.) All autosegmental theories, whether phonological or morphological, agree in assuming that there is some set of rules or conventions which effect this synchronization of tiers, which map one tier onto another such that something like (3a) or (3b)[1] is produced from (2):

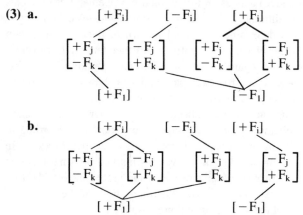

(3) a.

b.

As to the exact nature of these association rules or conventions, as they are called, many autosegmental analyses differ (see section 1.4 below). All are in agreement, however, about their general nature:

    (i) Association of tiers generally starts at one margin of a word or morpheme (left or right) and links features on one tier to features on another one to one, proceeding away from the margin. (The status of right to left spreading is somewhat controversial, however. See discussion below 1.4.)

    (ii) Most autosegmental analyses allow one to many mappings as illustrated in (3), that is, cases in which a segment on one tier is associated with several segments on another tier. Such cases are often referred to as "spreading" of association lines. (Particular analyses differ as to the amount and direction of spreading and the conditions under which it can occur.)

    (iii) All autosegmental theories espouse some form of the principle in (4): originally proposed by Goldsmith (1976).

    (4) Association lines may not cross.

This convention ensures that autosegmental tiers are properly synchronized. In a sense, it guarantees that the mapping between individual tiers is a temporal possibility. According to this convention, the feature $[+F_i]$ in (5) cannot precede the $[-F_i]$ feature and simultaneously be associated with the $[-F_j, +F_k]$ features that follow the ones with which $[-F_i]$ is associated:

    (5)
$$\begin{bmatrix} +F_j \\ -F_k \end{bmatrix} \qquad \begin{bmatrix} -F_j \\ +F_k \end{bmatrix}$$
$$[+F_i] \qquad\qquad [-F_i]$$

1.1.3 Morphological Tiers

Finally, most autosegmental analyses assume that individual tiers can constitute independent morphemes. The following are a number of examples that have appeared in recent literature. Welmers (1973), for example, notes a case in Igbo where a particular tonal pattern acts as an inflectional morpheme. Verb radicals and suffixes in Igbo are traditionally divided into two tone classes called "high" and "low." The tone class determines the tonal pattern of the verb in certain tenses—for example, in the Narrative Negative. In other tenses, however, a uniform tone pattern appears, regardless of the tone class of individual verbs. In the SVF I Main Clause form, for example, verbs are always low toned. In other words, the SVF I Main Clause form is a low tone.[2]

    The feature [nasal] when autosegmentalized on its own tier can also constitute an independent morpheme in some languages. For example, according to Poser (1980a-ms), [nasal] has morphological status in Coatzospan Mixtec: "In Coatzospan the second person singular of the verb is marked by a nasalization 'prosody.' The word-final vowel is nasalized, as are the preceding vowels if no voiceless obstruent intervenes." Thus, as (6) illustrates, both of the vowels of the second person singular of the verb 'to drink' are nasalized:

(6) kò?ŏ   'to drink'   →   kŏ?ŏ   'you-sg. will drink'

The feature [+nasal] is therefore an inflectional morpheme in Coatzospan Mixtec.

According to McCarthy (1983), the feature [+round] (labialization) and the features [+high, −back] (palatalization) constitute morphological tiers in the Semitic language Chaha. In this language, palatalization "marks the verb for agreement with a second person feminine singular subject." The features [+high, −back] attach to the last root consonant, as in (7):

(7) Imperative
2nd pers. masc. sg. = gʸækʸət
2nd pers. fem. sg. = gʸækʸətʸ

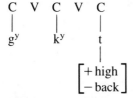

The feature [+round] also constitutes a morpheme in this language. According to McCarthy, "Among other categories, labialization marks (with the suffix +n) a third person masculine singular object." The labial feature attaches to the rightmost labializable consonant in the root (see chapter 2 for a fuller discussion):

(8) Perfective
3rd pers. masc. sg. without object: dænæg
with 3rd pers. masc. sg. object: dænægʷ

Other familiar examples of tiers which are also morphemes come from Mc-Carthy's work (1979, 1981) on the Semitic languages. In Classical Arabic, for example, roots are represented as melody tiers consisting of three (usually) consonantal melody segments—for example, **ktb** 'write'. Certain inflectional morphemes, such as the perfective active (**a**), are represented as vocalic melody segments. Skeletons—that is, arrays of Cs and Vs—are also morphemes. Each Binyan, or modification of the verbal meaning or diathesis, in the verbal system of Classical Arabic is represented as a skeleton; CVCCVC is the skeleton for Binyanim II and IV, both of which are associated with a causative meaning.

It thus seems likely that any feature or bundle of features that can be autosegmentalized can in some language constitute an independent morpheme. I will have more to say below about the distribution of particular features onto tiers. This discussion will lead to a more specific prediction as to the features which may count as morphemes and those which may not.

1.2 A DIVERGENCE IN THEORY: DUPLICATION OF FEATURES

As section 1.1 suggests, a large part of the general outline of autosegmental theory is held in common by all analyses done under the autosegmental rubric: there are tiers composed of features, some of which can be morphemes and each of which acts independently in some way; tiers are synchronized with one another by some set of rules or conventions, and so on. It is in the details of the theory, however, that differences among analyses have arisen. Here I wish to focus on one of these differences and to use its resolution as a departure point for a truly integrated theory of autosegmental representations.

Autosegmental theory, as I asserted above, is at base a theory of distinctive feature representations, that is, of possible and impossible configurations of distinctive features. Many phonological analyses done within autosegmental theory seem to have assumed that distinctive features can only be distributed among tiers in a highly restricted way; (9) is meant to be a pretheoretic or informal statement of this assumption:

(9) Principle of Exhaustive Partitioning
   The distinctive feature bundle of each segment is exhaustively partitioned among tiers such that each distinctive feature appears on exactly one tier.

In other words, many phonological analyses within autosegmental theory have assumed that a single distinctive feature may not be projected on more than one tier (see, for example, Clements 1980 a, b, 1984, 1985; Halle 1986). However, morphological analyses putatively done within the same framework often make the opposite assumption, namely, that a single distinctive feature can appear simultaneously on several tiers (see, for example, McCarthy 1979, 1981, 1986). I will first substantiate the claim that phonological and morphological analyses make contradictory assumptions about the duplication of features. I will then go on to show how this apparent difference can be resolved.

Take as a typical phonological analysis within autosegmental theory Clements's (1984) analysis of the Kikuyu tone system.[3] According to Clements, each morpheme in a Kikuyu verb has a characteristic lexical tone. However, a rule (repeated as [10] here) which Clements calls Tone Shift regularly operates to link the tone lexically associated with the first tone-bearing unit one syllable to the right. This phenomenon is illustrated in (11).

(10) Kikuyu Tone Shift (Clements 1984)   t = tone-bearing unit, T = tone

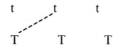

(11) Current Habitual   ma mo rɔr aɣ   a   'they look at him/her'

H   L   L   L
↓
ma mo rɔr aɣ   a

H   L   L   L

Such a rule works only on the assumption that tones are linearly ordered on a single tier regardless of the morpheme they belong to. In fact, almost all autosegmental treatments of tone that I am aware of take it for granted that there is a single tonal tier.[4]

A similar assumption is also inherent in all autosegmental treatments of harmony with which I am familiar. For example, Clements (1980a) has analyzed rounding harmony in Turkish autosegmentally. In Turkish, high noninitial vowels agree in rounding with preceding vowels. In a polymorphemic word, the initial vowel is specified for roundness, as are any succeeding nonhigh vowels. Spreading proceeds from left to right, as illustrated in (12), on the assumption that the feature [round] is projected on the same tier for each morpheme:

(12) Turkish Rounding Harmony   (Clements 1980a)

g i d + I y o r + I m → g i d + I y o r + I m

[−rd]   [+rd]   [−rd]   [+rd]

= gidiyorum

In other words, many autosegmental tone and harmony analyses have assumed that tone features or rounding features are not duplicated on more than one tier. This, of course, does not mean that they explicitly rule out the possibility that there might be some language, for example, exactly like Turkish except that the feature [round] needs to be projected on two tiers:

(13) Pseudo-Turkish

[+rd]   [+rd]

g i d + I y o r + I m → g i d + I y o r + I m

[−rd]   [−rd]

However, there is good reason to believe that representations like (13), Pseudo-Turkish, should be explicitly ruled out; if they were allowed, they would lead to a serious weakening of autosegmental theory.

As mentioned in section 1.1, all autosegmental analyses, regardless of other differences, assume that association lines may not cross. This convention would, of course, rule out a representation like (14):

(14) *C V C V C

[+ rd]   [− rd]

The prohibition on crossing association lines claims, in effect, that the two tiers in (14) are improperly synchronized. But if the feature [round] can be projected on more than one tier, the [round] features are no longer linearly ordered, and the prohibition on crossing association lines no longer governs their association to vowels. Given a representation like (15a), either (15b) or (15c) could result without any crossing of association lines.

(15) a.   [+ rd]   **b.**   [+ rd]   **c.**   [+ rd]

C V C V   C V C V   C V C V

[− rd]   [− rd]   [− rd]

In other words, allowing representations like (13) and (15) also allows us to circumvent freely the prohibition on crossing of association lines. Since this convention does a great deal of work in autosegmental theory, this suggests that the prohibition on duplication of distinctive features, or something like it, should be made an explicit principle of autosegmental theory.

There is also empirical evidence which supports the need for a principle like (9) in autosegmental theory. An autosegmental theory which prohibits or highly restricts the duplication of a given distinctive feature on more than one tier predicts that processes of consonant mutation should be local.[5] Consonant mutation is a morphological phenomenon in which lexical stems exhibit two or more allomorphs that differ only in their initial, or less frequently final, consonants and appear in distinct morphological environments, for example, one in the past tense, the other in the present, or one in one noun class and the other in a second noun class.[6] The West Atlantic language Fula, for example, has a noun classifier system in which nouns are divided among twenty-five possible classes such that each noun stem belongs to a singular class, a plural class, and up to five diminutive and augmentative classes for a possible maximum of seven classes. Class membership is signaled in a number of ways, one of which is a change in initial consonant, as illustrated by the paradigm in (16):[7]

(16) 'monkey'   (data and numbering system from Arnott 1970)

Class   11   waa-ndu
        25   baa-ɗi

3   baa-ŋgel
5   baa-ŋgum
6   mbaa-kon
7   mbaa-ŋga
8   mbaa-ko

For example, the class 3 form of all nouns begins with a stop, the class 11 form with a corresponding continuant, and the class 6, 7, or 8 form with the corresponding prenasalized stop (see chapter 2 for a full analysis of Fula).

Consonant mutation can be analyzed autosegmentally as follows.[8] Since the changes in the form of the initial consonant concern the features [continuant] and [nasal], these will be projected on an independent tier in Fula. The initial consonant of the stem of the noun 'monkey' will be underspecified for these features (in general) and will be represented as in (17):

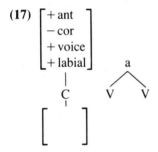

(17)

(The empty bracket below the C is merely meant to suggest the presence of a separate tier for [continuant] and [nasal], the mutation features. These brackets, in other words, are purely heuristic.) Each noun class will have a characteristic morpheme that will prefix to the stem form; this morpheme will not be a complete segment, but rather will consist of the features [continuant] and [nasal]. The class 3 and class 24 morpheme will, for example, be [− cont, − nas]:

(18)

$$
\left[\begin{array}{l} +\,\text{ant} \\ -\,\text{cor} \\ +\,\text{voice} \\ +\,\text{labial} \end{array}\right] \quad a
$$

C   V   V

$$
\left[\begin{array}{l} -\,\text{cont} \\ -\,\text{nas} \end{array}\right] \left[\quad\quad\right]
$$

Let us say that mutation is actually a process of linking the prefix, which consists only of a floating autosegment, to the underspecified stem (actually, we will see in chapter 2 that there is sometimes more to mutation than this):

(19)

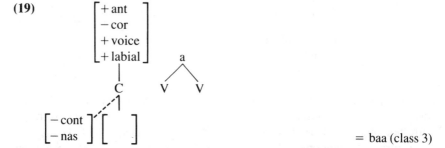

= baa (class 3)

Within an autosegmental theory that prohibits duplication of features on more than one tier, a rule like consonant mutation must be local. The [continuant, nasal] floating autosegment of the class prefix cannot associate to a noninitial consonant in the stem without resulting in a crossing of association lines:

(20) yardu   'calabash'   (class 24 form = jardu)

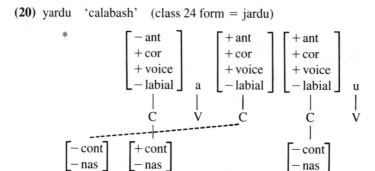

The class prefix can attach only to an immediately adjacent consonant which is underspecified. Consonant mutation is therefore predicted to be strictly local.

But any framework which allows free duplication of distinctive features on different tiers will predict that languages ought to exhibit nonlocal mutations. If, for example, [continuant] and [nasal] could be projected on two tiers for two different morphemes, we would predict the existence of a language like Pseudo-Fula, where, given the underlying representation in (21a), either (21b) or (21c) could be well formed in the same language:

(21) rim-   'free man'

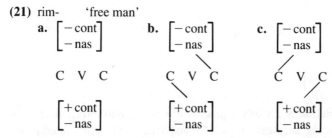

(I have suppressed the melody tier in [21] since two-dimensional representation prevents us from drawing these three-dimensional structures with ease.) In this case, the prefix could associate with either an initial or a noninitial consonant with impunity. But to my knowledge, no language precisely like Pseudo-Fula exists (see, however, note 5 and section 2.2 below). I have argued elsewhere (Lieber 1983b) that processes of umlaut and mutation do in fact appear to be local. Mutations occur only at the beginnings and ends of morphemes, and if triggered by an adjacent element, initial mutations are always triggered by something immediately to their left and final mutations by some element immediately to their right. If this is true, then a framework lacking some sort of prohibition on the duplication of distinctive features appears to make false predictions.

An autosegmental theory which includes the Principle of Exhaustive Partitioning or something like it appears to be desirable on both theory-internal and empirical grounds. And clearly it is a restrictive theory, since it rules out a whole range of configurations like (13), (15), and (21) which appear not to be necessary. Still, as I indicated at the beginning of this section, at least one important development in recent years in the realm of autosegmental morphology suggests that a theory prohibiting **all** duplication of features is too restrictive.

Our major problem arises first in accounting for the root and pattern morphology of the Semitic languages. McCarthy (1979, 1981) has shown quite convincingly for Semitic that consonantal roots and vocalic inflections constitute different morphemes and that they must be projected on different tiers and interpolated with a skeleton which is itself a morpheme:

(22)

The root **ktb** which appears in (22) also occurs in a whole array of other verbal forms and nominalizations. Different Binyanim are represented in McCarthy's analysis as different skeletons which modify the verbal meaning or diathesis. McCarthy shows that adopting this sort of representation not only allows a simple characterization of the majority of roots—the triliteral ones—but also explains the behavior of biliteral and quadriliteral roots as well. It is thus an extremely well-motivated analysis.

Yet all distinctive feature theories to date assume that consonants and vowels consist largely of the same distinctive features. If we were to expand the representation in (22) by replacing the phonetic symbols with the distinctive feature bundles for which they stand, it would be easy to see the duplication of features on the two melody tiers:[9]

(22′)

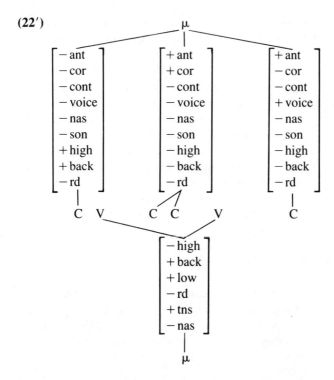

It seems, then, that for the Semitic languages at least, some distinctive features must be projected on more than one tier, contrary to the Principle of Exhaustive Partitioning. In other words, given a strict prohibition on the duplication of distinctive features, we would have to abandon an elegant and explanatory analysis of Semitic morphology.

McCarthy's analysis of Arabic also reveals an even stronger sort of case in which duplication of features appears to be required. In addition to consonantal roots, vocalic inflections and skeleton morphemes which represent each Binyan, the Arabic verbal system also involves several processes of infixation. For example, in the XIIth Binyan, which according to McCarthy has the skeleton CCVCCVC, a special association rule attaches the infix **w** to the third C slot:

(23) C   C   V   C   C   V   C
$$\qquad\qquad\qquad\quad |$$
$$\qquad\qquad\qquad\quad \text{w}$$
$$\qquad\qquad\qquad\quad |$$
$$\qquad\qquad\qquad\quad \mu$$

This infix melody cannot appear on the same tier as the root melody; if it did, the proper attachment of the root segments would be blocked by the prohibition on crossing of association lines:

(24)

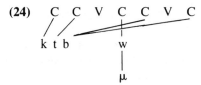

Instead, the infix melody must represent an entirely different tier. Association of the root tier will then proceed smoothly (McCarthy [1981, p. 395] assumes a special Erasure rule which delinks the last root consonant from the fourth C slot and allows the second root consonant to reassociate):

(25)

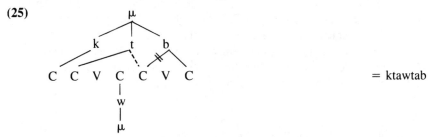

= ktawtab

Of course, this analysis necessitates the duplication of **all** consonantal features on two tiers;[10] that is, once we again replace phonetic symbols with feature bundles, as in (25′), it becomes obvious that Arabic requires the sort of feature duplication that the Principle of Exhaustive Partitioning would rule out:

(25′)

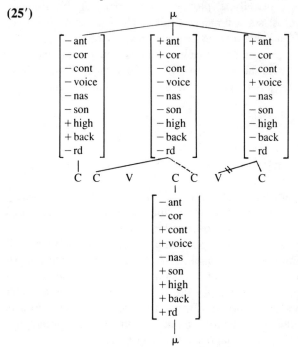

Distilled to its essence, our problem is this: we must find a way to allow the duplication of features we seem to need for Arabic without simultaneously permitting unconstrained duplication of features on different tiers—the sort of duplication, in other words, like that in (13), (15), and (21), which would undermine the prohibition on the crossing of association lines.

The key to solving our dilemma comes in noticing that whereas autosegmental phonology and the autosegmental analysis of Arabic morphology seem to differ in the number of tiers on which they allow a given distinctive feature to be projected, they do not differ in the number of specifications each segment gets for an individual feature; each segment receives only a single specification for each feature. In other words, although the feature [voice] may appear both on the consonantal root tier and on the tier of the vocalic inflection in (22), no segment ever gets more than one value for this feature. Represented formally, it appears that configurations like that schematized in (26) are prohibited in both autosegmental phonology and autosegmental morphology:[11]

(26) $*[\alpha\ F_i]$
$$|$$
$[\beta\ F_j]$
$$|$$
$[\gamma\ F_i]$

(26) is meant to be taken literally; it prohibits two (or more) **simultaneous** values for a given feature. As such, it makes intuitive phonetic sense: if a given feature $[F_i]$ represents an articulatory gesture, say position of the velum (that is, $[F_i]$ = [nasal]), then a given segment cannot simultaneously be pronounced with the velum open and with the velum closed; (26) in effect rules out physical impossibilities. It does not, however, rule out a representation like that in (27):

(27) $[\alpha\ F_i]$ $[\beta\ F_i]$

$[\gamma F_j]$

In (27) the values of $[F_i]$ are not simultaneous but successive. If $[F_i]$ = [nasal], then (27) represents a segment in which the velum is first opened then closed or vice versa—in other words, a pre- or postnasalized segment.

I would like to argue here that autosegmental phonology and autosegmental morphology need not differ from one another in the assumptions they make about duplication of features. Instead, let us assume that features may be freely duplicated on different tiers (that is, that the Principle of Exhaustive Partitioning is **not** a part of autosegmental theory at all), and that something like (26) acts as a filter on autosegmental representations in both phonology and morphology. Henceforth I will refer to (26) as the *Duplicate Features Filter* (the DFF).

It is, of course, not immediately obvious how the Duplicate Features Filter can serve to replace the Principle of Exhaustive Partitioning. Remember that the latter constraint automatically ruled out representations like (13), (15), and (21), which allowed us to circumvent the prohibition on crossing of association lines, and which are not in fact necessary for representing natural languages. I must therefore show that (26) not only permits the duplication of features that we need for Semitic and for infixing, but also rules out the duplication of features that will result in (13), (15), and (21); in other words, I must show that the DFF has all of the positive effects of the Principle of Exhaustive Partitioning, but none of its negative effects.

In order to show that the DFF is sufficiently restrictive, however, I must first make explicit some preliminary assumptions about what it means to say that features may be freely duplicated on different tiers and about the ways in which segments on one tier become linked to segments on other tiers. Section 1.3 will be devoted to the former issue, and section 1.4 to the latter. We will return to the DFF in section 1.5.

1.3 PROJECTIONS

It has remained implicit in much of previous autosegmental theory that the phonology of each language must contain some statement of the tiers to be projected and of the distribution of distinctive features among tiers. But such statements are rarely given explicitly. Nor are the principles governing such statements made explicit in many works on autosegmental theory. In this section I will try to address a number of issues surrounding the projection of features onto tiers. In section 1.3.1, I will consider whether any tiers are universal and will propose an unmarked distribution of features onto tiers. Section 1.3.2 will make explicit the ways in which features may be duplicated on different tiers in the present theory, and section 1.3.3 will consider ways in which tiers may be underspecified.

1.3.1 Universal Tiers

Although it is relatively difficult to find evidence bearing on the issue of universal tiers, it does seem possible to argue that every language projects at least melody and skeleton, the two tiers that make up the phonological core. One bit of suggestive evidence for this argument comes from languages like English and French, whose phonologies lack any of the obvious processes that would lead linguists (and native speakers) to postulate independent tiers—that is, harmony, tone, mutation, reduplication, and infixation. Significantly, speakers of English and French still invent play languages that use separate melody and skeleton tiers.

(28a), for example, illustrates a French-based language game called "Ge-De":[12]

(28) a. Le livre est illustré. -→

[ləgədə ligidivrəgədə egede igidilögödöstregede]

In Ge-De, the syllables gVdV are inserted between the nucleus and the coda of every syllable. The original vowel of the syllable then spreads. That the extra syllables go between the nucleus and the coda can be seen in a word like *format*, whose first syllable is closed; the Ge-De equivalent for *format* is [fogodormagada]. This sort of game can easily be represented if we assume that French has separate melody and skeleton tiers as illustrated in (28b).

(28) b.

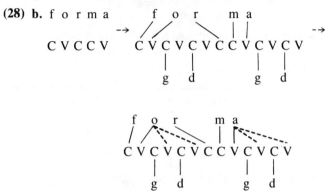

In other words, the existence of a play language like Ge-De implies that speakers of French can make use of the two-tiered phonological core. But if French lacks any of the regular autosegmental processes, these speakers receive no direct evidence for the two-tiered structure in the course of language acquisition. If they are nevertheless using such a structure in a language game, the only alternative is to say that it is innate, hence universal.[13]

Let us say, then, that each language L projects at least melody and skeleton tiers (T_m and T_s, respectively) and may in addition project other tiers. Let us say also that if L has only the two core tiers, distinctive features will be distributed as in (29); nothing crucial hinges on the precise inventory of features here:

(29) T_m = $\begin{bmatrix} \text{anterior} \\ \text{coronal} \\ \text{voice} \\ \text{nasal} \\ \text{continuant} \\ \text{distributed} \\ \text{high} \\ \text{back} \\ \text{low} \\ \text{tense} \\ \text{round} \\ \text{ATR} \end{bmatrix}$ T_s = $\begin{bmatrix} \text{syllabic} \\ \text{consonantal} \end{bmatrix}$

In short, the melody will contain place and manner features, the skeleton the major class features.

The former proposal is relatively uncontroversial; it is what autosegmental theories seem to have assumed all along. An interesting but still open question is whether the melody tier has any internal organization of its own. Steriade (1982) has proposed, for example, that this tier be divided into two subtiers corresponding to traditional notions of 'place of articulation' and 'manner of articulation'. Some support for this notion comes from a variable fast speech rule applied by speakers of Venezuelan Spanish (Gonzalez 1982). Gonzalez reports that in certain speech styles a rhyme-final consonant followed by another consonant loses its place of articulation features, whatever they are, and becomes velar, so that underlying **apto** is pronounced in this speech style as **akto**. Gonzalez's derivation is illustrated in (30):

(30)

This sort of rule would be especially easy to state if a phonological rule could refer specifically to the place of articulation subtier (T_p); that is, the rule could delete T_p in a rhyme-final consonant preceding another consonant.[14]

The proposal to identify the skeleton tier with the major class features is, of course, a much more controversial choice (see Levin 1982-ms, Yip 1983-ms). I will return to this proposal in section 1.4.3, where I will examine the role of the skeleton in association. Some support for this proposal will emerge in that discussion.

Some languages will, of course, project one or more tiers in addition to T_m and T_s. Let us say that for every tier which a language L projects in addition to T_m and T_s, there will need to be an explicit PROJECTION STATEMENT in the grammar of L indicating what feature or features are autosegmentalized. Fula, for example, might have the extra Projection Statement in (31), where T_{mut} is a tier of features relevant to the consonant mutation process:

(31) Fula T_{mut} = $\begin{bmatrix} \text{continuant} \\ \text{nasal} \end{bmatrix}$

Let us assume, as well, that once a feature is mentioned in a Projection Statement in L, it is normally removed from the melody or skeleton of L (we will see below that there are some features which cannot be removed from T_m or T_s by a Projection Statement).

1.3.2 Duplication of Features

I argued above that we must allow free duplication of features on different tiers and that the DFF would provide sufficient restriction to rule out unwanted representations. In effect, free duplication of features can result in at least two distinct sorts of configurations. First, and most obvious, a language could conceivably have two (or more) Projection Statements which mention the same feature or features. This occurrence would result in representations like those in (32):[15]

(32) a. [+round]   b. H L H   c. $\begin{bmatrix} +\text{cont} \\ -\text{nas} \end{bmatrix}$

     C V C   C V C

                                     C V C

   [−round]   L H

                                        $\begin{bmatrix} -\text{cont} \\ -\text{nas} \end{bmatrix}$

These, in fact, are exactly the sorts of cases that we looked at in (13), (15), and (21).

This is also a sort of duplication of features that we need for Arabic. In Arabic, in fact, there would have to be at least two Projection Statements for melody tiers, one for roots and another for vocalic morphemes. As mentioned in note 9, not all melody features would necessarily have to be duplicated, since some features necessary for distinguishing consonants could be filled in on the vowel melody tier by late redundancy rules. Still, some features necessary for distinguishing both consonants and vowels ([high], [back], [round]) would need to be duplicated. In section 1.6.4.1 I will go into the case of Arabic infixes in some detail and discuss whether this sort of duplication (or the one to be discussed immediately below) is needed for infixes too.

There is also another perhaps less obvious way of letting features be duplicated on more than one tier. A language might, for example, allow selective violations of a particular Projection Statement such that a feature F_i which is normally projected on a tier T_i in that language might appear on a different tier T_j in special circumstances, say, on a particular segment in a particular lexical item. Suppose, for example, that L is a hypothetical language which projects the feature [high] on a distinct tier. Most lexical entries in L would be like the one in (33a):[16]

(33) **a.** p $\begin{bmatrix} -bk \\ -rd \\ +tns \end{bmatrix}$ t $\begin{bmatrix} +bk \\ +rd \\ +tns \end{bmatrix}$ **b.** p $\begin{bmatrix} -bk \\ -rd \\ +tns \end{bmatrix}$ t $\begin{bmatrix} +bk \\ +rd \\ +tns \end{bmatrix}$ k $\begin{bmatrix} +bk \\ -rd \\ +tns \\ -high \end{bmatrix}$

    C   V   C   V   C   V   C   V   C   V

       [+high]   [+high]

If distribution of features is allowed to be truly free, however, something like (33b) might be permitted to occur. In (33b) the feature [high] is still projected on its own tier, but it also appears idiosyncratically on the last segment of the melody. Let us call this sort of idiosyncratic duplication of features PRESPECIFI-CATION.

There is one important thing to note about prespecification, namely, that this sort of duplication of features explicitly violates a Projection Statement in the language in question. Thus, this sort of duplication of features must come at some cost within the grammar of that language, and if we allow it to occur, we must count it as a marked phenomenon.

It is of course possible to rule out prespecification entirely while still allowing the other sort of feature duplication, multiple projection of a single feature. We might, for example, choose to interpret each Projection Statement as a strict statement to the effect that F_i in L must always be projected on T_i, rather than as a weaker statement that F_i can be and normally is projected on T_i in L. Here I propose that we should interpret Projection Statements in the weaker way, in other words, that we should allow prespecification **as a marked option**.[17] As this work progresses, I will try to show that doing so has rather interesting theoretical consequences.

1.3.3 Underspecification

We have seen in the previous section that the same feature may be duplicated on more than one tier leading to what might look like overspecified representations. I will also adopt here an assumption of many previous autosegmental theories, namely, that representations may be **underspecified** as well as overspecified.[18] Underspecification deserves a much more detailed discussion than I will be able to provide here. However, I will clarify below what I mean by underspecification, and show that it is not subject to the classic criticism of underspecification in linear phonological theory, that is, that it leads to ternary-valued distinctive features (Lightner 1963, Stanley 1967). I will rely heavily on arguments of Clements (1980a) below.

In linear segmental theories of phonology, it was quite clear what was meant by underspecification. Since each segment consisted of a single indivisible bundle of features, an underspecified segment was one which in underlying representation lacked values for one or more features. In the autosegmental theory, there are a number of ways in which the term *underspecification* can be and has been used.

For example, in autosegmental representations prior to association, we have a number of segments on a number of tiers. All are in some sense underspecified since they are not at this point independently pronounceable (that is, each "segment" is only a partial feature bundle). Of course, assuming that segments on independent tiers are linked together through the operation of association rules, they **can** end up fully specified at the end of an autosegmental derivation. Clements (1980a) argues that this sort of underspecification is not subject to the usual objections to underspecification; I refer the reader to that work for the relevant argument.

I will be using the term *underspecification* in two other ways, however. First, if, in a language whose melody tier normally projects all place and manner features, some segments in underlying form lack a specification for, say, [voice] or [nasal], we might say that they are "underspecified segments." Unlike the sort of underspecification mentioned above, which is a sort of **absolute** underspecification (**all** underlying segments are underspecified in that sense), this is a kind of **relative** underspecification; such segments are incomplete relative to what is normally projected on the tier in question in that language.

We may also refer to a representation as underspecified under the following circumstances. If, through delinking, incomplete spreading, or some other autosegmental process, a segment has been left without a value for some feature or features, that segment will also be underspecified relative to other segments. In other words, at the derivational stage in question—postlinking—the underspecified segment has fewer features than normal segments.

Within linear phonological theory, underspecification was criticized on the following grounds. (I borrow both the form of the argument and the examples from Clements [1980a,49]. See Pulleyblank [1983] and [1984] for similar arguments.) Given a set of rules like those in (34a) and the underlying matrices in (34b), the initially underspecified segment will turn out differently than its fully specified counterparts:

(**34**) **a.** i. $\quad$ $+a$ $\rightarrow$ $+c$
$\quad\quad\quad$ ii. $\quad$ $-a$ $\rightarrow$ $+d$
$\quad\quad\quad$ iii. $\quad$ $+b$ $\rightarrow$ $-a$

b.	(f)	(g)	(h)
Feature a	+	$\emptyset$	−
Feature b	+	+	+
Feature c	−	−	−
Feature d	−	−	−

Although (g) starts out as nondistinct from (f) and (h), after the operation of the rules in (34a) it ends up distinct from both:

(**34**) **c.**	(f)	(g)	(h)
Feature a	−	−	−
Feature b	+	+	+
Feature c	+	−	−
Feature d	−	−	+

Clements (1980a) shows, however, that this sort of derivation is based on a rather questionable assumption, namely, that feature-changing phonological rules can precede the morpheme structure rules (MSRs) that were meant to fill in missing features within the linear theory. Clements argues persuasively that if filling in must precede feature changing, underspecification cannot lead to ternary-valued features; originally underspecified segments will no longer be underspecified when rules like those in (34a) apply.

Although Clements (1980a) does not talk about the sorts of relative autosegmental underspecification that I have set out above, the same argument can apply to them as well. This is because the original use of the term *underspecification* in linear theory was a relative use. Segments had fewer features than were expected. For relative autosegmental underspecification, we need only assume that all missing features must be filled in (by linking and/or default— see section 1.7) before any feature-changing rule applies. If so, then underspecified segments could never be treated differently than fully specified features (where "fully specified" means "having the normal array of features for a segment at that stage of a derivation"). To summarize, regardless of how we define underspecification in autosegmental theory, there is no reason to believe that it results in ternary-valued features. I will therefore continue to assume underspecification in the various ways it has been used in autosegmental theory.

1.4 ASSOCIATION RULES

Once we have determined the distribution of features onto tiers in a given language, we must provide a way to link these tiers together. It seems safe to say that of all the issues raised by the theory of multitiered representations within the last ten years, the proper statement of association has generated the most controversy. Yet in a way it is an issue which has escaped serious comparative examination. By this I mean that there has been little attempt to make association principles within tonal systems consistent with association principles within harmony systems or nonconcatenative morphology, or to see if there are ways in which they differ systematically. Little attempt has been made to isolate the parameters by which association rules for different tiers can differ from one another in a single language and from one language to the next.

I will start with a discussion of association in the lexicon (section 1.4.1) and proceed to the regular associations between tiers: first the association of the phonological core to autosegmental tiers in section 1.4.2, and then the association of melody to skeleton in section 1.4.3. I will then discuss the rules or conventions by which autosegmental associations will spread (section 1.4.4). Section 1.4.5 will illustrate the operation of these rules, specifically their intrinsically unordered nature. Finally, in section 1.5 I will return to the question of duplicate features and will show how the DFF, working together with our association rules, resolves the dilemma set out in section 1.2.

Before I begin, I will first eliminate from discussion an issue I will not be concerned with here. One of the major points of controversy in autosegmental theory has been whether association is effected by conventions—that is, by mechanisms that operate at any point in the derivation so as to produce well-formed representations—or by rules operating at a specified point in the derivation. Since the development of the issue is covered thoroughly in Halle and Vergnaud (1982), I will not review it here. I will, however, note that Halle and Vergnaud, Clements and Ford (1979), and Pulleyblank (1983) have argued convincingly that association rules are needed even if well-formedness conventions are assumed and that in a number of cases—for example, the analysis of Tonga in Halle and Vergnaud (1982)—autosegmental analyses are simplified by assuming rules rather than conventions. Therefore, in the autosegmental framework I am developing here, association will be accomplished by rule.

1.4.1 Lexical Association

It is clear, first of all, that while an independent tier can constitute a morpheme in some languages, in many languages (perhaps in most) morphemes consist of two or more tiers. In English, for example, morphemes consist of both melody and skeleton. In Igbo, nouns have lexical tone; each noun has its own distinctive tone melody (Clark in preparation):

(35)   ákwúkwọ́   'paper'   ákàbọ́   'hedgehog'
       àghìghá   'needle'   úv̄únè   'kind of fruit'
       òkúkọ̀   'hen'   ŋgàjì   'spoon'
       ŋkúkú   'gourd cup'   úbọ̀cì   'day'

The lexical entries for such nouns will consist of three tiers: melody, skeleton, and tonal tier. In languages exhibiting vowel or consonant harmony, morphemes may also consist of three tiers. In Akan, for example, some verb roots (but not prefixes or suffixes) may consist of melody, skeleton, and [ATR] tiers, as illustrated in (36):

(36)
$$
\begin{bmatrix}
[+\text{ATR}] \\
\text{f} \quad \text{i} \quad \text{t} \quad \text{i} \\
\text{C} \quad \text{V} \quad \text{C} \quad \text{V}
\end{bmatrix}
$$
V root

The phonological representation in the lexical entry for the verb root **fiti** will be a three-tiered one. We might assume, then, in the simplest case possible that any single tier or any combination of two or more tiers could in some language constitute a morpheme.

If the phonological representations in some morphemes are multitiered, we must consider how these tiers are related to one another in lexical entries: are they fully linked as in (37a), entirely unlinked as in (37b), or partially linked in some other way?

(37) a.   [+ATR]   b.   [+ATR]

     f   i   t   i   f   i   t   i

     C   V   C   V   C   V   C   V

Clements (1980a) discusses this issue in detail; here I will briefly summarize his argument, and accept his conclusions in what follows.

Clements favors the sort of unlinked representation in (37b), primarily on the grounds of simplicity. The most economical approach to the issue of lexical association is to say that multiple-tiered lexical entries are actually linked together in the lexicon only if their association could not be predicted by a general rule. Most autosegmental theorists who accept the rule approach to association assume a rule or rules which link elements of T_i to elements of T_j one to one (and usually left to right, but see below). Rules of this form occur in Williams (1976), Haraguchi (1977), Halle and Vergnaud (1982), McCarthy (1979, 1981), Clements and Ford (1979), and elsewhere.[19] Given some such one-to-one linking rule and the hypothetical lexical representation in (38a) (where capital letters = skeleton slots, small letters = melody segments, and Ts = tones), (38b) would automatically result:

(38) a.   c   v   c   v   b.   c   v   c   v

       C   V   C   V   C   V   C   V

         T   T   T   T

In other words, linking the tiers in (38a) in the lexicon would be redundant, assuming that some sort of one-to-one mapping rule is needed anyway.

But if, for some reason, a particular tone or harmony feature is a special characteristic of a particular segment in the skeleton or melody string, this may be indicated in the lexical entry of the morpheme with a line linking these elements. Clements uses harmony in Akan as an example. The vowel **a** in Akan is called an "opaque" vowel. It is always [−ATR] itself regardless of where it occurs in a morpheme, and it induces the feature [−ATR] on vowels to its right (unlike other vowels, which take on the value of [ATR] of the root morpheme, whatever that value is). The root **bIsa** which contains the opaque vowel, can be represented autosegmentally as in (39):

(39) [+ATR]   [−ATR]
                         |

    b   I   s   a

    C   V   C   V

By including the association line between the **a** and the [−ATR] feature in the lexical entry, we are indicating that the feature is an idiosyncratic characteristic of the vowel **a** and not a general characteristic of the morpheme as a whole. Similarly, it can be argued (see chapter 4) that two classes of roots in Zulu differ idiosyncratically in that one has the first tone of the tone melody lexically bound to the first two vowels, whereas the other class has no lexical linking at all between the tone and skeleton tiers:

(40) Zulu

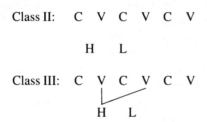

    Class II: C V C V C V

                      H   L

    Class III: C V C V C V

                      H   L

Again, actual association lines occur in the lexical entry only in case of some sort of lexical idiosyncrasy.

This view of lexical association has one major advantage. As Clements (1980a) has pointed out, it eliminates a great deal of indeterminacy in lexical representations. If all tiers in all lexical entries had to be linked, a case like the following would be problematic. In the lexical entry for the Igbo noun **ákwúkwó** 'paper', all of whose vowels bear H tone, we would have at least four choices for lexical representations:[20]

(41) a. akwukwo   **b.** akwukwo   **c.** akwukwo   **d.** akwukwo
    | | |
    H   H   H   H

Although the H tone seems to be a property of the whole word, we would have to commit ourselves to one sort of lexical linking or another between the tone tier and the melody. Assuming that association lines appear in the lexicon only in cases of lexical idiosyncrasy, the noun **akwụkwọ** in Igbo would have a unique representation, one in which the core and the tonal tier are completely unlinked, similar to the examples in (37b) and (38a). We would be spared the necessity of making an arbitrary choice among (41a–d).

1.4.2   Regular Association of Autosegmental Tiers

If association lines appear in the lexicon only in cases of idiosyncrasy, then the majority of associations between tiers must be effected by regular association rules. I will turn first to the sort of rules needed to link such autosegmental tiers as harmony tiers or tone tiers to the phonological core; a number of analyses within the autosegmental framework make their nature clear. The most important observation that emerges here is that there is no universal association rule linking autosegmental tiers to the core. Rather, associations of this sort can differ from language to language and from rule to rule in two ways: (i) each association rule must specify what units in the core the relevant autosegmental tier attaches to, and (ii) each association rule must specify the direction of mapping. In other words, given the association rule schema in (42), each language must fill in the features (and in some cases specific values of the features) and the direction of the rule for each autosegment in addition to the core:

(42)   Attach $[\alpha F_i]$ to $[\beta F_j]$ one to one, $\left\{ \begin{matrix} L \text{ to } R \\ R \text{ to } L \end{matrix} \right\}$

Languages with harmony processes provide excellent illustrations of the need to set F_i and F_j individually for each language. For example, both Classical Mongolian (Lightner 1967) and Turkish (Clements 1980a) have backness prosodies. In Turkish only vowels undergo backness harmony, whereas in Mongolian both vowels and velar consonants are affected. Therefore the rule creating the associations between the feature [back] and the core tiers must be different in the two languages. In the former case [back] attaches only to $[+syl]$ segments and in the latter to a disjunction of features: $[-ant, -cor]$ or $[+syl]$. Similarly, both Coatzospan Mixtec and Tereña have nasal harmony, according to Poser (1980a-ms), but since the harmony affects different classes of segments, the rules linking [nasal] to the core tiers must be different. In Coatzospan, nasal harmony affects vowels. It operates across sonorants and voiced obstruents but does not nasalize them. We might therefore say that in this language initial association between [nasal] tier and the core attaches [nasal] to $[+syl]$ segments and nowhere else. In contrast, nasalization in Tereña affects consonants in addition to vowels. Then nasalization harmony does not spread beyond an obstruent, but it does affect obstruents, causing them to become prenasalized. It both spreads beyond and affects all sonorants. The initial association rule must therefore allow the feature [nasal] to attach to any segment in the core.

Languages with additional tiers must apparently also be allowed to differ in the direction of association, that is, whether the additional tier is mapped onto the core from left to right or from right to left. Mende, for example, maps its tonal tier onto its tone-bearing tier from left to right. According to Leben (1978), most monomorphemic words in Mende exhibit one of the following tone patterns: H, L, HL, LH, LHL. When a bisyllabic word has the tone melody LHL, for example, its first syllable receives the first tone, and its second syllable the second:

(43) n   y   a   h   a
               | |
               L   H   L

Since Mende allows contour tones, the final tone is mapped onto the second syllable by a separate rule:

(44) n   y   a   h   a
               | ⌐⟍
               L   H   L

If the mapping had proceeded in the opposite direction, we would have produced the incorrect result nyaha with the extra tone remaining before the first
              L H L
syllable.

   According to Clark (forthcoming), the opposite sort of initial mapping is necessary for Japanese. Clark argues that Tokyo Japanese can be analyzed as a tone language, rather than as a pitch-accent language as has been done in the past (Haraguchi 1977). For "accented" verbs, a low tone is inserted at the point in the derivation after the present tense suffix has been attached, but before other inflectional suffixes are inserted (Clark assumes a model of Lexical Phonology in which rules of morphology operate at different levels, followed at each point by phonological rules). An initial association rule (her Free Tone Association) links the low tone to the rightmost mora of the verb stem, where the present tense suffix **-ru** counts as part of the stem:

(45) t   a   b   e   t   a   b   e – r   u
                    | |
                    L   L

Later in the derivation, a high tone is inserted at the beginning of the tone melody (in both this and other cases), and this tone also associates to the rightmost free vowel:

(46) t   a   b   e   t   a   b   e – r   u
                    | |
         H   L   H   L

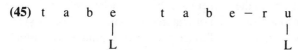

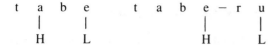

Finally, the high tone spreads leftward onto an unassociated mora. Note that a left-to-right rule of association would complicate the description of Tokyo Japanese; if we said that tone assignment universally proceeded from left to right, we would have to add an extra idiosyncratic rule to the grammar of Tokyo Japanese which would dock the low tone in accented verbs to the rightmost mora, and a second idiosyncratic rule which would then dock the H tone to the next rightmost mora. In other words, we would need two rules explicitly violating the normal association rule.

The nasalization harmony of Coatzospan Mixtec (Poser 1980a-ms) apparently provides another example in which an autosegmental tier is attached to the phonological core starting at the right margin of the word. As the data in (47) illustrate, in the second person singular, vowels are nasalized from the right margin of the verb to a voiceless obstruent, if one exists. As mentioned above, the nasalization process is not blocked by sonorants or voiced obstruents, but it also does not affect these segments:

(47) **a.** kò?ò
    'to drink'

kò̃?õ̀
'you-sg. will drink'

   b. kúðíí
    'to become angry'

kṹðí́ĩ́
'you-sg. will become angry'

   c. kótóndÉÉ
    'to examine'

kótṍndÉ̃É̃
'you-sg. will examine'

The process illustrated in (47) is easily explained by saying: (i) that the second person singular morpheme is the feature [+ nasal], (ii) that it associates to the rightmost segment, and (iii) that it spreads leftwards, stopping at a voiceless obstruent.

If we were to insist that initial association must start at the left margin of the word, however, Coatzospan Mixtec would require a rather peculiar sort of initial association rule, namely, one which attached the feature [+ nasal] to the right of the last voiceless obstruent in the word. Such a rule is a rather powerful device; not only does it require us to state a context for the initial association (that is, attach [+ nasal] to [+ syl] following [− voice, − son]), but it also requires the initial association rule to be able to **count** (that is, attach [+ nasal] to [+ syl] following the **last** [− voice, − son] segment in the word). Allowing a directional parameter to initial association would thus allow us to avoid this sort of complication.[21]

Thus it appears that rules associating autosegmental tiers to the phonological core differ according to two parameters: features relevant to linking and direction of linking.

1.4.3 Regular Association of Melody to Skeleton

That the rules associating autosegmental tiers to the core are not universal but rather conform to a schema like that in (42) is perhaps somewhat controversial. What is much more controversial, however, is the way of stating the association rule linking melody to skeleton; this latter rule has been the subject of dispute primarily because there has been little agreement on the exact composition of the melody and skeleton tiers. I will argue here that if both melody and skeleton are projections of distinctive features—specifically, if the skeleton consists of major class features and the melody of the remaining nonautosegmentalized features—the rule linking melody and skeleton will conform to the schema in (42) just like other association rules.

First, I will review briefly the controversy that has arisen over the nature of the skeleton tier. Originally, when McCarthy (1979, 1981) developed the idea of separating out a skeleton and a melody from the phonological core of distinctive features, he conceived of all tiers as being composed of distinctive features. The skeleton, although represented for convenience as an array of Cs and Vs, was actually a projection of the feature [syllabic]. Melodies contained the remaining features. However, given this picture of melody and skeleton, McCarthy saw no way of getting the association rules to attach consonantal melody segments to C slots and vocalic melody segments to V slots. To solve this problem, McCarthy was forced to duplicate the feature [syllabic] on the melody tier so that the association rules could simply match up [+ syllabic] skeleton slots with [+ syllabic] melody segments, and so on. This solution admitted an unattractive redundancy into the theory.

Others, like Halle and Vergnaud (mss), perceived this sort of duplication of the feature [syllabic] as an embarrassment and sought to eliminate it. Their solution was to represent the skeleton tier as an array of Cs and Vs which do not stand for distinctive feature values, but rather for an array of slots which were in some unspecified way "consonantal" and " vocalic." Melodies were a projection of all distinctive features, including [syllabic]. Given these assumptions, the rule associating melody and skeleton tiers could match up melody segments containing the feature [+ syllabic] with V slots and melody segments containing [− syllabic] with C slots.

Two distinct outgrowths of this sort of analysis have recently emerged; the first is represented by the work of Levin (1982-ms) and Yip (1983-ms), and the second by Clements and Keyser (1983).[22] I will consider each of these in turn.

In the analyses of Levin (1982-ms) and Yip (1983-ms), the skeleton consists of what Levin calls "empty time sequence" slots, represented as an array of Xs; these slots are not projections of a distinctive feature, but rather are the terminal elements of syllabic structure. Yip in fact argues that major class features like [syllabic] and [vocalic][23] can be abandoned in favor of hierarchical syllable structure, in part lexically specified and in part built upon the empty time sequence skeleton by universal and language-particular syllable structure rules. For example, according to Yip (1983-ms), the skeleton of the Arabic XIth Binyan, represented in terms of a C-V skeleton like (48a), would be represented as (48b) in the syllable structure skeleton framework:

(48) Arabic XIth Binyan

a. C   C   V   V   C   V   C   b. X   X   X   X   X   X   X

Xs dominated by R are skeleton positions that are lexically designated as the nuclear position in the syllabic rhyme. In this framework, melodies contain most of the distinctive features, including [consonantal]. The actual rules matching up melody and skeleton must apply in a specific order. A rule must first attach vowels (that is, melodies containing [-cons]) to slots dominated by R. Other rules, both universal and language particular, then build further syllable structure on top of the skeleton, and finally nonvocalic melodies (that is, consonants and glides) are linked to the skeleton. Since we will compare this analysis shortly to the one I will give below, I will briefly sketch the mechanics of the X skeleton framework. Yip (1983-ms) analyzes the IIIrd Binyan Arabic verb **kaatab** as follows. Its skeleton is illustrated in (49a):

(49) IIIrd Binyan   **a.**

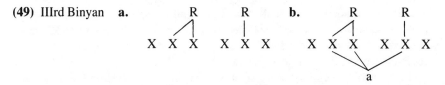

Vowel association applies first and attaches the vocalic melody **a** to all slots dominated by R, as is shown in (49b). Subsequently, Yip's rules of syllable structure construction, which are repeated in (50), build more structure on top of the skeleton:

(50) Yip   (1983-ms, 9)

   a. Onset Formation   R   O   R   (probably universal)
                              | | |
                          X   X   →   X   X

   b. Adjunction   (i)   R ⎤   R
                                | ⎥   →   ⎰⟍⟍
                            X   X ⎦   X   X

                         (ii) ⎡   O   O
                               ⎢ | →   ⟋⟍
                               ⎣X X   X   X

   c. Syllabify

Application of these rules to (49a) yields (51):

(51)

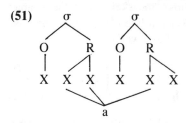

Consonants are then linked to the remaining slots, as indicated in (52):

(52)

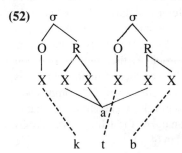

Note that the association of melody and skeleton must be broken into two separate steps; vowels must be associated first, since after the rules in (50) have
operated, the rhyme of the second syllable has become indistinguishable from
the first rhyme. Only then can consonants be linked.

Levin and Yip claim that the empty time sequence skeleton has a number
of advantages over a specified skeleton. First, it eliminates some redundancy
from the theory which results from having both a major class feature [syllabic]
and hierarchical syllable structure. The X-skeleton framework makes use of only
the latter theoretical mechanism. And because it allows for skeleton slots which
are initially unspecified for content, it obviates the need for so-called special
provisos which change Cs to Vs and vice versa as a consequence of rules like
Compensatory Lengthening.

Still, there are a number of problems with the current X-skeleton proposals.
First, and most important, these proposals in fact fail to provide sufficient means
for distinguishing all four major classes of segments, namely, consonants, syllabic consonants, glides, and vowels; in the effort to reduce redundancy, they
appear to be too parsimonious. For example, within Yip's framework, vowels
and glides can be distinguished in underlying representations: the former are X
slots dominated by R and attached to "vocalic" melody segments, and the latter
are "vocalic" melodies attached to Xs and not dominated by R. However, after
adjunction of rhymes occurs (I am assuming that some languages may have both
(50b-i) and its mirror image), a vowel-glide sequence like **uy** (u̯i) would be
phonetically indistinguishable from a glide-vowel sequence like **wi** (u̯i). Since

Harris (1983) has suggested that such a distinction exists in Spanish ([mui̯] versus [cu̯i-da]), the X-skeleton approach would not be adequate to represent it.

In addition, within these X-skeleton approaches, syllabic consonants require a separate association rule which would attach a "consonantal" melody to an X dominated by R. Still another disadvantage of the X-skeleton proposals is the one alluded to above: although they claim to simplify autosegmental theory by eliminating the special provisos changing Cs to Vs and Vs to Cs, they introduce new complexities into the theory in the form of the extrinsic ordering of association rules.

Clements and Keyser (1983) argue for a rather different view of the skeleton. Like Levin (1982-ms) and Yip (1983-ms), Clements and Keyser view the skeleton as a timing tier, but unlike them, they propose that this tier consists of differentiated elements C and V. C and V do not, however, correspond to values of the feature [syllabic] as they did in McCarthy (1979); rather, V is meant to stand for "syllable peak" and C for "syllable margin." Clements and Keyser's proposal, like Yip's, is embedded in a theory of the syllable. Specifically, Clements and Keyser propose nonhierarchically organized syllables; C and V are gathered directly into syllables according to a number of universal and language-particular principles, the precise nature of which need not concern us here.

Clements and Keyser's skeleton proposal is attractive in at least two respects. First, within this framework, association of melody and skeleton can be accomplished with great simplicity. V slots are attached to [− consonantal] segments, C slots to either [+ consonantal] or [− consonantal, + high] segments. Association rules linking vocalic melodies to V and consonantal melodies to C appear to require no extrinsic ordering. Second, Clements and Keyser appear to do without special provisos which change Cs to Vs in rules like Compensatory Lengthening. Since they claim that C does not stand for "consonant" in this framework, they can also claim that the representation in (53) that results from Compensatory Lengthening is simply interpreted as a vowel:

(53)

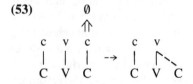

This sort of interpretation is also crucial to their analysis of Klamath, in which they propose that long vowels can have the two distinct representations illustrated in (54):

(54) **a.** u
      ∧
     V V

b. u
      ∧
     V C

The phonology of Klamath makes use of the distinction between (54a) and (54b) in their analysis, but the rules of phonetic interpretation treat them identically; both surface as long vowels.

It is on this level, the level of phonetic interpretation, that Clements and Keyser's proposal runs into difficulties. Early on (1983,9), Clements and Keyser propose that glides be represented as vocalic melody features (that is, those melody segments containing [+ high, − cons]) linked to Cs. But given the treatments of Compensatory Lengthening and Klamath long vowels shown above, it is clear that not **all** such segments are counted as glides. Rather, Clements and Keyser must take the position that phonetic interpretation rules can be language particular and that they can count some [+ high, − cons] attached to C slots as vowels and others as glides. To be precise, in Klamath presumably the first C slot in (55) must be counted as a glide, and the second as a vowel:

(55)
$$
\begin{bmatrix} +\text{hi} \\ -\text{lo} \\ -\text{bk} \\ -\text{cons} \end{bmatrix}
\begin{bmatrix} +\text{hi} \\ -\text{lo} \\ +\text{bk} \\ -\text{cons} \end{bmatrix}
$$

C V C

σ

But any phonetic interpretation rule that could do this would have to have a rather peculiar property: that is, the phonetic interpretation rules in Klamath would have to state that (i) if a single set of melody features containing [+ high, − cons] is attached to both a V and C, this configuration is interpreted as a vowel, whereas (ii) if [+ high, − cons] is attached solely to a C, this is considered a glide. This statement presupposes a relatively nontrivial component of phonetic interpretation rules, one in which these rules do far more than add up the sum total of distinctive features attached to each skeleton slot. Within Clements and Keyser's proposed framework, phonetic interpretation rules would have to scan whole configurations of features and association lines and to distinguish among them on the basis of linkings. In other words, although defining V as 'peak' and C as 'margin' results in some simplification, it reintroduces complexity in the form of phonetic interpretation rules of a powerful sort. It is not clear whether this added power is desirable (see Liberman and Pierrehumbert [1984] for a discussion of phonetic implementation rules).

I would like to propose that a specified skeleton of a form to be developed below will overcome these difficulties, and will do so without too many unwanted side effects. Given this sort of skeleton, association rules will not need to be extrinsically ordered, and in fact will all be able to apply simultaneously. No peculiar phonetic interpretation rules will be needed. And I will argue in section 1.4.4.2 that although "special provisos" changing C to V and V to C may be necessary in the theory being developed here, this necessity will actually have a positive consequence. At least one additional argument in favor of my proposal will emerge as this chapter progresses.

Suppose, then, that the skeleton tier is a projection of the major class features [consonantal] and [syllabic].[24] Four sorts of elements will be represented directly on the skeleton tier: vowels, consonants, glides, and syllabic consonants, as illustrated in (56):

(56)   + cons   + cons   − cons   − cons
        − syl   + syl   − syl   + syl

        = C   = C   = G   = V
                       |

I am assuming that skeleton slots will be gathered into perhaps hierarchically organized syllables according to some theory of syllable structure (perhaps Steriade's [1982] or Clements and Keyser's [1983]), although nothing in what follows hinges on the particular choice of syllable structure.[25]

As mentioned in section 1.3, within this framework, melodies will contain most place-and-manner-of-articulation features, that is, those which have not been autosegmentalized. They will not contain any specifications for the major class features, since these are projected on the skeleton tier. The question then immediately arises of how we are to match up the right melody segments with the right skeleton slots, or, in other words, how we are to tell "consonantal" melody segments from "vocalic" ones in the absence of the features [consonantal] and [syllabic] on the melody tier. The answer is a relatively simple one. In order to match up the right melody and skeleton slots, we need only assume that there is some additional characteristic of "consonantal" melody segments that distinguishes them from "vocalic" melody segments, and that the association rule can be made sensitive to that distinction.

That there is some difference between consonants and vowels and that this difference is reflected in their melodies (that is, in their place and manner of articulation features) is not an implausible claim. It is in fact consistent with the assumptions of traditional phoneticians and with more recent work. As Chomsky and Halle (1968) point out in SPE, it is implicit in the IPA itself that the parameters used in describing the place and manner of articulation of consonants are different from those used in describing vowels. While Jakobson, in contrast, argues for a feature system that is identical for consonants and vowels, SPE takes a position between the two extremes; Chomsky and Halle (1968, 303) suggest that "the complete identification of vowel and consonant features seems in retrospect to have been too radical a solution." Specifically, phonological evidence suggests that the features [diffuse], [grave], and [compact] used by Jakobson to specify position of articulation in both consonants and vowels are inadequate to characterize both primary and secondary articulations in consonants. SPE, in fact, opts for specifying primary place of articulation for vowels and consonants with entirely different features. The features [high], [back], [low] give primary place of articulation for vowels, whereas [anterior] and [coronal] are used for primary articulations in consonants. Of these five features, [high], [back], and [low] are used for secondary articulations in consonants, and [coronal] for a secondary articulation—retroflexion—in vowels. But [anterior] has no use at all in characterizing vowels.

Acoustic evidence also suggests that there is a fundamental difference in the articulation of consonants and vowels and that this difference rests upon the place of articulation information embodied in the feature [anterior]. Stevens (1968, p. 20–21) discusses the issue:

> Examination of the four sets of acoustic attributes corresponding to these four places of articulation [i.e., labial, alveolar, palatal, velar—R.L.] suggests that they can be classified in terms of two features. For the two posterior constriction positions, there is a major spectral energy concentration in the central frequency range that is of importance for vowel production (up to, say, 3500 cps in this case). The two anterior positions on the other hand, have no such energy concentration. The latter two have been labeled with the feature *anterior*.

In other words, all vowels share acoustic properties with [− anterior] consonants. Put slightly differently, while it seems necessary in every language to use the feature [anterior] to distinguish consonants from one another, the feature is completely superfluous in the description of vowels. This fact is taken in SPE to mean that vowels are always specified redundantly as [− anterior], but the phonological and phonetic evidence is in fact consistent with another interpretation.

Suppose instead that all "consonantal" melodies have some underlying specification for the value of the feature [anterior] but that "vocalic" melodies lack this feature entirely. "Consonantal" melodies would therefore differ from "vocalic" ones in having exactly one more feature. Suppose further that the melody-skeleton association rule is sensitive to this minimal distinction so that it matches up [+ consonantal] slots in the skeleton only with matrices that have the feature [anterior]. Such a rule is stated in (57):

(57) Melody-Skeleton Association

Associate segments with [anterior] to [+ cons], other segments to [− cons] one to one, $\left\{ \begin{array}{l} \text{L to R} \\ \text{R to L} \end{array} \right\}$

Note that (57) conforms to the association rule schema in (42); it is a single rule, and it is exactly like all other association rules. Note also that I have left open the directional parameter in (57). While it seems that for most languages a left-to-right rule is sufficient, others seem to require a right-to-left rule. Marantz (1982) indicates, for example, that the rule associating melody to skeleton in Dakota must operate from right to left. This is especially apparent when we look at reduplication. According to Marantz, reduplication in Dakota involves the suffixation of a CCVC skeleton to the root. When the melody is copied, it associates to the skeleton starting with the rightmost melody segment:

(58) **a.** h   ą   s   k   a   h   ą   s   k   a
    | | | | |
    C   V   C   C   V+   C   C   V   C   →

   b. h   ą   s   k   a   h   ą   s   k   a
      | | | | | / / /
      C   V   C   C   V   C   C   V   C

   = hąskaska

Thus it seems that this association rule, like others, must be available in universal grammar with a directional parameter.

Rule (57) has a number of advantages over other proposals. Unlike McCarthy's original association rule, it requires no duplication of the feature [syllabic] (or indeed of any feature) on more than one tier. And unlike the sort of rules needed within Levin's and Yip's frameworks, it is a single rule; (57) attaches both consonantal melodies and vocalic melodies to the skeleton in the same operation (we will see more of how the rule operates in section 1.4.5). Finally, because it attaches matrices with the feature [anterior] to [+ cons] skeleton slots, it accounts at the same time for both syllabic and nonsyllabic consonants: that is, (57) will attach consonantal melody matrices either to [+ cons, − syl] skeleton slots, resulting in true consonants, or to [+ cons, + syl] skeleton slots, giving syllabic consonants.[26] Although neither Yip nor Levin discusses the issue directly, as I have mentioned earlier, syllabic consonants require a special association rule in the X-skeleton framework.

Rule (57) also has another interesting consequence. Since it specifies that attachment of melody and skeleton depends upon the feature [anterior], it requires that the feature [anterior] always be a part of the melody tier; that is, unlike the features [high], [back], [round], etc., which are part of the melody tier in some languages and in others are autosegmentalized, the feature [anterior] cannot be autosegmentalized. While this may seem a rather bizarre state of affairs, it does yield an interesting prediction: there should be no language which has a harmony process or a rule of consonant mutation which is based on the feature [anterior]. This prediction is of some interest precisely because there is at least one case that has been cited in recent literature—Chumash (Poser 1980b-ms)—which is claimed to be a case of [anterior] harmony. I will return to this prediction in chapter 2, where I will argue that Chumash is not a true example of [anterior] harmony at all, and that the prediction made by our theory appears to be correct.

1.4.4 Spreading

1.4.4.1 Regular Spreading

Given the possibility of lexical association between tiers and the initial association rules discussed in section 1.4.3, configurations may still arise in which elements on one tier are not associated with elements on any other tier. Such representations are illustrated in (59):

(59) a.
```
        x                b.    x      y   z
        |                      |      |   |
    X   Y   Z   W          X   Y   Z   W
```

As was the case with the association rules that accomplished the initial linking of tiers, the rules that govern the spreading of prior association lines to create one to many mappings may vary from language to language (see also Pulleyblank [1983] on this subject). Once again, each language must choose the direction(s) in which association lines can spread.

Configuration (59a) arises when there are unattached segments at the margins of words or morphemes and a possible locus of spreading somewhere within the word or morpheme. In some languages, association lines may spread bidirectionally in such a case. This appears to happen in the [ATR] harmony of Akan:

(60)
```
o  +  f i t i  +  i    →      o  +  f i t i  +  i
         |                            
      [+ATR]                        [+ATR]
```

The root **fiti** is always [+ATR]. By an initial association rule, this feature will be associated with the first vowel of the root. Then the feature will spread bidirectionally from the root.

In other languages, association lines may spread exclusively in one direction or another. For example, in Zulu, spreading of tone to the margins of words apparently occurs only in a left-to-right direction (see chapter 4 for a full analysis of Zulu). The representation in (61) results from initial association of the tonal tier to the core and from a special rule shifting the high tone on the prefix from the first to the second vowel. Given this representation, spreading proceeds rightward:

(61)
```
[ i  s  i [ h  l  a  l  o ]] → [ i  s  i [ h  l  a  l  o ]]
      |          |                    |          |
      HL         L                    HL         L
```

However, the high tone of the prefix does not spread leftward to the first vowel of the prefix. Instead, at the end of the derivation a low tone is assigned by a default mechanism to the first vowel.

In the nasalization harmony of Coatzospan Mixtec (Poser 1980a-ms), spreading apparently occurs only in a right-to-left direction. As mentioned above, the second person singular morpheme is the feature [+nasal] which is attached to the rightmost vowel. This feature then spreads from right to left, halting at voiceless obstruents:

(62) k o t o n d E E → k o t o n d E E   kotōndĒĒ
         | ⌐⌐⌐⌐⌐↘   'you-sg. examine'
       [+nas]   [+nas]

Note that in (62) the [+nasal] feature spreads over the prenasalized stop.

In addition to being the second person singular marker, the [+nasal] feature may also arise when it follows a nasal consonant:

(63) m i ? n d E
        |
      [+nas]

If the feature arises in this way, it will not spread to the right even though nothing in Coatzospan specifically prevents the spread of a nasal feature over glottal stops or prenasalized stops; see (62) and (47). Therefore, in (63) only the first vowel is nasalized.

Configuration (59b) arises when, through a combination of initial associations, lexical linkings, and language-particular rules, an eligible segment or segments on one tier are not linked to another tier, and possible loci of spreading exist to either side. As Clark (1982-ms, forthcoming) shows, Igbo and Kikuyu choose different directions of spreading:[27]

(64) *Igbo*: c i̧ f u̧ s i̧ l a   →   c i̧ f u̧ s i̧ l a
                 | | | | | | ⌐⌐⌐↘
                 H   L   H   H   L   H

        Kikuyu: n d i n a r ɔ r a k e ŋ a ŋ i   →
                   | ╲ ╲↓╱ |
                   L   H   LH

                   n d i n a r ɔ r a k e ŋ a ŋ i
                   | ╲ ╲↓╱‑‑‑‑‑‑‑‑‑‑‑‑‑‑ |
                   L   H   LH

Given these representations, Igbo chooses to spread from right to left and Kikuyu from left to right.

This evidence thus suggests that direction is a parameter left open in a universal schema for spreading rules as well as in initial one-to-one associations. As for the precise statement of spreading rules, let us assume that for each tier which requires a spreading rule (not every pair of tiers will necessarily require one), that rule will normally spread association lines from the autosegmental tier to an item in the core to which it could have been associated by initial association rule; that is, if in a given language the [nasal] tier can associate only to [+syllabic] elements by a rule of the form of (42), then [nasal] will not be allowed to spread to items other than [+syllabic]. One sort of systematic exception to this rule will be allowed and will be discussed in the next section.

1.4.4.2 Special Provisos

Before we leave the subject of spreading of association lines, there is one more sort of problem to consider, namely, the problem of the so-called special provisos mentioned earlier. Special provisos are needed within any framework using specified skeletons for cases in which, as a result of phonological deletions or morphological rules, segments on the melody tier seem to associate with slots on the skeleton tier to which the melody-skeleton linking rule in (57) could not have linked them. (65) illustrates schematically the sort of process I have in mind:

(65) a.

$$
\begin{array}{ccc}
 & & \emptyset \\
 & & \uparrow \\
c & v & c \\
| & | & | \\
C & V & C
\end{array}
\quad \rightarrow \quad
\begin{array}{ccc}
c & v & \\
| & |\!\!\diagdown & \\
C & V & C
\end{array}
$$

b.

$$
\begin{array}{ccc}
\emptyset & & \\
\uparrow & & \\
v & v & c \\
| & | & | \\
V & V & C
\end{array}
\quad \rightarrow \quad
\begin{array}{ccc}
v & & c \\
| & & |\!\!\diagdown \\
V & V & C
\end{array}
$$

Case (65a) is traditionally referred to as "Compensatory Lengthening." (65b) is the reverse sort of case, where the deletion of a vowel results in a concomitant lengthening of an adjacent consonant. As far as I know, it has no convenient label of its own, so I will refer to it here as "reverse Compensatory Lengthening."

Suppose now that languages have the option of having special provisos, like the ones stated in (66) below, that operate on the representations in (65).

(66) a. $C \rightarrow V \ / \ \begin{array}{c} v \\ |\!\!\diagdown \\ V \ \underline{\hspace{1em}} \end{array}$ or mirror image

b. $V \rightarrow C \ / \ \begin{array}{c} c \\ |\!\!\diagdown \\ C\underline{\hspace{1em}} \end{array}$ or mirror image

(66) states in effect that if a vocalic melody has spread to a [+cons, −syl] skeleton slot, that slot is changed to [−cons, +syl], and conversely, if a consonantal melody has spread to a [−cons, +syl] skeleton slot, that slot is changed to [+cons, −syl]. Let us assume as well that languages which have Compensatory Lengthening or its reverse also allow the aberrant spreading that is illustrated in (66).

If this is a reasonable derivation for rules of Compensatory Lengthening and its reverse, it also suggests an interesting prediction about such rules. The spreading rule which would attach a v-melody to [+cons, −syl] in (65a) is marked, but it is not especially peculiar, in that it results in a phonetic feature matrix which is **like** a consonant except that it is missing the feature [anterior]: that is, the matrix is underspecified, but the actual combination of features present is nothing unusual. However, the spreading rule which would attach a c-melody to a [−cons, +syl] slot in (66b) is more highly marked; in fact, it produces an aberration, namely, a vowel marked with the feature [anterior]. In some sense, the language with the latter type of spreading is highly marked, the language with the former type of spreading less marked, and the language with no aberrant spreading of either sort the least marked of all. From this it should follow that languages with rules like (65b)–(66b) should be extremely rare, languages with rules like (65a)–(66a) (Compensatory Lengthening) less rare, and languages without either sort of process most common of all.

On the whole, this prediction seems to be on the right track, although the total number of relevant cases that we can bring to bear on the question is quite small. There are many languages which have neither Compensatory Lengthening nor its reverse, although they have representations with unassociated skeleton slots. For example, in Agta reduplication (Marantz 1982), a skeletal prefix of the form CVC is attached to a noun to form its plural, as in (67):

(67) takki   t a k k i   t a k k i   = taktakki 'legs'
     'leg'   \\ \\ \\ | | | | |
             C V C   C V C C V

If the noun stem is vowel initial, however, association lines never spread from the initial vowel to the initial consonant slot of the skeleton prefix:

(68) ulu   u l u   u l u   = ululu 'heads'
     'head'   \\ \\ | | |
             C V C V C V

Similar sorts of examples can be found in many languages.

There are a number of languages that have discussed in the literature that have Compensatory Lengthening, among them Latin, Greek, and Old English. DeChene and Anderson (1979) mention a number of cases other than these. Still, there are far fewer languages with Compensatory Lengthening than there are languages without it.

Moreover, cases involving the reverse of Compensatory Lengthening, that is, the case in (66b), do appear to be very rare indeed, just as we have predicted. Indeed, to my knowledge there is only one such example in the literature.[28] In Clements's (1982) analysis of Luganda, he gives the following derivation:[29]

(69) σ σ σ   σ σ σ
    /\ /\ /\   /\ /\ /\
    V V C V C V → V V C V C V
    | | | | | | | \ | | |
    e i k u m i   e   k u m i   = [ekkumi]

Apparently, with the loss of the vowel **i**, the neighboring **k** is lengthened by spreading to the dissociated V. I know of no other analyses making use of comparable processes.

Thus the prediction we have drawn from these problematic cases appears to be correct, at least on the basis of the currently available data. Note that this prediction is available **only** within a theory which makes use of labeled skeletons. Within a framework that advocates X skeletons, for example, no such prediction is available. In the event, then, that languages with the reverse of Compensatory Lengthening turn out to be rarer than those with Compensatory Lengthening, a theory like the present one, which requires so-called special provisos, actually turns out to be superior to one which does not.

1.4.5 Operation of Association Rules

Our theory now admits the following range of theoretical devices. Distinctive features are projected on a number of tiers: major class features on the skeleton tier, [anterior] and other place and manner features on the melody tier, and possibly a number of other features individually or in groups on separate autosegmental tiers. Two sorts of idiosyncrasy are permitted. In one sort, prespecification, a feature F_i, which is normally projected on T_i in some language appears on T_j in some segments in some lexical items. In the other sort of idiosyncrasy, one tier may be linked partially or completely to another in the lexicon. Otherwise tiers are linked to one another by the melody-skeleton linking rule in (57) and possibly by some number of rules conforming to the schema in (42) (for each tier, in addition to melody and skeleton, there will be one additional rule of the form [42]). Finally, for each tier in a given language, we have the possibility of having an additional rule which sanctions spreading, that is, the creation of one to many mappings between tiers.

These devices will operate as follows. As far as I can tell, since each association rule in a language will operate in a distinct domain, all association rules may apply simultaneously. There seems to be no need to order (57) and rules of the form (42) with respect to one another. Thus, given the hypothetical representation (70b) and the hypothetical association rules (70a), (70c) will result:

(70) a. (i) = (57) Associate segments with [anterior] to [+cons], other segments to [−cons] one to one, L to R.[30]

(ii) Attach [+nasal] to [+syl], one ot one, L to R.

(iii) Attach tonal features to [+syl], one to one, L to R.

b.   c   v   c   v   (where c,v stand for melody segments)

$$\begin{bmatrix} +\text{cons} \\ -\text{syl} \end{bmatrix} \quad \begin{bmatrix} -\text{cons} \\ +\text{syl} \end{bmatrix} \quad \begin{bmatrix} +\text{cons} \\ -\text{syl} \end{bmatrix} \quad \begin{bmatrix} -\text{cons} \\ +\text{syl} \end{bmatrix}$$

[+nasal]

H   L   H

c.

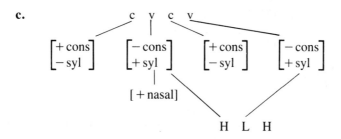

If the hypothetical language in (70) also has the spreading rules in (70d), then (70e) will result:

(70) d.   (i)   Spread [+ nasal] to [+ syl] L to R.
(ii)   Spread tonal features to [+ syl] L to R.

e.

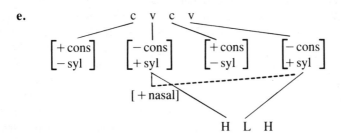

By definition, spreading rules must follow the regular association rules. This intrinsic ordering leaves open the possibility that other phonological rules (for example, segmental rules, delinking rules, or tone shift rules) might apply to intermediate representations like (70c) before the spreading rules apply. I will explore this possibility below and will show in chapter 4 that this in fact occurs.

1.5   THE DFF AND MULTIPLY PROJECTED FEATURES

We have now reached the point at which we can begin to resolve the dilemma I raised at the beginning of this chapter. To reiterate, our problem was that autosegmental phonology had apparently diverged from autosegmental morphology in that the former required that there be no duplication of distinctive features on different tiers (lest the prohibition on crossing of association lines be undermined), while the latter made extensive and necessary use of feature duplication. I asserted at the end of section 1.2 that autosegmental theory should not contain a constraint like the Principle of Exhaustive Partitioning in (9), that is, should not directly prohibit the duplication of features on different tiers, but rather should contain a prohibition on the simultaneous attachment of the same feature from two different tiers to a single element. I repeat this restriction, the DFF, in (71):

(71) Duplicate Features Filter (= (26))

$$* \quad \begin{array}{c} [\alpha F_i] \\ | \\ [\beta F_j] \\ | \\ [\gamma F_i] \end{array}$$

In this section I will discuss logical possibilities in which a language might project the same feature or features on two or more tiers. As we saw in section 1.3, this possibility is not excluded directly within the present theory. Rather, the virtual nonexistence of duplicate tiers will be made to follow from the DFF. Making use of the association rules developed in earlier sections, we will be able to see how the DFF restricts the duplication of features so that unwanted representations like Pseudo-Turkish (13) and Pseudo Fula (21) are ruled out, but necessary duplications like those required for Semitic are permitted. I will go on to show in the following section how the DFF operates in cases where features are prespecified on tiers other than those on which they are normally projected. We shall see how the DFF not only allows us to maintain exactly the same autosegmental theory for phonology and morphology, but also that it has interesting ramifications in other areas of autosegmental theory as well.

Let us suppose from now on that distinctive features may be duplicated on different tiers, and further that our theory contains association rules like (42), (57), Spreading, and (71), the DFF. A number of examples will suffice to show that this constellation of principles restricts our representations in precisely the desired way. Look first at (72b), which represents a morpheme in a hypothetical language with the association rule (72a):

(72) **a.** Associate [round] to [+ syl] one to one, L to R.

    b. [+ round]

      C V C V

      [− round]

    c.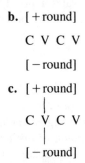

In this hypothetical language the feature [round] has been projected on two tiers. Given the association rule (72a), the representation in (72b) and our assumptions about the operation of association, the only possible outcome linking these three tiers is (72c); in other words, (72a) would have no choice but to apply blindly to both [round] tiers at once, attaching each [round] feature to the leftmost vowel. This outcome violates the DFF. In other words, although the grammar of a language might generate the representation in (72b), such a representation would not be allowed to surface.

The example of Pseudo-Turkish (13), which I argued earlier should in principle be ruled out, is not too different from (72). Let us assume that Pseudo-Turkish contains association rule (72a) and also a rule which will spread the feature [round] to unassociated [+ syl] segments from left to right. Let us assume again that in Pseudo-Turkish the initial vowel of each morpheme is specified for the feature [round] as is any succeeding nonhigh vowel:

(73) Pseudo-Turkish

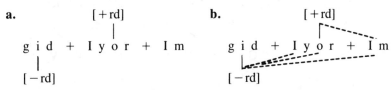

a.   [+ rd]

g i d + I y o r + I m

[− rd]

b.   [+ rd]

g i d + I y o r + I m

[− rd]

Association rule (72a) does not apply to the Pseudo-Turkish representation in (73a), since both [round] features are lexically associated. Spreading, however, does apply. Again, as in the earlier case, given our assumptions, spreading could not help but apply simultaneously and blindly to both round tiers. Given this sort of simultaneous application, the two final vowels in (73b) will each get two simultaneous values for the feature [round], and the representation will be blocked by the DFF.

Also blocked would be a representation like the hypothetical one in (74), where C and V stand for the obvious values of the major class features and c and v, respectively, for consonantal and vocalic melody segments:

(74) a.   c   v   c   v

C   V   C   V   C   V

c   v

b.   c   v   c   v

C   V   C   V   C   V

c   v

Given rule (57), both melodies would be attached simultaneously to the skeleton (let us assume from left to right), and the result (74b) would violate the DFF many times over.

Pseudo-Fula is again only slightly more complicated than the example in (74). Assuming that Pseudo-Fula has an association rule which links [cont, nas] to [− syl] one to one, left to right, and a rule which spreads rightward, a representation like (75a) would be ruled out in the following way:

(75) a. $\begin{bmatrix} -\text{cont} \\ -\text{nas} \end{bmatrix}$

C   V   C

$\begin{bmatrix} +\text{cont} \\ -\text{nas} \end{bmatrix}$ $\begin{bmatrix} -\text{cont} \\ +\text{nas} \end{bmatrix}$

b. $\begin{bmatrix} -\text{cont} \\ -\text{nas} \end{bmatrix}$

C   V   C

$\begin{bmatrix} +\text{cont} \\ -\text{nas} \end{bmatrix}$ $\begin{bmatrix} -\text{cont} \\ +\text{nas} \end{bmatrix}$

rim − 'free man'

The upper [cont, nas] tier, which represents the class 3 diminutive morpheme, will be associated with the initial consonant of the stem at the same time as the other specification for these features. Once again, this association violates the DFF, and the representation will be ruled out.

No problem occurs in the derivation of Semitic morphology, however, even though many distinctive features (all of the melody features) are duplicated on different tiers. Consider the schematic representation of Arabic morphology in (76), where small letters again are melodies and capital letters skeleton slots:

(76)

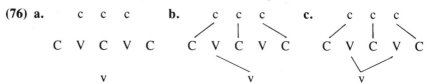

Association rule (57) will produce (76b) from (76a). It will operate on both melody tiers simultaneously, but it will never attach duplicate sets of features to the same skeleton slot, since the melodies on the upper skeleton tier contain the feature [anterior] and will attach to Cs on the skeleton tier, and the segments on the lower melody tier will lack [anterior] and therefore will attach only to Vs. Presumably Arabic also has a left-to-right spreading rule for melodies. This will produce the form in (76c). Although features are duplicated on the two melody tiers, the DFF is never violated.

To summarize, the claim here amounts to this. Given a reasonable set of association rules and conventions governing their operation, and the DFF, which amounts to another sort of condition on the operation of these rules, we will allow only the sorts of representations we seem to need for both phonological and morphological analyses within autosegmental theory. What our theory says, in effect, is something that makes good phonetic sense: we cannot set up phonological representations in such a way that the association rules will provide the same feature twice, simultaneously, to a single segment. In this theory we get all of the positive effects which the informal Principle of Exhaustive Partitioning had for phonology and none of the negative effects it had for morphology. Most multiple projections of features will in fact be ruled out.

1.6   THE DFF AND PRESPECIFICATION

We saw above how the DFF worked in cases where the same features had been projected regularly on more than one tier. As we saw earlier, however, it is possible within the present theory to have a feature (or features) duplicated on more than one tier without having multiple Projection Statements for that feature. The relevant case is what I called "prespecification," where a feature F_i, which is normally projected on a tier T_i in some language, is idiosyncratically (for some segment in some lexical item) projected on T_j. In section 1.6.1, I will consider the cases of Fula and Akan where prespecification is needed and make a proposal as to how the DFF should operate there. This proposal will have extensive ramifications, as following sections will show.

1.6.1 Fula and Akan

Let us examine first the case of lexical idiosyncrasy in Fula. Most nouns in Fula behave like the one illustrated in (16); that is, the initial consonant of most nouns mutates depending on the class of the noun, so that in class 3, for example, a noun will be stop-initial, in class 7 prenasalized stop-initial, and so on. In such cases, as I argued earlier, mutation was the result of the prefixation of a class morpheme consisting of the features [continuant, nasal] which associated to the normally underspecified first consonant of the stem. The derivation of **baa**, the class 3 form of the noun 'monkey', is repeated in (77):

(77)

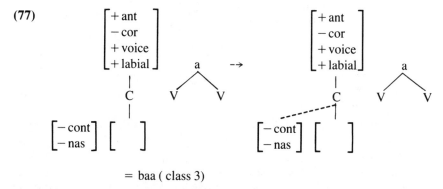

= baa (class 3)

In addition to the regular nouns in Fula whose initial consonants mutate depending upon the noun class they are in, there are a number of nouns in Fula which never undergo mutation, regardless of their noun class. The noun **beebe** 'deafmute', for example, retains its initial stop throughout its paradigm. Invariant nouns like **beebe** can easily be accounted for if we assume that the features [continuant, nasal] are idiosyncratically prespecified in the lexical entry of the noun. As (78) shows, where most nouns in Fula are underspecified for [continuant, nasal] on their initial segments, **beebe** and like nouns have these features lexically prespecified:

(78) beebe 'deafmute' lexical entry:

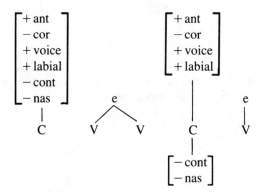

What happens when a class morpheme like the class 2 [+cont, −nas] prefix is attached? It appears that the features idiosyncratically specified in the lexical entry take precedence over those supplied by the regular class morpheme, so that the rules of association will not operate in a representation like (79) to attach prefix features:

(79)

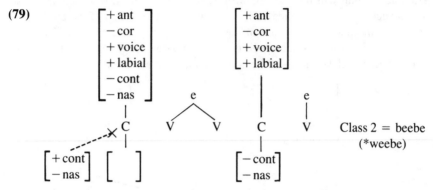

Class 2 = beebe
(*weebe)

In other words, prespecified features are features that reflect a special case in the Paninian sense, and as in Panini, the special case takes precedence over the more general case.

This priority relation can be built into the theory that we have been developing with almost no additional complexity. We already have the DFF, which prohibits the simultaneous linking of duplicate features to the same segment. Assume in addition that association rules like (42) and (57) and spreading rules will fail to attach a given feature T_i if it is already visible on T_j, to which T_i is being attached. Assume, in other words, that the association and spreading rules work so as not to violate the DFF. It is crucial to note that since all other association rules operate simultaneously, followed by the spreading rules, the only conditions under which a feature will already be visible on T_j will be in cases of prespecification.[31]

Akan provides another example in which the DFF operates in exactly this way. Marantz (1982) noted that in the sort of reduplication that occurred in Akan verbs, the first CV of the verb stem was copied, and in addition the vowel was raised to [+high]:

(80) se?   'say'   -→   sise?

sɔ?   'light'   -→   sʊsɔ?

According to Marantz, Akan reduplication could be analyzed as the prefixation of CV to the skeleton of the verb; what is unusual about the V of this skeletal affix is that it is prespecified with the feature [+high].[32]

(81) s   e   ?   s   e   ?
                        | | |
          C   V   C   V   C
          [+hi]

If the reduplicative skeleton is already prespecified for the feature [+high], when association of the copied melody occurs, the association rules will attach all of the melody features except [high] to the V slot. Again, they will work so as not to violate the DFF.[33]

Note that this development necessitates a slight revision in our derivation of Pseudo-Turkish in (73). In that case, we assumed that both the initial vowel and the nonhigh vowel were lexically specified for the feature [round] and that spreading caused two violations of the DFF. However, if spreading and association avoid attaching a feature to a slot already specified on a different tier for that feature, the Pseudo-Turkish example will be derived as in (82):

(82)

```
            [+rd]          Spreading          [+rd]
             |                                  ┌──────────
g i d  +  I y o r  +  I m      ->      g i d  +  I y o r  +  I m
 |                                      └────────────────────
[−rd]                                  [−rd]
```

The difference between (73) and (82) is that in (82) Spreading will skip the slot for which [+rd] is already specified. It will still, however, spread both [round] features simultaneously to the last vowel, violating the DFF and once again blocking the representation.

1.6.2 Excursus: the DFF and the Elsewhere Condition

As mentioned above, this interpretation of the DFF ensures that the more specific case of feature specification—lexically prespecified features—overrides the more general case—features which are provided by the regular association rules. Since there is another commonly accepted condition in phonological theory which gives the specific case priority over the general case, namely, the Elsewhere Condition (Kiparsky 1982), it seems appropriate to compare the two conditions and to see if perhaps the DFF is superfluous. I will argue below that it is not superfluous for two reasons, and that the DFF rather than the Elsewhere Condition should apply to autosegmental representations.

Kiparsky (1982, pp. 136–37) defines the Elsewhere Condition as in (83):

(83) Rules A, B in the same component apply disjunctively to a form ϕ if and only if
   (i) The structural description of A (the special rule) properly includes the structural description of B (the general rule)
   (ii) The result of applying A to ϕ is distinct from the result of applying B to ϕ
   In that case, A is applied first, and if it takes effect, then B is not applied.

We must first examine how the Elsewhere Condition would apply to autosegmental representations. We will then see if the Elsewhere Condition excludes the sort of representations that we want to rule out.

The canonical case in which the Elsewhere Condition would apply is one in which a language L has two association rules like A and B in (84):

(84) A: Attach [αnasal] to [+ syl, + high], L to R.
   B: Attach [βnasal] to [+ syl], L to R.

If such a situation existed in L, then the Elsewhere Condition would clearly dictate that A, the more specific rule, would apply to forms containing [+ high] vowels, and B elsewhere. Significantly, I know of no languages which have pairs of association rules like A and B, and therefore no languages which would need the Elsewhere Condition to apply in exactly this way.

Where the Elsewhere Condition **would** be needed if we dispense with the DFF is in cases where features are lexically prespecified. Kiparsky (1982, p. 137) proposes that each lexical entry be taken as a sort of rule: "Suppose then we construe each lexical entry L as a rule, namely the identity rule L, whose structural description and structural change are both = L." For us, this statement means that if a lexical entry is already specified for F_i, this specification counts as a special rule overriding whatever association and/or spreading rule normally distributes F_i. Counting lexical specification as a "rule" would, in fact, give the right results in the Fula case discussed in section 1.6.1. If the invariant noun **beebe** is lexically prespecified for [− cont, − nas] and if this counts as a lexical identity rule in Kiparsky's sense, then this "rule" will preempt the regular Fula rule supplying the [cont, nas] features. So the Elsewhere Condition appears to be equivalent to the DFF in this sort of case.

But there is evidence that the Elsewhere Condition would work too thoroughly if we used it in place of the DFF. It would rule out processes that we need to allow in autosegmental theory. Consider the sort of nasalization process that occurs in Tereña. As mentioned in section 1.4.2, in this language nasalization affects both consonants and vowels. In the first person singular of a verb or first person singular possessor of a noun, the harmony nasalizes both sonorants and vowels. It stops at obstruents, but, significantly, it causes an obstruent which stops it to become prenasalized (Poser 1980a-ms, 15):

(85)

nokone	'need'	-→	nõŋgone
ituke	'poss. pronoun'	-→	ĩnduke
owoku	'house'	-→	õw̃õŋgu
piho	'went'	-→	mbiho
arine	'sickness'	-→	ãrĩñẽ

Following Poser (1980a-ms), we can analyze the data as follows. The first person singular morpheme and the first person singular possessive morpheme consist solely of the feature [+ nasal]. This feature prefixes to the verb or noun stem and spreads left to right, attaching to all segments. We may assume as well that all obstruents are lexically attached to the feature [− nasal] which appears on the regular nasal tier. The first and third forms in (85) can therefore be derived straightforwardly as in (86):

(86)

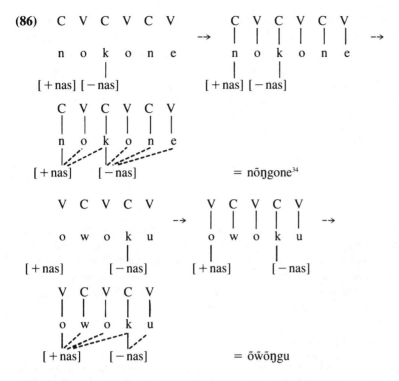

As (86) shows, the [+nasal] prefix in Tereña will spread even to the obstruent lexically preattached to the [−nasal] feature, but it can spread no further, since to do so would force it to cross an association line. This appears to be a reasonable and well-motivated analysis of the nasalization harmony in Tereña.

If we adopted the Elsewhere Condition, such an analysis would be explicitly ruled out, however. The lexical preattachment of the feature [−nasal] to obstruents would constitute a special case which ought to override the general nasal spreading process that creates the harmony. In other words, since each obstruent in Tereña must be lexically preattached to a [−nasal] feature prior to the spreading rule, these segments ought to be immune from getting a feature specification via spreading. If the Elsewhere Condition were in effect, they ought to remain nonnasal. Yet, as we have seen, the nasal spreading rule needs to affect them.

The DFF, in contrast, would not rule out this analysis of Tereña. As I pointed out in section 1.2, the DFF works to rule out **simultaneous** specifications of some feature on more than one tier. It does not rule out **sequential** specifications of a feature attached to a single segment, the sort of specification that we need for prenasalized stops or affricates. The DFF thus permits the sort of analysis that we need for Tereña, whereas the Elsewhere Condition rules it out. This is one reason to believe that the Elsewhere Condition cannot take the place of the DFF.

The other reason concerns the sort of representations we discussed in section 1.5. There it was argued that the DFF served to constrain representations that could be generated in a framework in which features could be simultaneously projected on two or more tiers. In other words, given a language which projected two [round] tiers and an association rule linking [round] to [+syl] L to R, representations like (87a) would result in representations like (87b), and the DFF would rule the latter representation out:

(87) a. [+rd]   b.   [+rd]
                             |
     C V C V   C V C V
                             |
     [−rd]   [−rd]

In the representation in (87), what we have is not the sort of specific versus general case to which the Elsewhere Condition is tailored, but rather two identical, simultaneous applications of a single regular association rule. The DFF applies in these cases. The Elsewhere Condition does not. The conclusion we must draw is that the DFF rather than the Elsewhere Condition is appropriate to constraining autosegmental representations.

1.6.3 Neutral Segments

To reiterate our conclusions so far, we have opted for allowing the association rules to operate so as to pass over or ignore segments which have already received a particular feature in the lexicon. This move, in turn, has further consequences in that it can also be invoked to explain the behavior of a certain type of segment which is occasionally found in harmony systems, namely, those segments which have been called "neutral" segments. In languages with vowel or consonant harmony, neutral segments are those which neither trigger harmony nor undergo it nor block its spread. They are segments which appear to be entirely invisible to the harmony process.

A good example can be found in Classical Mongolian (Lightner 1967). Classical Mongolian has a backness harmony which affects both vowels and velar consonants. All vowels in a word and all velar consonants must agree in backness, as the examples in (88) illustrate:

(88) [+back]   uγuta   'bag'
     [−back]   köbegün   'son, boy'

However, the segment [i] in Classical Mongolian is neutral in the sense described above—it does not itself trigger harmony, it does not undergo harmony, and it does not block the spread of harmony. Thus, we have examples like those in (89) in Classical Mongolian in which [i] exists both in words with [−back] segments and in words with [+back] segments:

(89) [+back]   qubilγan   'transformation'
     [−back]   kötelbüri   'instruction'

Within this framework, Classical Mongolian can be accounted for as follows. Morphemes in Classical Mongolian consist of three tiers—skeleton, melody, and a harmony tier containing the feature [back]. The noun 'bag', for example, will have the lexical entry in (90a). This entry (and others) will be subject to the association and spreading rules in (90b), as well as to (57), producing (90c):[35]

(90) a. Lexical entry
'bag'

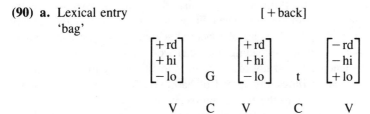

b. Attach [back] to [+ syl] and [− ant, − cor] one to one, L to R.

c.

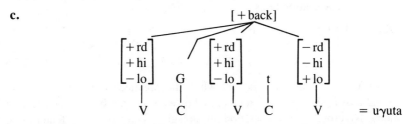

Let us say now that neutral segments in harmony systems are segments in which the harmonizing feature is lexically prespecified in the core, let us say, for concreteness, in the melody.[36] Given this assumption, the noun 'transformation' will have the lexical entry in (91a):

(91) a.

b.

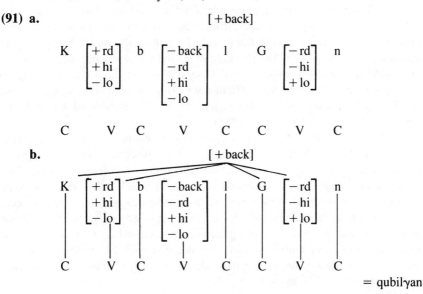

(90b) and (57) will operate on (91a) to give (91b). Note that the spreading rule will skip over the fourth segment since it already has a specification for the feature [back].

The behavior of neutral segments in harmony follows directly if they are treated as cases of prespecification. As we will see in chapter 3, a harmony occurs when an autosegmentalized feature is spread to segments in the core. Neutral segments do not undergo harmony because they already have a value for the harmonizing feature in the core. The DFF prevents them from getting doubly specified. The prespecified feature of a neutral segment does not itself spread because the association and spreading rules that would do this refer exclusively to the autosegmental tier and not to the core. And finally, neutral segments as construed here cannot **block** the spread of harmony; blocking occurs when a segment creates a barrier to the further propagation of the harmony. In effect, this happens, as illustrated schematically in (92), where the spreading feature meets a **preattached** feature. In this case, continued spreading would cause a crossing of association lines:

(92) $[+F_i]$ $[-F_i]$ $*[+F_i]$ $[-F_i]$

   C   V   C   V   C   V   C   V   →   C   V   C   V   C   V   C   V

As (92) shows, blocking occurs when the preattached feature $[+F_i]$ cannot spread past $[-F_i]$. Neutral segments, however, cannot block the spread of harmony. No crossing of association lines results when a harmony feature is spread past a neutral segment (see [91b]).[37]

Note that our theory offers a prediction as to the markedness of neutral segments. Since neutral segments represent a type of prespecification, and since prespecification comes at some cost to the grammar, neutral segments ought to be highly marked and therefore relatively infrequent in the languages that have harmonies. A survey of some languages with harmonies indicates that this prediction seems to be on the right track: Finnish (Halle and Vergnaud 1981) and Hungarian (Vago 1980) appear to have neutral segments, but such languages as Mixtec (Poser 1980a-ms), Tereña (Poser 1980a-ms), Igbo (Green and Igwe 1963), Guaraní (Poser 1982), Hindustani (Hoenigswald 1948), Capanahua (Halle and Vergnaud 1981), Akan (Clements 1980a), Kirghiz (Johnson 1980) and Turkish (Halle and Vergnaud 1981) do not.

Let us digress for a moment to compare the treatment of neutral segments with that of so-called **opaque** segments within autosegmental theory. Opaque segments are those which do not themselves harmonize (Clements 1980a, 24), although they do control the harmony in segments which follow them. In other words, opaque segments define new harmony domains within a word or morpheme. We have in fact already seen an example of an opaque segment in our brief discussion of Turkish rounding harmony in section 1.2. There it was stated that initial vowels of morphemes in Turkish are specified lexically for the feature [round] as are any succeeding nonhigh vowels. A typical example was given in (12), repeated below as (93):

(93) Turkish   g i d + I y o r + I m

   [− rd]   [+ rd]

Nonhigh vowels in Turkish are in fact opaque with respect to rounding harmony. In formal terms, we have represented this as a lexically linked (**preattached**) [round] feature **on the harmonizing tier**. This proposal was originally made in Clements (1980a). Because this feature is part of the harmony tier, it is subject to spreading. In other words, it determines the value of the feature [round] on succeeding segments.

The difference between neutral and opaque segments in harmony systems therefore amounts to the following. Neutral segments are those with the harmonizing feature prespecified in the phonological core. Opaque segments have the harmonizing feature lexically linked on the harmony tier. The former are invisible to the harmony process, whereas the latter are not. But both neutral and opaque segments in a way represent forms of lexical idiosyncrasy.

1.6.4 Infixation Revisited

The notion of prespecification has still further ramifications in that it suggests a way of simplifying McCarthy's treatment of infixation in the Arabic verbal paradigm, and of accounting for one of the major characteristics of infixation. In the next section, I will review and reanalyze infixation in the Arabic verbal system, and in section 1.6.4.2, I will extend the analysis to other, more representative, cases of infixation—one in Tagalog and another that occurs in the American English play language Alfalfalal.

1.6.4.1 Arabic Infixation

McCarthy's analysis of infixation was mentioned in section 1.2. To flesh out the details, infixing occurs in the triliteral Binyanim XII–XV,[38] which all have the basic skeleton CCVCCVC. In addition, Binyanim XII and XIII have the consonant **w** infixed to the third C of the skeleton, Binyan XIV has the consonant **n** infixed to the same slot, and XV has **n** infixed to the third C and **y** suffixed to the last C:

(94) (McCarthy 1981, 393)

XII & XII   w

          C   C   V   C   C   V   C

   XIV   n

          C   C   V   C   C   V   C

XV
$$\begin{matrix} & & & n & & y \\ & & & | & & | \\ C & C & V & C & C & V & C \end{matrix}$$

Although McCarthy does not give the exact form of the infixation rules, he does state that "the additional complication of these very rare conjugations is that the rules of association must indicate where the affixes are to be fixed on the prosodic template" (1981, 393). Although they are marginal rules, these association rules would still have to have a rather strange property; as regularly applying association rules, they would have to be able to count Cs in the skeleton: that is, in each case they would have to "look for" the third C slot. Since no other "counting" rules appear to be necessary in autosegmental theory (or in any other phonological or morphological theory, for that matter), it would be a good idea to dispense with them if possible.

Clearly what we have in the case of the Arabic XII–XV Binyanim are examples of lexical idiosyncrasy. Each of the skeletons in (94) must be listed in the lexicon in any case, along with its meaning or effect on the verbal diathesis; the fact that each of these binyanim already has one slot filled with melody features is simply another aspect of its lexical idiosyncrasy.

As we have seen earlier, however, there are actually two different ways that this lexical idiosyncrasy might be represented in this framework. That is, the XIIth Binyan, for example, could be represented either as (95a) or as (95b) in the lexicon:

(**95**) XIIth Binyan

a. $\begin{matrix} C & C & V & C & C & V & C \\ | & & & & & & \\ w \end{matrix}$ b. $\begin{matrix} & & & & w & & \\ C & C & V & C & C & V & C \end{matrix}$

In (95a) the infixed **w** is meant to be analogous to an opaque segment in a harmony process; it is on its own tier, but it is lexically linked to a specified skeleton slot. In contrast, in (95b) the infix is meant to be analogous to a neutral segment; $\overset{w}{C}$ is meant to be a convenient abbreviation for the major class features [−cons, −syl] plus the distinctive features of **w**. (95b) thus represents another case of prespecification. Although it may, at first glance, seem as if the two representations are equivalent in this case, there is at least one reason, although it is a theory-internal one, to believe that (95b) is the preferable one.[39]

Remember that neutral and opaque segments in harmony processes differed from one another in that the former segments did not take part in harmony at all—they were invisible to it—whereas the latter defined their own harmony domains. Since opaque segments had the harmonizing feature specified on the harmony tier, this feature was subject to spreading. Consider in this light the two possible derivations of the XIIth Binyan verb **ktawtab:**

(96) a.   k t b   Erasure   k t b   Spreading   k t b

C C V C C V C → C C V C C V C → C C V C C V C

| |

w   w   w

b.   k t b   Erasure   k t b   Spreading   k t b

C C V C C V C → C C V C C V C → C C V C C V C
  w   w   w

If the infix were a separate melody lexically linked to the skeleton, as in (96a), after the Erasure rule broke the first link between the third root consonant and the skeleton, both the root melody **t** and the infix melody **w** would simultaneously reassociate to the unfilled C slot, thereby violating the DFF. In the representation in (96b), however, no such violation occurs; like the neutral segments, the infixed **w** is inert by virtue of being lexically prespecified on the skeleton.[40]

Let us say, then, that Semitic infixation is a form of prespecification of features. This analysis seems especially plausible for Semitic, since it is easily argued that the melody features for **w** do not themselves constitute a morpheme; they do not carry any meaning apart from the XIIth Binyan skeleton. Rather, it makes more sense to say that the whole skeleton, prespecified features and all, is a morpheme.

1.6.4.2 Other Cases

Not all cases of infixation can be treated purely as prespecification of features, as the Arabic case was. However, prespecification of features seems at least to be one component in the analysis of other cases of infixation. Here I will provide two more examples; the first is a play language which involves a process of infixation, and the second is perhaps the classic type of infixation, that found in Tagalog.

Alfalfalal,[41] an English-based play language, is illustrated, in (97):

(97) *English*   *Alfalfalal*
quack [kwæk]   qualfack [kwælfæk]
wagon   walfagon
hunting   hulfunting
decided [dəsaydəd]   decilfided [dəsalfaydəd]

In this play language, the infix **Vlf** is inserted after the onset of the stressed syllable, where the V represents a copy of the vocalic nucleus of this syllable.

In autosegmental terms, the rules for Alfalfalal can be stated as follows:

(98) Rules for Alfalfalal

  a. Delink stressed syllable.
  b. Insert VCC after onset, and resyllabify.
     l f
  c. Apply association rules and spreading.

Given these rules, the Alfalfalal forms of **hunting** and **decided** will be derived as in (99):

(99) a.

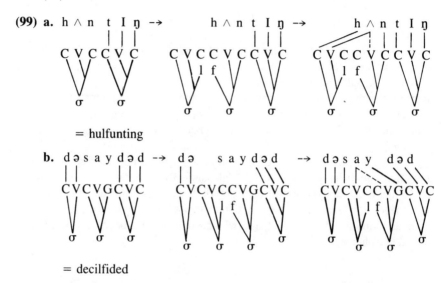

= hulfunting

b.

= decilfided

In other words, if the Alfalfalal morpheme is represented as a skeleton with two slots containing the prespecified features for the consonant melodies **lf**, and if this morpheme is inserted into the stressed syllable, the regular rules of association and spreading will account for the copied vowel. The Alfalfalal example differs from the Semitic one in the following respect. Although the prespecified skeleton is itself a sort of morpheme as it was in Arabic, unlike Arabic it must be inserted by special rule into another morpheme which itself has melody and skeleton, and it must be attached to a phonological constituent within that morpheme. In other words, Alfalfalal infixation consists of two components—prespecification and insertion—only one of which it shares with Arabic infixation.

    These two components, exist in the classic case of Tagalog infixation as well. Tagalog has two infixes; **-um-**, which creates an agentive form from a stem, and **-in-**, which denotes the object which is the result of an action. Both infixes appear after the onset of the initial syllable of the stem:

(100) su:lat   'a writing'   sumu:lat   'one who wrote'
                            sinu:lat   'that which was written'

In the theory being developed here, these morphemes can be represented as a VC skeleton on which the melody features for -**um**- and -**in**- are prespecified. These morphemes are inserted into the first syllable (which has been delinked from the original skeleton), and resyllabification subsequently occurs. The form **sumu:lat** will be derived as in (101):

(101)

```
        s  u  l  a  t          s     u  l  a  t
  u m   C  V  V  C  V  C   →   C  V  C  V V C  V  C
  V C +                  u m
        \ /     \ /           \ /    \ /   \ /
         σ       σ             σ      σ     σ
```

Tagalog will be like both Arabic and Alfalfalal in having skeleton morphemes prespecified with melody features. It will be like Alfalfalal in having an infix insertion rule. Its sole distinction lies in its having infix skeletons in which all slots contain prespecified features (in fact, all features are fully specified on the skeleton). What is important to note here is that there is no unitary phenomenon which we can call "infixation,"[42] nor is there a sharp break between the cases that have been referred to as infixation and the apparently more phonological cases prespecification. Neutral segments in harmony, Fula invariant nouns, Akan reduplication, Semitic infixation, Alfalfalal, and Tagalog infixation represent what might be seen as a continuum of autosegmental processes, all containing the essential element of prespecification.

1.7 SUMMARY AND CONCLUSIONS

In this chapter I have begun to build up a theory of autosegmental representations on the basis of a few simple principles. These principles are summarized in (102):

(102) **a.** Distinctive features are projected onto a number of different tiers, as discussed in section 1.3. Features may be duplicated on different tiers.

b. Two sorts of lexical idiosyncrasy are sanctioned:

(i) Lexical Linking (**preattachment**): where morphemes consist of more than one tier, say T_i and T_j, an element on T_i can be lexically linked to an element on T_j in cases of lexical idiosyncrasy (e.g., a certain arbitrary vowel in a harmony system always induces a certain value of the harmonizing feature on succeeding vowels).

(ii) Prespecification: a morpheme which consists of T_i can be lexically specified for distinctive features that are normally projected on T_j in that language (e.g., neutral segments in harmony systems).

    c. Association
      (i) Attach [αF_i] to [βF_j] one to one, L to R/ R to L.
      (ii) Attach [anterior] to [+cons], other segments to [−cons], one to one, L to R/ R to L.
      (iii) Spreading: none/ L to R/ R to L / bidirectional.
    d. Duplicate Features Filter (DFF)

    e. Operating Assumptions
      (i) If [F_i] is projected as an autosegment on more than one tier, association rules will operate simultaneously wherever [F_i] is projected (in fact, it is probably only necessary to say that association rules operate simultaneously).
      (ii) Association and spreading rules operate so as to avoid violations of the DFF. That is, if [F_i] is present on a segment (due to prespecification) prior to the simultaneous application of the association rules, then these rules will not attach another [F_i] to this segment.

Adopting the principles in (102) allows us to resolve what appeared to be an inconsistency in the treatment of autosegmental representations between typically phonological analyses (harmony and tone) and typically morphological ones (root and pattern word formation, reduplication, and infixation); duplication of features appeared to be necessary for the latter, but if allowed in the former case, seemed to undermine the prohibition on crossing of association lines and to make false empirical predictions. We have seen, however, that free duplication of features can be allowed in all cases. If we assume association and spreading rules based on the schema in (102c) and the filter on representations, the DFF, we can rule out all unwanted cases of duplication. In fact, most cases of multiple projections of features are excluded.

The principles in (102) are those in which the present framework differs from others that have been proposed. Specifically, they are also those which form the universal core of autosegmental representation. That is, although particular languages can set parameters differently, all languages must set those parameters—they must specify how features are projected, how independent tiers are associated, whether or not there is spreading, and if so, in what direction. We will see in the chapters that follow that autosegmental analyses of mutation, harmony, and tone also frequently make use of two sorts of language-particular rules:

Delinking Rules: McCarthy (1979, 1981), Pulleyblank (1983), Laughren (1980), and others have shown that it is sometimes necessary to posit rules which break an association line already created by regular association or spreading rules. We will also have occasion to make use of such rules below.

Shift Rules: Autosegmental analyses of tonal systems have made use of a second sort of language-particular rule as well, one in which a tone melody associated with one syllable (or sequence of syllables) is shifted to another syllable (or sequence of syllables). Above we have already seen one example of this sort of rule, Kikuyu Tone Shift (Clements and Ford 1979, Clements 1984), and we will see further examples in Chapter 4.

The only other theoretical assumption I will make here is that there is, in addition to the universal principles and language-particular rules mentioned above, some sort of perhaps universal default mechanism which fills in unmarked distinctive features on segments which have remained unspecified for some feature or features after the operation of all other autosegmental rules and principles. Several recent tone analyses (Clark forthcoming, Pulleyblank 1983) argue that, in a language with two tones, segments which remain toneless at the end of a derivation surface with a default L tone. (Pulleyblank also argues that in three-tone languages the default tone is M.) Broselow (1984ms) shows that in Amharic a consonant slot that remains underspecified at the end of the derivation surfaces as a t; she argues that the features of t are supplied by default. The exact mechanics of the default mechanism have yet to be completely worked out and it is beyond the scope of the present work to do so in any great detail.[43] Still, since a good deal of justification for their use exists in current literature, I will also make use of them here. We will see in the following chapters that default values of [voice], [continuant], [nasal], and [ATR] are needed in mutation and harmony analyses.

The theory I have begun to develop in this chapter is neither a phonological theory nor a morphological one. Rather, it is a theory of distinctive feature representations and their interpretation. It allows me to make a further point as well. Given the theory of autosegmental representations that I have begun to develop here, I can begin to break down what have always appeared to be different processes and different phenomena into similar component parts. Thus we saw in section 1.6 that infixation, neutral segments in harmony systems, Fula invariant nouns, and Akan reduplication all shared a component of prespecification in their analyses. In other words, it is possible to begin to argue here that the traditional names for these phenomena have misled us into believing that they **are** different phenomena; disparate names suggest disparate problems and disparate solutions. It is my contention that the traditional labels *harmony, tone, mutation, reduplication, infixation*, and so on obscure pervasive similarities among these phenomena, and that a correctly and explicitly articulated autosegmental theory will give us a way of revealing them. The next three chapters will be devoted to a more extensive proof of this point.

The major goal of each of the following chapters, however, will be to show that for particular phenomena like mutation, harmony, and tone, we require no formalism but the autosegmental formalism developed here. I will argue for each of these phenomena that the present autosegmental framework, with its theory of precedence for duplicated features, its parameterized association and spreading rules, and its means of representing lexical idiosyncrasy, affords substantially simpler and more explanatory analyses than other formalisms (segmental or metrical) or other autosegmental frameworks.

NOTES: CHAPTER 1

1. Other configurations are, of course, possible if spreading does not occur.

2. Other languages in which tone constitutes a morpheme are the following. In Etsako (Elimelech 1976, cited in Schuh 1978), the present progressive negative is distinguished from the present progressive by the tone pattern on the subject pronoun—HL in the former, L in the latter. In Ngizim, the perfective aspect is signaled by a LH contour. In Dschang Bamileke, the associative marker is a tone, H or L, depending upon the class of the first noun in the construction (Tadadjeu 1974, cited in Schuh 1978).

3. This analysis is in many respects similar to that of Clements and Ford (1979).

4. Yip (1980) is an exception here. Yip argues that there are two tonal tiers, but that different features appear on each tier. The sort of proposal that has not, to my knowledge, been made is one in which the same tone features are projected on different tiers.

5. Here I am presenting the argument against free duplication of features in a somewhat simplified form, namely: mutations are local, but a theory with free duplication of features cannot predict this fact. In fact, as we will see in chapter 2, the argument will need to be given in a more sophisticated form and a number of assumptions of the present analysis will need to be spelled out. There does appear to be a very limited sort of nonlocal process which still might be called a "mutation" (it is not, however,like the one in [21]). If so, nonlocal mutations should be permitted, but they should also be counted as highly marked phenomena. Local mutations should be much more highly valued by the theory. Again, a theory with **no** restrictions on the duplication of features will not be able to predict the markedness of nonlocal mutations.

6. I will revise this definition in chapter 2.

7. Class membership in Fula is also signaled by suffix. Suffixes as well as stems participate in the consonant gradation system: that is, they display nearly the same array of initial mutations that stems do. See Skousen (1972), Anderson (1976), and Lieber (1984a) for a discussion of the facts, and the last-mentioned for an analysis of the suffixes within the autosegmental framework.

8. There are a number of assumptions implicit in this analysis that will be spelled out in chapter 2.

9. Although certain features—for an example, [voice], [sonorant], [continuant], and [nasal]—that are necessary to distinguish consonants from one another are predictable for the vowels (in the sense that they could be filled in by redundancy rules at a late stage in the derivation), and others —for example, [anterior] and [coronal]—are not necessary for distinguishing the vowels, nevertheless, some features—[high], [back], perhaps [round]—must be duplicated on both melody tiers.

10. A reanalysis of this case of infixation will be proposed in section 1.6.4.1.

11. Pulleyblank (1983) suggests something like this filter as a way of ruling out Halle and Vergnaud's (1982) analysis of Tonga, in which the default tone, L, is underlyingly present on the melody of all vowels and surfaces only if the vowel is not otherwise provided with a tonal autosegment in the course of the derivation. Pulleyblank makes no attempt to show how this constraint on feature representations works, however, or to work out its ramifications for autosegmental theory.

12. I am grateful to Gilles and Betty LeCompagnon for the Ge-De data.

13. A similar argument can be made for English, in which there exist play languages which demand a multitiered analysis, even though English lacks the sort of phonological or morphological processes which provide overt evidence for multiple tiers. The language Alfalfalal to be described below (1.6.4.2) is an example.

14. For other proposals concerning the internal structure of the melody, see Clements 1985 and Halle 1986. Clements (1985), for example, proposes a laryngeal tier and a supralaryngeal tier in addition to the place and manner tiers.

15. I am suppressing the melody in order to make these representations easier to read.

16. We will see below (1.4.1) that in lexical entries separate tiers are normally unlinked.

17. Such an assumption has been implicit in earlier works as well, for example, in Halle and Vergnaud (1981) and Marantz (1982).

18. The subject of underspecification of course deserves a much more detailed discussion than I am providing here. See Archangeli (1984) for a recent treatment of the topic.

19. I will work out my own version of these rules in the sections that follow.

20. If we abandoned the Obligatory Contour Principle (Leben 1978), there would, of course, be more possible representations.

21. It does appear that right-to-left initial association is rarer than left-to-right association. And as Goldsmith (1976) and others have pointed out, it appears that there are no languages with contour tones only on initial syllables corresponding to the languages with contour tones only on final syllables. One possible explanation of this asymmetry might be the following. As Marantz (1982) shows for reduplication, association in suffixes generally proceeds from the outside in, that is, from right to left. Let us say that right-to-left association (and spreading) is allowed, but it is considered marked except in the case of suffixation. The tones in the Japanese system described above, as well as the Coatzospan Mixtec second person singular suffix, could be counted as suffixes. Under this story, we would not expect languages with contour tones only in initial syllables. In languages like Mende, in which each stem consists of melody, skeleton, and tone tiers, that is, where the tone melody is **not** suffixal, the expected association would be left to right.

The above suggests that perhaps the schema in (42) should not be construed as a schema for language-particular rules, but rather as a universal schema in which certain settings count as default or unmarked settings. Thus, the expected direction of association would be left to right except in suffixal material, tones would be expected to attach to vowels, and so on.

22. Hyman (1985) presents another sort of proposal. He chooses to eliminate the skeleton entirely and to replace it with an X tier. But unlike the X-skeleton proposals to be discussed immediately below, Hyman's Xs stand for weight units (roughly, moras) and not for empty timing sequence slots (roughly, segments). Hyman is primarily concerned with the nature of the syllable and whether syllables per se are needed universally; he is less concerned with the sorts of processes in which the skeleton seems to be of primary importance, namely, processes of reduplication in which a portion of the skeleton appears to be a morpheme (Marantz 1982) or root and pattern processes in which again the skeleton seems to have morphological status. Hyman does suggest that the feature [consonantal] may be prelinked to WUs (weight units = Xs) to give the equivalent of the skeleton in a language like Arabic, but the proposal is not sketched in sufficient detail to be directly comparable to the other proposals discussed here.

Another treatment of the skeleton can be found in Kaye and Lowenstamm (1984), where use is made not only of timing slots (represented as dots, rather than as Xs), but also of lexically specified syllable structure and the major class features [vocalic] and [consonantal]. It is beyond the scope of this work to give a full critique of this proposal. It will suffice here to point out that

Kaye and Lowenstamm's proposal is theoretically quite rich, and also that it requires a use of the features [consonantal] and [vocalic] which separates vowels into two classes (high vowels are classed as [+cons] and nonhigh vowels as [-cons])—that is, within this proposal, there is no way of treating vowels as a natural class apart from other segments.

23. A question that is raised by this proposal is why the remaining major class feature [consonantal] is allowed to remain. Presumably Levin and Yip retain it because they need some way of distinguishing "vocalic" melody segments from "consonantal" ones. I will argue shortly, however, that there is an alternative, a way of determining from place features alone which melody segments are "consonantal" and which "vocalic." If this alternative turns out to be an acceptable one, then we arrive at an even more radical X-skeleton theory, one which has eliminated all major class features. And the issue becomes even clearer: is the major class of a segment (consonant, vowel, glide, syllabic consonant) purely a function of its position in the syllable structure or does it at least partially inhere in the nature of the segment itself?

24. Or perhaps [vocalic] rather than [syllabic.]

25. Ideally, given the correct theory of syllable structure (or of phonological weight—see Hyman [1985]), we may be able to do without the feature [syllabic]. Formulating a theory of syllable structure which allows all the necessary distinctions with a minimum of redundancy is beyond the scope of the present work, however. Until such a theory emerges, I have chosen to make use of [syllabic].

26. I am assuming that some independent set of markedness conventions will count syllabic consonants as more highly marked than nonsyllabic consonants.

27. Clark (1982) has argued that the verbal system of Igbo is accentual. The melody HL is added to accented verb forms with the L tone attaching to the accented vowel, in this example, **u**.

28. McCarthy (1982) gives what seems to be another example of a consonantal melody attaching to a V in his analysis of broken plural formation in Classical Arabic. McCarthy suggests that in forming such broken plurals, a medial consonant spreads to the preceding V and the vocalic melody dissociates:

The V slot changes to a C after this spreading. McCarthy rules out an alternative in which the second V slot is first changed to C, because in his framework, association lines can only spread from left to right—in the example above, this would give the wrong result, ***kuktab**. However, since right-to-left spreading is available within the present framework, McCarthy's alternative is not automatically ruled out for us. It is therefore possible that Classical Arabic broken plurals do not constitute another case of a consonantal melody spreading to a V slot.

29. Clements (1982) provides no explicit discussion of the derivation illustrated in (69). In Clements (in press), a more complete explanation of consonant gemination in LuGanda is provided within the general framework of Clements and Keyser (1983). There consonant gemination occurs when, as a result of the deletion of a preceding vocalic segment, a consonant spreads to a V slot. The example in (69) is one instance. Another instance occurs in the case of the class 5 nominal prefix **li-** (**ly-**), which is deleted before nongeminate obstruents. Clements (in press, 34) states the rule as follows:

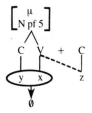

e.g., li + kubo → kkubo 'path'

Recall that in the framework of Clements and Keyser (1983) V stands for "syllable peak." A rule of phonetic interpretation counts a consonantal melody matrix attached to V as a consonant.

30. (57), of course, leaves the directional parameter open. Since this is meant to be a particular instantiation of (57), I have chosen the left-to-right direction.

31. In other words, association rules will only have visible to them the features on the tiers which they are supposed to link. If there are two [round] tiers and a rule associating [round] to [+ syl], the rule will "see" the tier with [+ syl], but will not see that it is about to attach two [round] features to the same [+ syl] segment. From the perspective of one [round] tier, the rule will therefore be unable to see the other [round] tier. But if [round] is lexically prespecified on the [syl] tier, or is already linked to that tier by lexical association, it will be visible to the association rule.

32. Marantz terms this sort of idiosyncrasy "preattachment" and represents **sise?** as follows:

I am calling this "prespecification" and representing it as in (81) because [high] appears outside of the melody where it is normally projected in Akan.

In addition, because Marantz (1982) has no generally articulated theory of the precedence of duplicated features, he requires a special condition for determining which [high] feature wins out (1982, 446):

> Condition C: The slots in a C-V skeleton may be preattached to distinctive features. These features take precedence over the features of any phonemes from a phonemic melody which may link to these slots.

Given the general assumption made above about the operation of the DFF, we may dispense with this special condition here.

33. This analysis presupposes that the association rules can in fact jettison a single feature of the melody when only that one feature is prespecified. I am not sure if the mechanics of this operation pose any special difficulty for the theory.

34. We must assume, as Poser does, that a rule follows spreading which voices the second part of the prenasalized stop.

35. Once again, the difficulties of fitting a three-dimensional representation into two dimensions prevents us from illustrating this example accurately. Technically, in (90c) the [+ back] feature should not be attached across the board to the melody tier, but rather should be attached to the V slots of the skeleton and to the [-ant, -cor] melody segments. The same difficulty exists in representing (91b).

36. Hart (1981) proposed a similar idea, but within a somewhat different autosegmental theory. See also Hyman (1985) for a similar proposal concerning neutral segments, again within a rather different framework.

37. It might be objected that allowing neutral segments to be treated in this way, and indeed allowing any sort of prespecification, undermines the prohibition on crossing of association lines. In a representation like (i), the $[+F_i]$ feature on the harmony tier can both precede and follow the prespecified $[F_i]$:

(i)

$$[+F_i]$$

C V C V C V

$$\left[-F_i \right]$$

But allowing this sort of representation does not truly undermine the prohibition on crossing association lines. This prohibition is important primarily because it eliminates indeterminacy in association. Given a representation like (ii), there is only one way to associate the tiers (assuming $[F_i]$ attaches to V slots) if we accept the prohibition on crossing association lines:

(ii) $[+F_i]$ $[-F_i]$ $[+F_i]$ $[-F_i]$

                               \ |

   C V C V   →   C V C V

Given representations like (iii) and without the DFF, the prohibition would truly be undermined because any association of tiers would be legitimate:

(iii) $[+F_i]$ $[+F_i]$ $[+F_i]$ $[+F_i]$

                        |

   C V C V   →   C V C V   OR   C V C V   →   C V C V

    $[-F_i]$ $[-F_i]$ $[-F_i]$ $[-F_i]$

Assuming the DFF and the simultaneous operation of all association rules, representations like (iii) would be disallowed in the present theory, however. Now, if we allow prespecification in cases of lexical idiosyncrasy and again assume the DFF, no indeterminacy in the operation of the association rules will result. Given the representation in (iv), there is only one possible means of association, namely, the linking illustrated in (i).

(iv) $[+F_i]$

   C V C V C V

        $\left[-F_i \right]$

Note in any case that prespecification is a marked phenomenon in the present theory.

38. It also occurs in Binyan VIII, where McCarthy uses a Flop rule. This can be treated easily in the present framework as well.

39. To put the same point in a slightly different way, the present theory forces us to choose representation (95b) over (95a). The choice between the two is **not** left open.

40. Note that there are infixed forms, for example, the XIIIth Binyan form **ktawwab**, which has **w** infixed to the third and fourth C slots, for which either the prespecified (ii) or the lexically linked representation (i) would work:

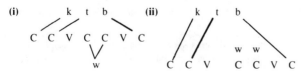

In other words, since the derivation of this form does not involve Erasure, reassociation, and the subsequent violation of the DFF as the example of **ktawtab** in (96) does, the theory could not choose between the two possible representations on the basis of **ktawwab**. The point, however, is that the form **ktawtab** does choose between the two types of lexical idiosyncrasy; it must be treated as in (96b). The infix in **ktawwab** and the other Arabic infixes will be represented for the sake of consistency as features prespecified on the skeleton. Note also that it is no more than a slight complication that the two skeleton slots will have to be prespecified with the features for **w** in **ktawwab**. We need to allow prespecification of two slots in any case for Binyan XV, which has an **n** specified for the third C slot and a **y** for the last.

41. I am not sure what the origins of the play language Alfalfalal are. I heard it first at a concert by the New Hampshire folk singers the Shaw Brothers in August, 1982, and have since tried to find out if it is a part of a local tradition. As far as I know, it is not, at least in southern New Hampshire. I have, however, come across a native speaker who learned the game as a child in Oklahoma. Data is from a recording of the Shaw Brothers' concert.

42. Broselow (1983) discusses another logically possible configuration for infixation, namely, one in which the infix consists only of skeleton slots—that is, insertion without prespecification. The example comes from an infixing reduplication process in the Salish languages Thompson and Shuswap.

43. See, however, Archangeli (1984) for a treatment of the default mechanism within a rather strict theory of underspecification.

Chapter 2

MUTATION

In this chapter I will examine a number of phenomena that have been called, variously, "mutations," "umlauts," and "consonant gradations." In my brief discussion of Fula in section 1.2, I began by defining mutation as "a morphological phenomenon in which lexical stems exhibit two or more allomorphs that differ only in their initial, or less frequently final, consonants and appear in distinct morphological environments." Actually, this definition is much too narrow. Some of these processes—those called "umlauts"—obviously refer to vowel alternations, and others are not really morphological at all, as we will see below. Perhaps a better definition of mutation would be the following (for convenience, I will refer to all of these processes as mutations): mutations are phenomena in which lexical stems exhibit two or more allomorphs that differ only in a single marginal segment (for example, an initial or final C or a vowel closest to either end of the word) and which appear in distinct morphological, syntactic, or phonological environments.

I have two reasons for looking closely at mutations here. First, they are among the most widely ignored phenomena in the generative literature. Although scattered analyses exist (umlaut in German and Fula consonant gradation, for example, have received some attention in the past), different mutations have never been carefully compared to one another. In fact, some of these mutation phenomena seem so bizarre and irregular as to defy serious comparisons. Second, where they have been analyzed at all within generative literature, they have been treated in at least three different ways: with redundancy rules, with segmental phonological or morphophonological rules, and more recently with autosegmental mechanisms. Here I will argue that all mutations and related phenomena—whether they affect consonants or vowels, whether they are purely morphological or not—can and should be analyzed as autosegmental processes. We will see that the present autosegmental framework both allows for the existing variations in mutation processes and also reveals their underlying similarities, and in addition makes correct predictions about the range of mutation phenomena that could exist in natural languages. Specifically, we will see that the present framework predicts two things: (i) that mutations ought to be local (in a sense to be made precise below) except in one sort of highly marked case, and (ii) that there are certain sorts of mutations that cannot occur.

This chapter will be organized as follows. Since mutations are among the least familiar of linguistic phenomena, I will start in section 2.1 with analyses of three typical cases: the consonant mutations of Fula, Nuer, and Chemehuevi. Here we will see how the present framework treats mutations. Section 2.2 will discuss the issue of locality. I will then present two reasons for preferring the autosegmental treatment of mutation to available segmental analyses. In section 2.3 I will argue that an autosegmental analysis of Umlaut in modern German eliminates two sorts of arbitrariness that occur in a typical segmental analysis of Umlaut (Lieber 1980). In section 2.4 I will show one of the benefits afforded by the device of prespecification and the general theory of precedence of features developed in chapter 1; by making use of this feature of our theory, we will not only be able to account neatly for the phonetically bizarre mutations that occur in Mende and Welsh, but we will also be able to predict what sorts of bizarre and phonetically irregular mutations could not occur in any language. We will see that this prediction is not available within any segmental analysis. Finally, in section 2.5 I will show that the apparently nonmorphological mutations of Mende and Chamorro are not in principle a problem for the autosegmental framework developed here, contrary to the claims of Rice and Cowper (1984).[1] Once again, we will see that since the present framework is neither a theory of phonology nor a theory of morphology but rather a theory of distinctive feature representations, there is no reason to expect that all mutation phenomena should be purely morphological.

2.1 CENTRAL CASES

Let us call "central cases" of mutation those cases that involve alternations of initial or final consonants in distinct morphological environments. Three cases— Fula, Nuer, and Chemehuevi—will be sufficient to show how these typical mutations work within the present framework. I will first present analyses of these three languages, and then in section 2.1.4 will discuss general characteristics of the analysis of mutation made available within the present theory.

2.1.1 Fula

The class system of Fula is actually somewhat more intricate than the sketchy picture given in section 1.2 suggests. As mentioned there, noun stems in Fula generally exhibit different allomorphs depending on the noun classes into which they fall. Noun stems which exhibit mutations generally display one of the series of variations illustrated in (1) (all Fula data from Arnott 1970).[2]

(1)		Labial		Alveolar		Palatal		Velar/glottal	
Continuant	w	f	r	s	y		y	w	h
Stop	b	p	d	sh	j		g	g	k
Prenasalized stop	mb	p	nd	sh	nj		ŋg	ŋg	k

Most stems beginning with voiced segments will have all three allomorphs; those beginning with voiceless segments exhibit nonnasalized stops where their voiced counterparts exhibit prenasalized ones. I will return to this pattern later.

Also mentioned in section 1.2 was the fact that Fula nouns can belong to up to seven out of a total of twenty-five noun classes; the seven typically include a singular form, a plural form, a diminutive and augmentative in both singular and plural, and a pejorative diminutive. Class membership is actually manifested on nouns in two ways: initial consonant mutations and characteristic suffixes. Elsewhere (Lieber 1983b, 1984a)[3] I have dealt with both the distribution of Fula class suffixes and with their participation in the consonant mutation system. Here I will concentrate on the initial mutations. (2) lists all of the possible noun classes and the mutation form that characteristically shows up there, with C standing for "continuant initial," S for "stop initial," and N for "prenasalized stop initial."[4]

(2) Class	1 S	6 N	11 C	16 S	21 S
	2 C	7 N	12 N	17 S	22 N
	3 S	8 N	13 C	18 N	23 S
	4 S	9 C	14 C	19 S	24 S
	5 S	10 N	15 N	20 C	25 S

(3) illustrates some typical Fula noun paradigms:

(3) a. VARIABLE		b. INVARIANT		c. PARTIALLY VARIABLE	
waa		beebe		bukka	
'monkey'		'deaf-mute'		'shelter'	
11	waa-ndu	1	beebee-jo	9	bukkaa-ru
25	baa-ɗi	2	beebe-'en	24	bukkaa-ji
3	baa-ŋgel	3	beebe-yel	3	bukka-yel
5	baa-ŋgum	5	beebe-yum	5	bukka-yum
6	mbaa-kon	6	beebe-hon	6	mbukka-hon
7	mbaa-ŋga	7	beebe-wa	7	mbukka-wa
8	mbaa-ko	8	beebe-ho	8	mbukka-ho

The paradigm in (3a) is typical of the majority of nouns in Fula, namely, those whose stems alternate. It might therefore be called a "variable" paradigm. But

Fula also has some nouns whose stems remain invariant regardless of the noun class in which they appear. Stems beginning with **t**, **l**, **m**, **n**, **ny**, **ɓ**, **ɗ**, **'y**, and **'** in fact never alternate, but as (3b) illustrates, normally alternating consonants remain invariant in a few stems. Finally, (3c) illustrates that there are some nouns which exhibit only partial alternations. These stems exhibit the stop-initial variant in both stop-initial and continuant-initial classes. The prenasalized allomorph appears where expected. Other patterns of partial alternation never occur.

As sketched in section 1.2, Fula nouns will generally be represented as the linking of a noun class prefix to a noun stem morpheme. The features [continuant] and [nasal] will in general be projected on an independent tier, which we will call the "mutation tier" (see section 2.1.4 for a general justification of this move). The noun class prefixes will consist solely of the features [continuant] and [nasal] as illustrated in (4):[5]

(4) a. Class prefix for classes 2, 9, 11, 13, 14, 20

$$\begin{bmatrix} +\,\text{cont} \\ -\,\text{nas} \end{bmatrix}$$

b. Class prefix for classes 1, 3, 4, 5, 16, 17, 19, 21, 23, 24, 25

$$\begin{bmatrix} -\,\text{cont} \\ -\,\text{nas} \end{bmatrix}$$

c. Class prefix for classes 6, 7, 8, 10, 12, 15, 18, 22

$$[+\,\text{nas}] \quad [-\,\text{nas}]$$
$$[-\,\text{cont}]$$

(4a) contains the manner features for continuants, (4b) those for stops, and (4c) those for prenasalized stops. In (4c) I have represented a prenasalized stop as a sequence of nasal features attached to the same [cont] segment.

The typically variable noun stems in Fula will be represented in the lexicon as morphemes which are underspecified on their initial segment for the manner features [continuant] and [nasal]. As illustrated in section 1.2, the noun stem for 'monkey' will be as in (5):

(5)

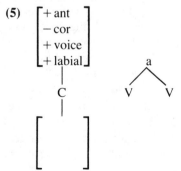

In its lexical entry this noun stem will have a listing of the classes it belongs to, since this information is almost completely arbitrary.[6]

Noun formation in Fula will consist of the prefixation of one of the class morphemes to a noun stem which selects it, as illustrated in (6):

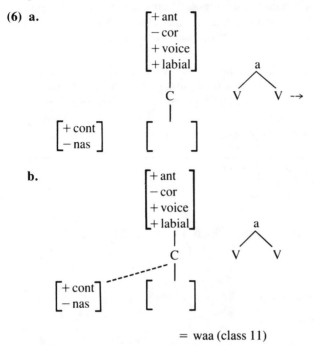

(6) a.

b.

= waa (class 11)

Assuming that Fula has an association rule which attaches [continuant, nasal] to [-syl] one to one, left to right, (6b) will be produced from (6a). I am assuming as well that the class prefix in (4c) with the sequential specification for [nasal] will attach in the same way that the other two class prefixes will.

This brief analysis of course accounts for only the fully variable Fula paradigms like the one in (3a). The invariant and partially variant paradigms can also be accounted for simply by making use of the device of prespecification. The derivation of completely invariant nouns like **beebe** was discussed in section 1.6.1, where it was shown that such nouns are already prespecified for the features [continuant] and [nasal] in the lexicon, rather than being underspecified. The normal class morphemes are then blocked from associating to such stems by the DFF. Partially variable nouns like the one in (3c) are rare, but they can also be handled easily within the present framework. In cases like (3c), nouns exhibit stop-initial forms in both continuant and stop-initial classes, but prenasalized stop-initial forms in those classes which normally begin with prenasalized stops. We can account for these nouns by saying that the stem has a prespecified [− continuant] feature but is normally underspecified for the feature [nasal]. When attachment of the prefix features occurs, then, the prefix supplies only the missing value for [nasal]. The value of [continuant] on the prefix is ignored in favor of that prespecified on the stem.

In fact, the notion of prespecification, together with a single observation about Fula phonetics, allows us to give a fairly restrictive characterization of the range of noun paradigms that should be possible in Fula. The relevant phonetic fact is that Fula allows no nasal or prenasalized continuants. We might therefore assume that Fula has some sort of redundancy rule like (7), which states that all [+ continuant] segments are [− nasal] and, conversely, that all [+ nasal] segments are [− continuant]:

(7) [+ cont]   -→   [− nasal]   ;   [+ nasal]   -→   [− cont]

If this is the case, then only a limited number of possible paradigms can occur in Fula, and these are listed in (8):

(8) a. If neither [continuant] nor [nasal] is prespecified, the paradigm will be fully variable, as in (3a).
b. If both [continuant] and [nasal] are prespecified, the resulting paradigm will be invariant, as in (3b).
c. If [− continuant] is prespecified, the partially variable paradigm in (3c) will result.
d. If [+ continuant] is prespecified, [− nasal] will automatically be supplied by the redundancy rule in (7). In other words, this case will be nondistinct from that in (8b).
e. If [+ nasal] is prespecified, [− continuant] will automatically be supplied by the redundancy rule in (7). Again, the result will be nondistinct from that in (8b).
f. If [− nasal] is prespecified, continuant-initial stems will occur in continuant-initial classes and stop-initial stems in both stop and prenasalized stop-initial classes.

Of these we have seen that cases (8a–c) exist,[7] and that (8d) and (8e) turn out to be indistinguishable from purely invariant nouns. The only predicted paradigm that we have not yet encountered is the one described in (8f). This possibility is in fact instantiated by the paradigm in (9):

(9) hufinee
      'cap'

9	hufinee-re
24	kufine-je
3	kufine-yel
5	kufine-yum
6	kufine-hon
7	kufine-wa
8	kufine-ho

In fact, as the chart in (1) indicates, **all** voiceless continuants which alternate in Fula lack prenasalized stop variants. We can express this fact by saying that all [− voice] segments in Fula are redundantly specified [− nasal]. It is, however, somewhat problematic for this analysis that no nouns with initial voiced consonants appear to be prespecified for [− nasal]; that is, there are no paradigms which have, for example, **w** in continuant classes and **b** in both stop and prenasalized stop-initial classes. But this is the **only** predicted paradigm that does not appear to exist. All of the paradigms that do apear in Fula are predicted by this analysis, and all other predicted paradigms occur; the fit between data and analysis is therefore fairly tight.[8]

Fula constitutes what I would call a central case of mutation, for two reasons. First, the mutation features of Fula can easily be identified and isolated. All the initial variations in Fula consonants concern continuancy and nasality, and they can easily be represented as a floating autosegment consisting of different values of [continuant] and [nasal]. Second, Fula is perhaps a classic example of morphological mutation. In fact, the mutation features are themselves morphemes in this case. The class prefixes in (4) are clearly the sort of item which belong in the lexicon with a lexical entry. The next case of mutation I will illustrate also qualifies as a classic case, but it is a case of final rather than initial mutation, and it illustrates another way in which mutation can be a purely morphological phenomenon.

2.1.2 Nuer

The consonant mutation system of Nuer, a Nilo-Saharan language, is very much like that of Fula, except that, as mentioned above, mutations in Nuer are final rather than initial.[9] Final consonants in Nuer display the following alternations:

(10)	Labial	Interdental	Alveolar	Palatal	Velar
Voiced	b	dh	d	y	γ
Voiceless continuant	f	th	ţ	ç	h
Voiceless stop	p	ţ	t	c	k

The transcription system in (10), which is Crazzolara's (1933), obviously needs some interpretation. **dh** and **th** are the interdental continuants [ð] and [θ], respectively. ţ is an interdental stop, and ţ a trilled alveolar continuant. According to Crazzolara, stems in Nuer can have up to three forms, one ending with a voiceless stop, one with a voiceless continuant, and the third with a voiced sound, which in most cases is a continuant. Crazzolara gives no clue that what he transcribes as **d** is anything but the noncontinuant [d], but he does suggest that what he writes as **b** is actually the continuant [β] in final position: "Of the **Bilabials** . . . b, f, p, the rare p is not very difficult to perceive . . . but whether a **b** or a **f** is pronounced is often hard to say" (1933, 6). In other words, it is possible that the distinction of which Crazzolara speaks is hard to discern because both sounds are continuant. If so, then only **d** is exceptional in the above consonant series.

Where final mutation occurs in the noun paradigms, it is more or less lexically idiosyncratic; some nouns mutate final consonants in the genitive or plural, others not. And where final mutation does occur in noun forms, it is not predictable which of the allomorphs (voiced, voiceless continuant, or voiceless stop final) will occur in which form. However, final mutation does seem to be regularly associated with various tenses and aspects in the verbal paradigms. Voiced consonant-final allomorphs occur in the singular present indicative active and the proper form of the noun agent. In the plural present indicative active, the indicative present passive, the past participle, and the imperative, the voiceless continuant-final allomorph occurs. Finally, the negative form of the present participle is signaled by the allomorph ending in a voiceless stop. (11) contains three partial paradigms illustrating the distribution of allomorphs (some of the verb stems also undergo vowel ablaut in certain forms, but I will have nothing to say about that here):

(11)

	'to overtake a person'	'to hit'	'to suck'
3rd sg. ind. pres. act.	cóbéjɛ	jaayὲ jὲ	lodhὲ jὲ
1st pl. ind. pres. act.	còɔfkɔ jɛ	jaçkɔ jɛ	loɔthkɔ jὲ
Pres. pple. neg.	còp	jaac	loṭ
Past pple.	cof	jaaç	loth

	'to sharpen'	'to throw away'
3rd sg. ind. pres. act.	paádὲ jɛ́	yá́ɣɛ́ jɛ́
1st pl. ind. pres. act.	páaṭkɔ́ jɛ	yὰkɔ jɛ
Pres. pple. neg.	paat	yäk
Past pple.	pàaṭ	yäh

Let us assume that in Nuer the features [voice] and [continuant] are projected on an independent tier. Nuer verbs, like Fula nouns, will consist of at least two morphemes, one a verb stem whose final consonant will be underspecified for the features [voice] and [continuant], and the other a tense marker, which will sometimes consist **only** of the features [voice] and [continuant], and sometimes of one or more fully specified segments in addition to the [voice] and [continuant] autosegments. The verb stems are illustrated in (12) and the tense markers in (13). For ease of representation, I have substituted the standard phonetic symbols for feature bundles except in the case of final consonants.

(12) a.

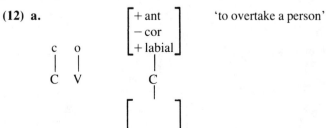

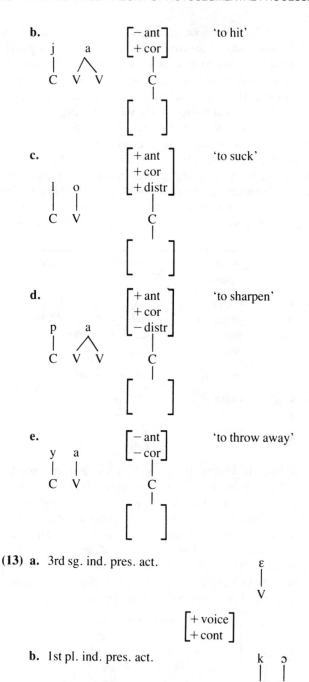

b.

$$\begin{bmatrix} -\text{ant} \\ +\text{cor} \end{bmatrix}$$ 'to hit'

c.

$$\begin{bmatrix} +\text{ant} \\ +\text{cor} \\ +\text{distr} \end{bmatrix}$$ 'to suck'

d.

$$\begin{bmatrix} +\text{ant} \\ +\text{cor} \\ -\text{distr} \end{bmatrix}$$ 'to sharpen'

e.

$$\begin{bmatrix} -\text{ant} \\ -\text{cor} \end{bmatrix}$$ 'to throw away'

(13) a. 3rd sg. ind. pres. act.

$$\begin{bmatrix} +\text{voice} \\ +\text{cont} \end{bmatrix}$$

b. 1st pl. ind. pres. act.

$$\begin{bmatrix} -\text{voice} \\ +\text{cont} \end{bmatrix}$$

c. Pres. pple. neg. $\begin{bmatrix} -\text{voice} \\ -\text{cont} \end{bmatrix}$

d. Past pple. $\begin{bmatrix} -\text{voice} \\ +\text{cont} \end{bmatrix}$

The derivations of these verb paradigms will be as follows. The morphemes in (13c) and (13d) will suffix to the verb stem and will fill in the features missing on the final consonant of the stem by associating with it. (14) illustrates the derivation of the present participle negative of the verb 'to hit':

(14)

In other words, for the present participle negative and the past participle at least, the floating autosegments are themselves morphemes, just like the class markers in Fula. The only difference between the two cases is that these are suffixes, whereas the autosegments in Fula were prefixes.

The other two morphemes in (13), (13a) and (13b), illustrate a slightly different, although still central, form that mutation takes. In these two cases, the mutation features are not morphemes in their own right, but are part of morphemes. In other words, the third singular indicative present active suffix and the first plural indicative present active suffix each consist of at least one complete segment in addition to the floating autosegment. The derivations for these forms are just as straightforward, however, as those for the participles were, as (15) illustrates:

(15)

This time the floating autosegment links to the left, filling in the underspecified features on the final consonant of the stem.

The verbs in (11) are fully variable verbs in Nuer. All three possible allomorphs appear. Like Fula, however, Nuer has a number of consonants which never take part in the mutation system, namely, **l, m, n, nh** (an interdental nasal), **ŋ, ny** (a palatal nasal), **r**, and **w**. To account for the invariance of these consonants, we will need to say that all [+ nasal] segments are redundantly specified [+ voice] and [− continuant], and all other sonorants except **y** [+ voice] and [+ continuant]. In terms of the autosegmental analysis of mutation, these features are prespecified on the final consonant of the verb stems ending with the above-listed consonants and will override the features provided by the regular mutation autosegments.

We might also expect Nuer to be like Fula in exhibiting invariant or partially variable verb paradigms—that is, paradigms in which a final consonant which normally alternates in regular verbs, in a few verbs does not alternate at all or does not alternate completely. Crazzolara (1933) in fact does cite a number of paradigms in which the expected alternations fail to occur:

(16)

	'to sing'	'to send'
3rd sg. ind. pres. act.	kíiṭɛ	jähɛ jɛ
1st pl. ind. pres. act.	kíieṭkɔ	jáko[10]
Pres. pple. neg.	kìiṭ	jä̀h
Past pple.	kìeeṭ	jä̀h

	'to know'	'to be timid'
3rd sg. ind. pres. act.	ŋäçɛ jɛ	lúthɛ̀ jɛ
1st pl. ind. pres. act.	ŋä́çkɔ jɛ	luɔthkɔ̀ jɛ
Pres. pple. neg.	ŋäç	luth
Past pple.	ŋäç	luɔth

Note, however, that the invariant examples in (16) all end with voiceless continuants in all verb forms.[11] We could analyze all these verbs as having the features [− voice, + cont] prespecified on the verb stem, but to do so and say nothing more would be to admit that this fact is an accident. Crazzolara, however, gives some indication that the pattern in (16) is not accidental. All the verbs in (16) are derived from other verb forms by taking the voiceless continuant final form (for example, the past participle) and using that as the base of the new verb form. If, in other words, the verbs in (16) are derived from other verbs by some process of morphological conversion or zero affixation, and if the verb base has already acquired its mutation features, then it no longer seems strange that all invariant verbs end in voiceless continuants.

One final example of mutation in Nuer should suffice to show that mutation can be seen as association of an autosegment to an underspecified stem. As mentioned above, mutation does not appear to distinguish nouns in Nuer with respect to case or number, but it does take place regularly on nouns which are followed by the demonstrative suffixes listed in (17);

(17) Nuer demonstratives (Crazzolara 1933, 73)

Common			Emphatic		
sg.		pl.	sg.	pl.	
− ɛ̀	(mɛ̀)	tì	− ɛ̀mɛ	tìtì	this (attached)
− ɔ̀	(mɔ̀)	tɔ̀	− ɔ̀mɔ	tɛ̀tɔ	this (detached)
− ì	(mì)	tì̈	− ìmi	tìtï	that (local)
− ëë		tëë	mëë	tëë	that (temporal)

The final consonants of nouns to which these demonstratives have been attached appear as voiceless continuants, as (18) illustrates:

(18) lòóc   'peg'   lòóçɔmɔ   'this peg'
lŭk   'tribunal'   lŭhɔ̀   'this tribunal'
dèép   'rope'   dèéfìmi   'that rope'
dí̈ìt   'bird'   dí̈ìt̪ɛ̀mɛ   'this bird'
jit   'ear'   jithɔmɔ   'this ear'

To account for this data, all we need to say, once again, is that the final consonants of the noun stems are underspecified for the features [voice] and [continuant] and that these features are supplied as part of the demonstrative suffixes themselves. (19) illustrates a typical derivation, including the lexical entries for the noun stem and the suffix.

(19) a. Noun stem 'peg'

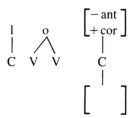

b. Demonstrative suffix: emphatic sg. 'this (detached)'

c.

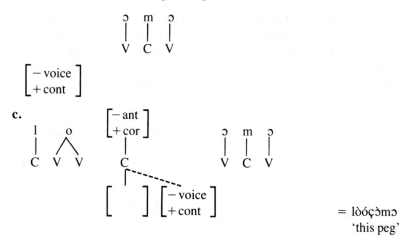

= lòóçɔmɔ
'this peg'

The floating autosegment of the demonstrative associates with the final consonant of the stem to fill in the missing features. If the noun stem remains unaffixed, the final consonant will be supplied with the features [− voice, − cont] by default.

Nuer, like Fula, is a central case of consonant mutation; the mutation features are easily isolable, and they either are morphemes in their own right or appear at the margin of other clearly definable morphemes.

2.1.3 Chemehuevi[12]

One more example will suffice to show how mutation typically works. Chemehuevi, a Shoshonean language closely related to Southern Paiute, exhibits alternations in the initial consonants of morphemes that strongly resemble the mutations we have seen in Fula and Nuer. Morphemes which show up with initial consonants from the stop series in (20) when they occur word initially or in citation form show up with corresponding voiced continuants or nasals when preceded by certain other morphemes.

(20)

Stop series	Voiced continuants	Nasal clusters
p	v	mp
t	r	nt
k	γ	ŋk
kʷ	γʷ	ŋkʷ
c	c (∼nc)	nc
s	s	s
m	w	m
n	n	n
ŋ	ŋ	ŋ

According to Press (1979), the reflexive morpheme **na** typically triggers a voiced continuant on the following morpheme, and the morpheme **ni** (glossed by Press as 'person') typically causes the following morpheme to begin with a nasal cluster. Still other morphemes, for example, **piŋka** 'keep on', have no effect at all on the following morpheme. This fact is illustrated in (21):

(21) a. Spirantizing

/na + punikai/ −→ navunika
reflex see

/na + tɨka/ −→ narɨka
eat

/na + koa/ −→ naγoa
cut

b. Nasalizing

/nɨ + poʔotuʔi/ → nɨmpoʔotuʔi
person teach   teach-intransitive

/nɨ + kuu/ → nɨŋkuu
bury   bury-intransitive

c. No effect

/pɨŋka + punikai/ → pɨŋkapunika
keep on   look

/pɨŋka + tɨka/ → pɨŋkatɨka
eat

As (21c) shows, the spirantizing of word-internal consonants cannot be explained as a purely morphological rule, since the appearance of word-internal intervocalic stops is possible. The data exhibited in (21) can, however, be accounted for easily as a classic case of mutation. Assume first that the features [continuant, voice, nasal] are projected on an independent mutation tier in Chemehuevi. In this analysis, the verb stems 'see', 'eat', 'cut', 'teach', '**bury**', etc., will be represented just as the Fula noun stems were, as morphemes with initial consonants underspecified for the features [continuant], [voice], and [nasal]. The lexical forms of '**see**', '**eat**', and '**bury**' are illustrated in (22). Once again, I substitute phonetic symbols for feature bundles for all but the relevant consonants.

(22) 'see'
$\begin{bmatrix} + \text{ant} \\ - \text{cor} \end{bmatrix}$ u n i k a i

C V C V C V V

[ ]

'eat'
$\begin{bmatrix} + \text{ant} \\ + \text{cor} \end{bmatrix}$ ɨ k a

C V C V

[ ]

'bury'
$\begin{bmatrix} - \text{ant} \\ - \text{cor} \end{bmatrix}$ u

C V V

[ ]

The prefixes in (21a–c) will be represented as in (23):

(23) a. Spirantizing prefixes   n   a

C   V

$$\begin{bmatrix} +\text{voice} \\ +\text{cont} \\ -\text{nas} \end{bmatrix}$$

b. Nasalizing prefixes   n   ɨ

C   V

$$\begin{bmatrix} -\text{cont} \\ +\text{voice} \end{bmatrix}$$

[+nas]   [−nas][13]

c. No effect prefixes   p   ɨ   ŋ   k   a

C   V   C   C   V

Derivations of the Chemehuevi verbs will go as follows. If an underspecified verb stem is concatenated with either a spirantizing or a nasalizing prefix, then the features missing from the verb stem will be provided by the prefix:

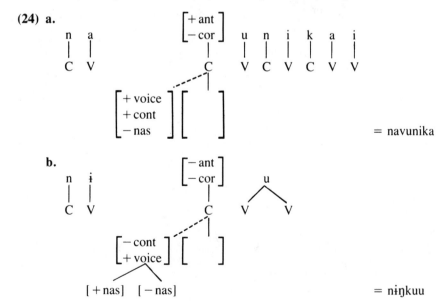

(24) a.

= navunika

b.

= nɨŋkuu

If these verb stems are concatenated with the "no effect" prefix **piŋka** or if the verb stem remains unprefixed, it will remain underspecified for the mutation features. We might assume that these cases are the default cases, and that our default convention fills in the features [−voice, −continuant, −nasal] as the unmarked features. This is shown in (25):

(25)

Chemehuevi, then, can be seen as another classic case of mutation.

2.1.4 General Characteristics of Mutation

Before we go on to look at cases of mutation which deviate from the central cases, I think that it would be worthwhile to extract from the three previous examples the main points of our analysis of mutation and to show why they could not be treated differently within the theory outlined in chapter 1. Remember that this is a theory in which certain parameters must be set for each language —projection of features onto tiers, nature and direction of Initial Association Rules, presence or absence of a Spreading rule (and if present its direction), and so on. Where the analysis of mutation involves setting parameters, I will try to show that all central cases set the parameters the same way, and that the way I have set the parameters is not arbitrary. I will also try to make explicit other assumptions involved in the analysis of mutation and to show that they are the simplest assumptions we can make. In the section which follows, I will try to show how the prediction of locality mentioned above follows from setting the parameters in the necessary way and making the simplest possible assumptions about mutation.

> *PARAMETERS*
> **(i)** Mutation features are projected on their own tier. They are not part of the melody or skeleton.
> **(ii)** Since mutation involves the projection of an autosegmental tier, there must be an Initial Association Rule in each case which attaches the mutation tier (usually) to the skeleton. There are, however, no Spreading rules for this tier in any of the central cases.

OTHER ASSUMPTIONS

(iii) Mutation in the central cases is triggered by floating features which either are or are part of prefixes or suffixes: that is, in central cases, mutation is nothing more than affixation. (We will see a case below where mutation is more like cliticization, however. See section 2.5 on Mende.)

(iv) In all central cases of mutation there is underspecification of an initial (or final) stem segment, but which stem segment, if any, is underspecified does not have to be stipulated within the theory.

Let us begin first with the most basic of all the autosegmental parameters, the projection of features. I have claimed in the analyses of Fula, Nuer, and Chemehuevi and in (i) that mutation features are always projected on a separate autosegmental tier. I will state my reasons for doing so, using Fula as a representative example (remember that in Fula the mutation was based on the features [continuant, nasal]). The same argument could be made for the other central cases as well.

Within the theory set up in chapter 1, either there is a separate projection statement for the features [continuant, nasal] or not. Suppose for a moment that there is no separate projection statement and thus no separate tier for the mutation feature. The features [continuant, nasal] would then have to be a part of the melody tier, along with the other melody features [anterior, coronal, sonorant, voice, distributed, . . .]; in other words, Fula would have only a melody and skeleton tier. In order to get the mutation to work, we would have to say that the melodies of initial consonants of stems were underspecified for the features [continuant, nasal]. But we would also have to say that the mutation prefixes are floating melodies, and that they are underspecified for all features **except** [continuant, nasal]. In other words, although we would have no choice except to call the prefixes "melodies" within this analysis, these "melodies" would invariably have to lack most of the melody features.

There are two problems with this move, besides its obvious inelegance. First, we would have to acknowledge it as accidental that all the prefixes show exactly the same pattern of underspecification; we would have no way of explaining why there are no prefixes which consist of melody features other than [continuant, nasal]. Second, and probably worse, if the prefixes in question lack the feature [anterior], they could actually not get associated to the stem by the melody-skeleton association rule at all, since this rule attaches melody segments with the feature [anterior] to C slots. So this prefixation would require a special rule of a sort not otherwise necessary within our theory.

Thus, not projecting [continuant, nasal] on a separate mutation tier leads to a number of undesirable consequences. It is much simpler to assume that in each language with a mutation there is a separate mutation tier, in other words, that there is a special projection statement separating off the mutation features from the melody. In Fula, of course, T_{mut} would consist of [continuant, nasal]. It would no longer be an accident that all class prefixes consist of these two features.

However, this move does have ramifications which need to be explored. Specifically, if we separate off an independent tier for [continuant, nasal], we do so for all consonants, not just the initial consonants that undergo mutation.

The lexical entry of a hypothetical variable stem **waba** ∼ **baba** ∼ **mbaba** would look like (26):[14]

(26)

$$\begin{bmatrix} +\text{ant} \\ -\text{cor} \\ +\text{voice} \end{bmatrix} \text{a} \quad \begin{bmatrix} +\text{ant} \\ -\text{cor} \\ +\text{voice} \end{bmatrix} \quad \text{a}$$

$$\begin{array}{cccc} \text{C} & \text{V} & \text{C} & \text{V} \\ | & & | & \\ [\quad] & & \begin{bmatrix} -\text{cont} \\ -\text{voice} \end{bmatrix} & \end{array}$$

I know of no negative consequences of representing lexical items in Fula and in other mutation languages this way; still, it might be asked whether the projection of the features [continuant, nasal] plays any role at all for noninitial consonants in Fula. For example, if the mutation tier is entirely independent, we might look to see if it behaves like the tonal tier in tone languages. In many of those languages, if a tone-bearing element is deleted, its tone remains behind and reassociates to a preceding or following tone-bearing unit. The stability of the tone follows from its independence. Unfortunately, mutation languages like Fula, Nuer, and Chemehuevi lack the sort of consonant-deletion processes which might reveal this sort of mutation tier stability.

Still, there is evidence that the mutation tier does play a role, at least in Fula, for consonants other than the initial one, just what we would expect if mutation features were independent. Arnott (1970, 50–51) mentions a number of processes that affect **final** consonants in some nominal stems. Significantly, these processes involve some of the same alternations as those that occur in initial mutations. In some nominal stems, like those in (27a), the final continuants become the corresponding stops when followed by certain vowel-initial suffixes. In other nominal stems which normally end in continuants, gemination occurs along with the change to the corresponding stop when these same suffixes follow. These are shown in (27b):

(27) a. (i) lees-o   'bed'   (ii) leesh-e   'beds'
             laaw-ol   'track'   laab-i   'tracks'

    b. (i) nof-ru   'ear'   nof-el   'little ear'   (ii) nopp-i   'ears'
             fow-ru   'hyena'   pow-el   'little hyena'   pobb-i   'hyenas'

Assuming that the mutation features are projected onto a separate tier for all consonants in Fula, and not just for the initial ones, an analysis of these facts is easily available within the present theory.

The forms in (27a-ii) and (27b-ii) will have the underlying representations in (28a) and (28b), respectively. The geminating stems will be distinguished from the nongeminating ones by having an extra C slot on the skeleton tier in stem-final position (note that **n** and **l** are nonalternating consonants, that is, consonants which have [continuant, nasal] prespecified on the melody tier):

(28) a.

$$
\begin{bmatrix} +\text{ant} \\ +\text{cor} \\ +\text{voice} \\ +\text{son} \\ -\text{nas} \\ +\text{cont} \end{bmatrix} \quad a \qquad \begin{bmatrix} +\text{ant} \\ -\text{cor} \\ +\text{voice} \end{bmatrix} \quad i
$$

$$
C \quad V \quad V \quad \underset{\displaystyle \begin{bmatrix} +\text{cont} \\ -\text{nas} \end{bmatrix}}{\overset{|}{C}} \quad + \quad V
$$

underlying form for **laab + i**

b.

$$
\begin{bmatrix} +\text{ant} \\ +\text{cor} \\ +\text{voice} \\ +\text{nas} \\ -\text{cont} \end{bmatrix} \quad o \qquad \begin{bmatrix} +\text{ant} \\ -\text{cor} \\ -\text{voice} \end{bmatrix} \quad i
$$

$$
C \quad V \quad \underset{\displaystyle \begin{bmatrix} +\text{cont} \\ -\text{nas} \end{bmatrix}}{\overset{|}{C}} \quad C \quad + \quad V
$$

underlying form for **nopp + i**

Let us assume that Fula has two lexically idiosyncratic rules. First, there is a rule which deletes a final [+cont, −nas] segment on lexically marked stems in the presence of lexically marked affixes like the suffix −i. Second, there is a rule which spreads the final melody segment to an unattached C on lexically marked stems in the presence of the same lexically marked suffixes. The first rule will work in both (28a) and (28b), deleting the final [+cont, −nas]. There is no spreading rule for this tier, so at the end of the derivation the default features [−cont, −nas] will be filled in, once for (28a) and twice for (28b). The end result will be stops. In addition, in (28b), the melody features will spread, and the result will be a geminate stop.[15] In a theory which projects the mutation features on an independent tier, we might expect this sort of continuant-stop alternation to occur noninitially. In a theory which does not project the mutation features across the board, the appearance of this same alternation on noninitial consonants would remain a mystery.

Thus there is good evidence that the mutation features constitute an independent tier. But once we have separated off these features onto their own tier, we must also set the parameters for Initial Association and Spreading. It is clear that we need an Initial Association Rule; for every tier in addition to melody and skeleton, there must be a way of attaching that tier to the core. For Fula, we would need an Initial Association Rule attaching [continuant, nasal] to [−syl] one to one, left to right. However, none of the languages discussed so far shows any evidence of spreading along the mutation tier. In the absence of such evidence, they will not have Spreading rules for this tier.

As for the other assumptions I am making in this analysis of mutation, they also appear to be the simplest assumptions possible. Assumption (iii), for example, seems relatively uncontroversial; in the central cases the mutation features are either morphemes in their own right or are part of morphemes which are clearly prefixes or suffixes. Therefore, it seems safe to say that in the general case mutation is nothing more than affixation.

Assumption (iv) is also the simplest possible assumption; if under-specification is not allowed to occur freely on the mutation tier, we must add to the analysis of mutation a special stipulation that only the initial (or final) segment is underspecified. It is, however, not immediately clear that we can do without this stipulation, and I will therefore go into this subject in some detail.

Let me first clarify the issue. Throughout this chapter I have been assuming that regular (that is, variable) lexical stems in Fula look like (5), or more precisely, if all consonants are spelled out in features, like (26). All fully variable stems lack the features [continuant, nasal] on initial consonants in their lexical representations. What, however, is to prevent Fula from having lexical stems like the ones in (29) (that is, stems in which **all** consonants are underspecified for the mutation features)? Note once again that the empty brackets are nothing more than heuristic devices to indicate that there is a mutation tier.

(29) a.

$$
\begin{bmatrix} +\text{ant} \\ -\text{cor} \\ +\text{voice} \end{bmatrix} \quad a \qquad \begin{bmatrix} +\text{ant} \\ -\text{cor} \\ +\text{voice} \end{bmatrix} \quad a
$$

$$
\text{C} \qquad \text{V} \qquad \text{C} \qquad \text{V}
$$

$$
\begin{bmatrix} \quad \\ \quad \end{bmatrix} \qquad\qquad \begin{bmatrix} \quad \\ \quad \end{bmatrix}
$$

b.

$$
\begin{bmatrix} +\text{ant} \\ -\text{cor} \\ +\text{voice} \end{bmatrix} \quad a \qquad \begin{bmatrix} +\text{ant} \\ -\text{cor} \\ +\text{voice} \end{bmatrix} \quad a
$$

$$
\overset{\textstyle\text{C}}{\vert} \qquad \text{V} \qquad \overset{\textstyle\text{C}}{\vert} \qquad \text{V}
$$

$$
\begin{bmatrix} \alpha\text{cont} \\ \beta\text{nas} \end{bmatrix} \qquad\qquad \begin{bmatrix} \quad \\ \quad \end{bmatrix}
$$

In (29a) all consonants in the (hypothetical) stem are underspecified. In (29b) it is the second, rather than the initial, segment that lacks the mutation features. The question then is, do we need to have a special provision that these sorts of representation are ruled out? And the answer, I would like to argue, is no— if such lexical items were generated, they would either be indistinguishable from already existing ones (29a), or they would be independently ruled out (29b).

Consider the case in (29a) first. The Initial Association Rule will attach the mutation prefix to (29a) as in (30). (The class 2 prefix is used here as representative.)

(30)

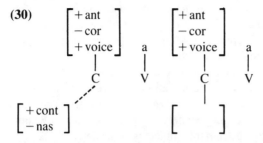

But Fula, as indicated above, has no Spreading rule, so the subsequent underspecified segment will not get the features [continuant, nasal] from the prefix. Since there is no other means for supplying these features during the derivation, we would expect that this internal underspecified segment would receive the default values of [continuant, nasal], namely, [−cont, −nas]. But if so, this stem would surface as **waba**, indistinguishable from a stem that was underlying specified [−cont, −nas]. In other words, given a surface lexical item like the hypothetical **waba** ~ **baba** ~ **mbaba**, we would at worst not be able to tell if its underlying representation were like (26) or (29a). At worst, to resolve this indeterminacy, we might have to develop a convention leaving out of underlying representations feature values that could later be filled in by the default mechanism. But this case causes no direct problem for the issue in question, namely, the analysis of mutation.

Nor does the sort of hypothetical representation in (29b) cause us any problems. If the Fula mutation prefixes attach to (29b), we will get the representations in (31):

(31) a.

b.

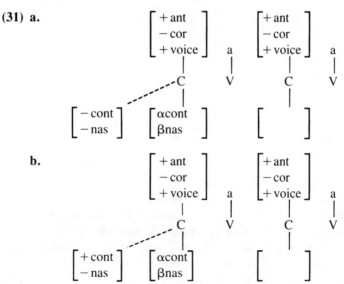

c.

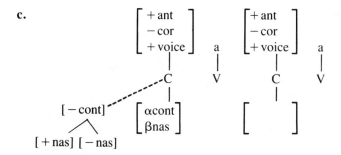

Two things need to be pointed out about the representations in (31): (i) the prefix features **will** attach to the initial consonant in (31a–c), and (ii) these features will not spread to the underspecified slot, for the same reason that the prefix features did not spread in (30). In fact, as far as the second consonant in (31a–c) is concerned, it will be supplied with default features; it again does not present a problem to the theory. What actually seems more problematic in (31) is that the initial consonant is **not** underspecified and seems to get too many [continuant, nasal] features. Recall that I argued in chapter 1 (specifically section 1.6.2) that the present theory prohibited two or more simultaneous specifications of a distinctive feature on a single segment, but did not rule out, across the board, sequential specifications of a feature. Thus, nothing a priori rules out the attachment of the prefix features to the already specified initial consonant. It might be thought at this point that we need an extra stipulation to **ensure** underspecification on initial segments. Still, I would like to argue that no such stipulation is necessary, and that the representations in (31) can be ruled out on independent grounds.

The independent grounds are as follows. It has been pointed out in some of the autosegmental literature on tone (Halle and Vergnaud mss, Clark 1983) that for each language with a tonal tier it needs to be stated what the maximum number of tones per tone-bearing unit is. Some languages (such as Yoruba) allow contour tones to be created in the course of autosegmental derivations, and others (such as Tonga) do not. For Yoruba it must be stated that the maximum number of tones per tone-bearing unit is two, for Tonga one.

If such a statement is needed for the tonal tier in languages, it would be reasonable to assume as well that this sort of statement will be needed for other autosegmental tiers in languages. The simplest assumption is that such statements are needed for each independent tier in each language. For a language with a [nasal] tier, we would need to state whether nasal contours are possible. In Tereña, for example, the maximum number of nasal features per segment is two; prenasalization is possible. In Mixtec there can be only one nasal feature per segment. Similarly, if a language had a [continuant] tier, then we would need to say whether more than one [continuant] feature per segment were allowed (that is, whether affricates were possible).

Let us assume, then, that such statements are independently necessary and that for Fula the only "contour" that is permitted is the sequence [+nas][−nas] attached to a single segment (prenasalization). If this is the case, the representation in (31c) will be ruled out regardless of the particular values of [continuant] and [nasal] on the initial segment; attaching the prefix in (31c) will result in three values of [nasal] on one segment.

The representation in (31b) is likewise ruled out no matter what values we choose for the [continuant, nasal] features of the first stem segment. If the initial segment is [−cont, −nas], a continuant contour will be created; but the contour [+cont][−cont] is not permitted in Fula. If the initial segment has the features [−cont, +nas], a postnasalized contour would be created, and these are also impossible. The initial segment cannot have the values [+cont, +nas]. This combination of features is ruled out independently, since Fula does not have nasal continuants. Finally, if the initial segment is [+cont, −nas], the initial segment specifications would be indistinguishable from the prefix specifications. We might assume in this case a convention which deletes the second of two identical sets of specifications on a single segment, reducing this case to the usual initially underspecified one.

Even the representation in (31a) can be ruled out regardless of what values of the features [continuant, nasal] appear on the initial stem segment. Suppose that this segment is [−cont, −nas]. Then the second of the two identical sets of features will be deleted by the convention mentioned immediately above. [+cont, +nas] is still independently ruled out. If the initial segment is [−cont, +nas], an inadmissible nasal contour is created, and this contour will be ruled out. The last possible case occurs if the initial stem segment is [+cont, −nas]. Here, if the [−cont, −nas] prefix attaches, an affricate would be created. But there are a number of reasons to believe that even this contour is generally ruled out in Fula.

Although there are two surface affricates in Fula, according to Arnott (1970), namely, the voiceless and voiced palatals [c] and [j], both have an odd status in the language. [c] occurs only in a few ideophones (**cak** 'completely', **coy** 'very (red)'). [j] occurs more frequently and in fact participates in the consonant mutation system, but, significantly, **in that system it functions as a stop** occurring in the classes where other stops occur (the palatal mutation series is **y~j~nj**). Also significant is the fact that **Fula has no surface palatal stops**. For the purposes of the mutation system, [j] is actually best treated as a pure stop. If we do not do so, we would have to postulate a special prefix for palatals for classes 1, 3, 4, 5, 16, 17, 19, 21, 23, 24, and 25 rather than the [−cont, −nas] prefix; the prefixes of these classes would then have to be made sensitive to the point of articulation of the initial consonant of the stem. It in fact seems simpler to say that Fula rules out [−cont] [+cont] (affricate) contours in general, that [c] and [j] **are** palatal stops throughout the derivation, and that a late, low-level phonetic rule applies after the phonological derivation to turn palatal stops to affricates. If, then, affricate contours are generally ruled out, the last case of (31a)—the one where the initial stem consonant bears the features [+cont, −nas]—will be ruled out. In other words, no matter what the prefix or the initial stem segment, independent features of the theory rule out the sort of representation in (29b).[16] In fact, it seems that it does not need to be stipulated within the present theory that all and only initial (or final) segments must be underspecified.

2.2 MUTATION AND LOCALITY

The central cases of mutation thus involve the following elements: (i) mutation features are projected on a separate tier, (ii) there is always a rule of Initial Association, but there is no rule of Spreading, (iii) each language has affixes that either are or contain floating features, and (iv) there is underspecification of an initial (or final) segment, but this fact does not need to be stipulated. Given this array of assumptions, all simple or independently necessary, it follows that in the unmarked case mutations ought to be local, that is, ought to affect only the initial (or final) segment of a stem. Again using Fula as an example, a representation like (32) could not arise:

(32)

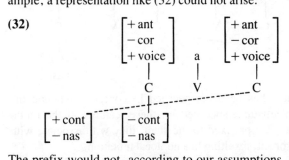

The prefix would not, according to our assumptions, cross association lines and attach to the second consonant; Initial Association would automatically attach it to the initial stem consonant, and the whole representation would be ruled out by the prohibition on continuant contours. Nor could the representation in (33) arise:

(33)

$$
\begin{bmatrix} +\text{ant} \\ -\text{cor} \\ +\text{voice} \end{bmatrix} \quad \text{a} \quad \begin{bmatrix} +\text{ant} \\ -\text{cor} \\ +\text{voice} \end{bmatrix}
$$

$$
\begin{array}{ccc}
| & | & | \\
C & V & C
\end{array}
$$

$$
\begin{bmatrix} +\text{cont} \\ -\text{nas} \end{bmatrix}
$$

There is no Spreading in mutation languages. The prefix in (33) would at most attach to the first consonant. The second could only be filled in by default. If the initial consonant alone is underspecified, mutation will work unproblematically. In a language with mutation prefixes, there is normally no way for anything but the initial consonant to mutate; for languages with mutation suffixes, only the final consonants can alternate.

The careful reader will notice that I have chosen to use the word **normally** in the sentence above.This is because there is in fact one condition under which a nonlocal mutation might be allowed to occur within the present theory. If, in some language with a mutation, the consonant nearest to the mutation affix were already prespecified for the mutation features and if a subsequent consonant were underspecified, the mutation features might be able to associate with a consonant not immediately adjacent to them. (34) illustrates a hypothetical example of this condition. Assume that the hypothetical language in question, the mutation tier, like Fula's, consists of the features [continuant]and [nasal]:

(34)

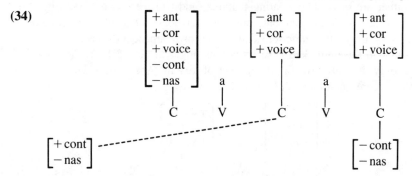

In (34), the initial consonant has been prespecified [−cont, −nas], and the medial consonant has been left underspecified for these features. If the mutation features [+cont, −nas] are prefixed to the stem, they will associate with impunity to the medial consonant, resulting in a nonlocal mutation.

To restate the point in more general terms, the present theory does not in fact predict that absolutely all mutations will be strictly local. Rather, it sanctions nonlocal mutations, but only under restricted circumstances. Remember that this theory treats prespecification as a possible but costly operation, since it involves violating Projection Statements (see section 1.3). If it is costly, we might expect a situation like that illustrated in (34) to occur only very infrequently in the languages of the world. In other words, nonlocal mutations might occur, but they ought to be very rare indeed, appearing only under the conjunction of initial (or final) prespecification and subsequent underspecification. Locality is predicted to be the **unmarked** and therefore the expected case.

Although Fula does have prespecification on some initial segments (that is, in invariant stems) and although we have argued that underspecification of consonants other than the initial one is not a priori ruled out, Fula apparently has no lexical entries of the appropriate sort to give rise to the marked nonlocal mutations. This fact might largely be explained by the nature of the invariant stems themselves.[17] As far as I can tell from Arnott (1970), many of the invariant stems are either (i) borrowed words or (ii) derived from other lexical categories. Words like **Hawsa** 'Hausaman' and **suley** 'shilling' are borrowings from Hausa (the latter originally borrowed into Hausa from English). We might speculate for these that foreign words taken into Fula maintain their original structures; that is, assuming that they come from languages like Hausa and English, which do not project [continuant, nasal] on a separate tier, they project these features on the melody tier for all consonants. If so, all consonants in borrowed words would be "prespecified," at least from the perspective of Fula phonology.They would not have any underspecified segments. Thus, we would not expect to find lexical items of the form of (34) among the borrowed words. As for the lexical items in the second category—adjectives derived from adverbials or nouns, nouns derived from other nouns or adverbials—we can only speculate that they are listed with the [continuant, nasal] features of their bases already prespecified on the initial segment, and that indeed in the prior derivation of the base items all [continuant, nasal] features have already been filled in. If so, we would not expect these either to meet the conditions of (34). Thus, while Fula does allow initial prespecification, it appears to allow it only under special circumstances in which the subsequent underspecification cannot also arise.

In fact, I know of only one case of a mutation that appears to parallel the hypothetical one illustrated in (34); this is the case of labialization in the Semitic language Chaha discussed by McCarthy (1983) and mentioned briefly in section 1.1.3. McCarthy (1983, 179) describes the mutation as follows: "Labialization . . . has a more unbounded character; it is applicable to any labializable root consonant, regardless of the distance from the end of the root. If the root contains more than one labializable radical, then the rightmost one is labialized.Among other categories, labialization marks (with the suffix $+\mathbf{n}$) a third person masculine singular object." In Chaha, all consonants but coronal ones are "labializable." The data in (35) (from McCarthy 1983) illustrates the labialization process:

(**35**) Perfective 3rd m. sg.

without object	with 3rd m. sg. object	
dænæg	dænæg^w	'hit'
nækæs	næk^{w}æs	'bite'
qætær	q^{w}ætær	'kill'
sædæd	sædæd	'chase'

As the last example shows, if all the consonants in the stem are [+ coronal], the stem remains unchanged in the third masculine singular object form.

The odd character of this mutation follows within the present theory if we make the following assumptions. First, let us assume, as McCarthy does, that the third masculine singular object morpheme is [+ round]. We will assume as well McCarthy's basic analysis of Chaha morphology; words in Chaha, like words in Arabic, have consonantal roots, vocalic melodies and skeletons. The [round] tier attaches to the consonantal melodies (see McCarthy 1983 for justification of this move), starting from the right. In our terms we might assume that [+round] is a suffix. As with Fula, Nuer, and Chemehuevi, there is no spreading of this tier in Chaha. We will depart from McCarthy's analysis in only one respect: coronal consonants will have the feature [−round] redundantly prespecified on their melody tiers. In other words, rather than stipulating, as McCarthy does, that [+round] will not attach to [+cor], we will make use of prespecification and the DFF to account for the labialization facts. The examples in (35) will therefore be derived as in (36):

(36)

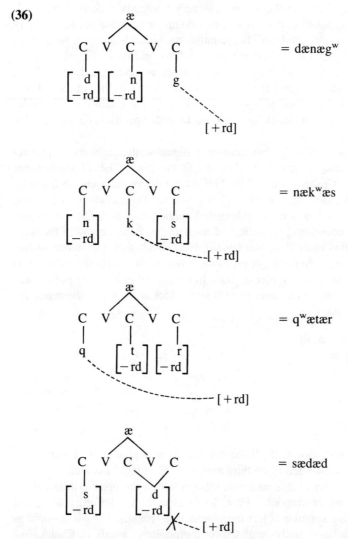

As (36) shows, the [+round] morpheme will attach to the rightmost consonant which is not prespecified for roundness; that is, which is [−coronal]. The DFF prevents association of the [+ round] morpheme to any segment already specified for roundness.

Thus, a sort of nonlocal mutation does appear to occur. Still, as I mentioned above, Chaha is the only example of nonlocal mutation of which I am aware. Conclusions must remain tentative, but it does appear that locality is the usual case, as predicted within the present framework.

2.3 UMLAUT

The three central cases we have looked at above are all handled neatly within the present autosegmental framework. For two of them, Nuer and Chemehuevi, no strong segmental analysis has been proposed. For Fula I have argued elsewhere (Lieber 1984a) that the autosegmental analysis is superior to earlier segmental analyses (Skousen 1982, Anderson 1976). Rather than repeat that argument here,[18] I will discuss another case of mutation, Umlaut in modern German, which has previously been analyzed segmentally. I will first try to show that although Umlaut deviates in one respect from the central cases of mutation described above, it should still be treated autosegmentally. In fact, I will try to show that an autosegmental analysis within the present framework is superior in two ways to my own previous (1980) segmental treatment of Umlaut; the autosegmental analysis will obviate the need for diacritic triggers, and in addition will predict the locality of Umlaut.

Umlaut is the process by which stem vowels in German are fronted in a number of different environments—before certain derivational suffixes, in some noun plurals, in a number of forms in the verb paradigms, in the comparative and superlative forms of some adjectives, and so on. Significantly, it is only one stem vowel which is umlauted—the one closest to the "triggering" morpheme (although we will see below that on the surface at least there is one exception to this generalization). It has been argued in some of my earlier work (Lieber 1980) and in the work of others (Wurzel 1970, Strauss 1976) that Umlaut is no longer a phonological process in German. The reader is referred to these works for complete arguments. However, to summarize briefly, while it may have been true historically that Umlaut was phonologically conditioned on a vowel by a front vowel in a following syllable, synchronically this is no longer true. There are underlyingly umlauted vowels in words like **Bär** 'bear' and **Tür** 'door' which are not followed by any vowels. In cases where Umlaut is an alternation, there no longer appears to be any clear phonological conditioning. Although the umlauted vowels in **bärtig** 'bearded' (cf. **Bart** 'beard') and **Hündin** 'bitch' (cf. **Hund** 'dog') look like they might be conditioned by the front vowel of the suffix, the front vowels of these same suffixes do not condition Umlaut in words like **wolkig** 'cloudy' or **Beamtin** 'woman official'. Other arguments against a phonological analysis of Umlaut exist as well; here I will start from the assumption that Umlaut in modern German is a morphologically conditioned process.

I will first give a list of environments in which Umlaut regularly or often appears and then show how these cases can be analyzed in the autosegmental framework.

(37) Umlaut environments

a. **Derivational affixes regularly conditioning Umlaut**
   (Umlaut conditioning)
   − **e** forming abstract nouns from adjectives (**gut** ~ **Güte**)
   Ge . . . e forming nouns from verbs (**bauen** ~ **Gebäude**)
   − **chen** forming diminutives (**Hund** ~ **Hündchen**)
   − **lein** forming diminutives (**Vogel** ~ **Vögelein**)
   − **ling** forming masculine (often pejorative) nouns (**dumm** ~ **Dümm-ling**)

b. **Derivational affixes sometimes conditioning Umlaut**
   (Umlaut variable)
   − **in** forming feminine nouns (**Hündin** vs. **Gattin**)
   − **er** forming agentive nouns (**Bäcker** vs. **Fahrer**)
   − **lich** forming adjectives (**ärztlich** vs. **amtlich**)
   − **ig** forming adjectives (**bärtig** vs. **wolkig**)

c. **Inflectional categories in which Umlaut appears**
   Plurals in − **er** (**Mann** ~ **Männer**)
   Some noun plurals ending in − **e** (**Fuchs** ~ **Füchse**)
   Subjunctive II of strong verbs
   Some comparative and superlative forms of adjectives

My analysis of Umlaut will adopt some of the assumptions made in my earlier (1980) analysis. First, I will assume the analysis of the nominal paradigms worked out there; exactly what this analysis entails will be spelled out shortly. Second, I will treat the Umlaut variable suffixes of (37b) in much the same way that I did in the earlier analysis. To reiterate briefly, the suffixes in (37b) are the ones that condition Umlaut in some forms but not in others. It is not at all predictable which stems will umlaut with which suffixes, nor will any given stem umlaut uniformly with all of the suffixes in (37b) (cf. **mündlich** ~ **(voll)mundig; örtlich** ~ **ortig**). Here, as in Lieber (1980), I will allow the morphological component to overgenerate both the umlauted and the unumlauted forms in all cases of variable suffixes (that is, both **mündlich** and **mundlich**, **mündig** and **mundig** will be generated), and I will not try to predict which of the two possible derivatives will be lexicalized in any given case. I refer the reader to Lieber (1980) for justification of this move.[19]

Since the environments in (37a) contain the simplest and clearest cases of Umlaut, let us begin with them. We will assume, first of all, that the feature [back] is autosegmentalized in German, that is, that it is projected on its own tier. We will have to assume, however, that the feature [back] is lexically linked to vowels in stems so that the adjectives **gut** and **frisch** will have the lexical representations in (38):[20]

(38)

$$g \begin{bmatrix} +\text{high} \\ -\text{low} \\ +\text{rd} \end{bmatrix} t \qquad\qquad f \quad r \begin{bmatrix} +\text{high} \\ -\text{low} \\ +\text{rd} \end{bmatrix} š$$

$$
\begin{array}{ccc}
C & V & C \\
 & | & \\
 & [+\text{bk}] & \\
\end{array} \quad = \text{gut} \qquad
\begin{array}{cccc}
C & C & V & C \\
 & & | & \\
 & & [-\text{bk}] & \\
\end{array} \quad = \text{frisch}
$$

Here we make a minor departure from the sort of analysis given for Fula, Nuer, and Chemehuevi: that is, in the classic cases in section 2.1, initial (or final) segments of lexical stems were normally underspecified for a number of features. In those languages, the value of the initial or final stem consonant for the features [nasal] or [voice] or [continuant] was always predictable for any morphological environment. But for the German stems, whether the stem vowel is [+back] or [−back] is not entirely predictable. Let us say, then, that in processes of mutation underspecification is permitted only where the values of the mutation features are completely predictable in all morphological environments. Otherwise lexical entries will have to be specified, as in German, for the value of the mutation feature(s).[21,22]

The suffixes in (37a) will have the lexical representations in (39):

(39)[23] **a.** Abstract noun forming −**e**

$$\begin{bmatrix} -\text{high} \\ -\text{low} \\ -\text{rd} \end{bmatrix}$$

$$
\begin{array}{c}
V \\
| \\
[-\text{bk}]\ [+\text{bk}]
\end{array}
$$

b. chen

$$x \begin{bmatrix} -\text{high} \\ -\text{low} \\ -\text{rd} \end{bmatrix} n$$

$$
\begin{array}{ccc}
C & V & C \\
 & | & \\
[-\text{bk}] & [+\text{bk}] & \\
\end{array}
$$

c. −**lein**

$$l \begin{bmatrix} -\text{high} \\ +\text{low} \\ -\text{rd} \end{bmatrix} \begin{bmatrix} +\text{high} \\ -\text{low} \\ -\text{rd} \end{bmatrix} n$$

$$
\begin{array}{cccc}
C & V & V & C \\
 & | & | & \\
[-\text{bk}] & [+\text{bk}] & [-\text{bk}] & \\
\end{array}
$$

d. **−ling**

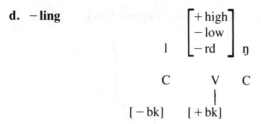

In other words, for each of these suffixes, in addition to the expected specification for the feature [back] on the [back] tier, there will be a floating [−bk] autosegment which will in effect serve as the trigger of Umlaut.

Now, since stem vowels in German start out fully specified for the feature [back], there will be one other difference between the derivation of umlauted forms in German and the derivation of mutation forms in Fula, Nuer, or Chemehuevi: that is, we must assume that German has a rule which delinks a single stem vowel. (40) is a possible formalization of this rule:

(40) German Delinking
(noniterative)

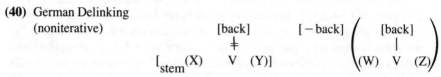

This rule will operate on stems in the presence of a floating [−back] feature and will delink a single specification for [back] on the stem. I will return to the operation of this rule below, but first in (41) I will illustrate the derivation of two typical cases, the deadjectival nouns **Güte** and **Frische**:

(41) **a.**

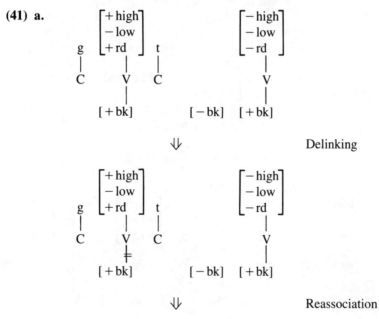

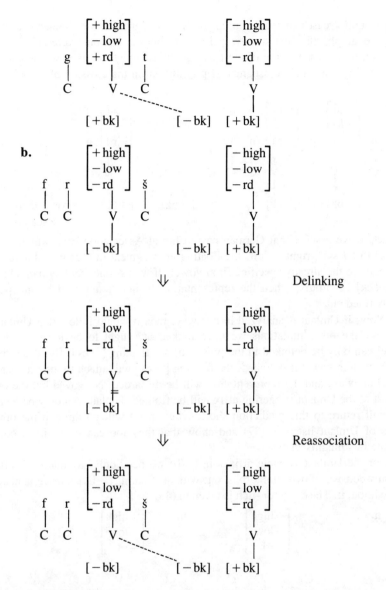

Once the Delinking rule has operated, the derivations in (41) will proceed just as those in Fula and Nuer did; an Initial Association rule will attach the floating [– back] segment to its left, causing the stem vowel to be fronted.

Two comments might now be made about the Delinking Rule (40). First, as (41b) shows, there is no reason to restrict Delinking to [+ back] stem vowels. If the rule applies blindly to front as well as to back vowels, the correct output is still obtained. Second, there is no more reason in this theory to stipulate that it is only the final stem vowel which is delinked than there was to stipulate in the central cases that only initial (or final) segments were underspecified. If, for example, the first stem vowel rather than the last one were delinked in (42) below, the association of the floating autosegment to this vowel would be ruled out by the usual autosegmental prohibition on the crossing of association lines:

(42)

$$
\begin{array}{ccccccccc}
& \begin{bmatrix} -\text{hi} \\ -\text{lo} \\ +\text{rd} \end{bmatrix} & & \begin{bmatrix} -\text{hi} \\ +\text{lo} \\ -\text{rd} \end{bmatrix} & & & & & \begin{bmatrix} -\text{hi} \\ -\text{lo} \\ -\text{rd} \end{bmatrix} \\
\text{p} & | & \text{p} & | & \text{n} & \text{t} & \text{s} & \text{x} & | & \text{n} \\
| & | & | & | & | & | & | & | & | & | \\
\text{C} & \text{V} \!-\! \text{C} & & \text{V} & \text{C} & \text{C} & \text{C} & & \text{C} & \text{V} \; \text{C}
\end{array}
$$

$$
\text{[+ bk]} \qquad \text{[+ bk]} \qquad \text{[- bk]} \qquad \text{[+ bk]} \qquad \text{*Pöpanzchen}
$$
'little scarecrow'

In fact, if we assume that German has an Initial Association Rule which links [back] to [+ syl], right to left, the floating autosegment in (42) would actually be linked to the already specified **final** vowel. If we assume that German allows no [back] "contours," then the representation in question would be independently ruled out.[24]

Now, if Umlaut is analyzed in this way, then it would follow that Umlaut, just like the other mutations we have looked at, ought to be local. A stem vowel can only be delinked in the presence of a floating [− bk]. But if any but the final stem vowel is delinked, the floating [− bk] will attach to the final stem vowel anyway, and the representation will be discarded. No vowel but the one closest to the Umlaut-triggering affix will be fronted. Umlaut can only be local. We will return to this prediction shortly, but first I will go through the other cases of Umlaut listed in (37) and show that they too can be easily accommodated within this analysis.

For the Umlaut variable affixes in (37b) we need only say that each affix actually consists of two allomorphs, one with the floating [− bk] autosegment and one without it. The entry for -**lich** is given in (43):

(43) a.

$$
\begin{array}{cccc}
& \begin{bmatrix} +\text{high} \\ -\text{low} \\ -\text{rd} \end{bmatrix} & & \\
\text{l} & & \text{x} & \\
\\
\text{C} & \text{V} & \text{C} & \\
& | & & \\
\text{[− bk]} & \text{[− bk]} & &
\end{array}
\qquad
\textbf{b.}
\begin{array}{cccc}
& \begin{bmatrix} +\text{high} \\ -\text{low} \\ -\text{rd} \end{bmatrix} & & \\
\text{l} & & \text{x} & \\
\\
\text{C} & \text{V} & \text{C} & \\
& | & & \\
& \text{[− bk]} & &
\end{array}
$$

As mentioned above, I am assuming that these allomorphs may attach freely to any appropriate noun stem, producing both an umlauted and an unumlauted form. I assume as well that one or another of the resulting derivatives, or very occasionally both, typically gets lexicalized and becomes the dominant form.

Inflected forms also fit easily within the autosegmental analysis. I will deal here only with Umlaut in the adjective and noun paradigms. Given these analyses, Umlaut in the verb forms could be dealt with in a similar fashion. Umlaut in the adjective paradigms is very similar to the sort of Umlaut observed in derivational affixes. (44) illustrates the comparative and superlative forms of some typical adjectives:

(**44**) **a.** alt   älter   ältest
       arg   ärger   ärgest
       arm   ärmer   ärmest

     b. bar   barer   barest
           froh   froher   frohest
           dumm   dummer   dummest

     c. bang $\begin{cases} \text{banger} \\ \text{bänger} \end{cases}$ $\begin{cases} \text{bangst} \\ \text{bängst} \end{cases}$
           blass $\begin{cases} \text{blasser} \\ \text{blässer} \end{cases}$ $\begin{cases} \text{blassest} \\ \text{blässest} \end{cases}$
           fromm $\begin{cases} \text{frommer} \\ \text{frömmer} \end{cases}$ $\begin{cases} \text{frommst} \\ \text{frömmst} \end{cases}$

As the examples in (44) show, some adjectives are always umlauted in their comparative and superlative forms, others never umlaut in either form, and still others display both umlauted and unumlauted variants. These patterns can be accounted for if we place the -**r** comparative suffix and the -**st** superlative suffix into the category of Umlaut variable suffixes. Each will therefore have two allomorphs, one with a floating [− bk] autosegment and the other without:

(**45**) **a.** Comparative   r   r

$$
\begin{array}{ccc}
& C & ; & C \\
[-\text{bk}] &&&
\end{array}
$$

     b. Superlative   s   t   s   t

$$
\begin{array}{ccccc}
& C & C & ; & C & C \\
[-\text{bk}] &&&&&
\end{array}
$$

As was the case with the other Umlaut variable suffixes, we will allow both allomorphs to attach to stems freely, and will assume that in most cases one or the other of the resulting derivatives is normally lexicalized.[25] Adjective paradigms are therefore no problem for the autosegmental analysis.

Noun paradigms present a slightly different case, however. In Lieber (1980) I accepted Wurzel's (1970) conclusion that the case inflections for nouns are normally the ones in (46):

(**46**)

	Sg.	Pl.
Nominative		-e
Accusative		-e
Genitive	-s (M,N)	-e
Dative		-n

In other words, the case endings are themselves more or less regular. Most idiosyncrasy in German nouns is to be attributed to allomorphy in noun stems; most nouns in German have at least two allomorphs, one of which typically appears in the singular and the other in the plural. Thus the noun **Staat** has an allomorph **Staaten**, the noun **Affe** the allomorph **Affen**, and so on. Both allomorphs are listed in the lexicon, and both are available for derivation. The plural noun inflections are subcategorized to attach to the latter allomorph in each pair. According to Wurzel (1970), the combination of stem allomorph and inflectional ending is then subject to three segmental phonological rules: (i) e-Epenthesis, which inserts an **e** between two consonants separated by a morpheme boundary (in most cases this **e** is then reduced to schwa), (ii) a general rule of Degemination, and (iii) a rule of e-Deletion which deletes an **-e** if it follows an unstressed **e** plus sonorant. The dative plural of the noun **Affe** 'ape' would be derived as in (47):

(47) Affe   Plural stem   Affen

              Dative pl.   Affen + n[26]

              Degemination   Affen

For many German nouns, one allomorph appears to be umlauted, and it is these that I will concentrate on here. First, there is a class of nouns whose plural allomorphs contain both Umlaut and an **-r** stem extension: **Mann ~ Männer**. Second, there is a class of nouns whose plural forms differ from the singular allomorph **only** in the presence of Umlaut on the former: **Bach ~ Bäch**[27]; **Vater ~ Väter**. In neither of these classes of noun stems is there any evidence that the umlaut is triggered by a floating autosegment on another morpheme. In the case of the stems listed above, there is no obvious morpheme from which an autosegment can come, nor is [− bk] really a morpheme in its own right—although the second allomorph in each pair is used in deriving the plural, it is also used in forming compounds and derived words of various sorts, so it would be incorrect to call [− bk] a "plural morpheme."

Our alternative is to say that the source of Umlaut is the lexical form of the allomorph itself. Both allomorphs of a noun, as shown in Lieber (1980), must be listed in a lexical entry.[28] Let us say that, for each of the classes mentioned above, nouns exhibit two allomorphs. The one that is used in the plural forms will have a floating [− bk] feature, as illustrated in (48b):

(48) a.
$$
m \begin{bmatrix} -\text{high} \\ +\text{low} \\ -\text{rd} \end{bmatrix} n
$$

b.
$$
m \begin{bmatrix} -\text{high} \\ +\text{low} \\ -\text{rd} \end{bmatrix} n \qquad r
$$

C   V   C   C   V   C   C

      | |

   [+ bk]   [+ bk]   [− bk]

Delinking will occur in stems like the one in (48b), and the floating [−bk] will be linked to the stem vowel. In other words, these cases will be treated on analogy to the Umlaut-inducing suffixes in (37); in fact, we might count these as cases in which an originally independent umlauting suffix has been lexicalized as part of a stem.

We can see then that it is possible to analyze Umlaut as an autosegmental process. In fact, it appears that this analysis is preferable to a segmental one for a number of reasons. First, it allows for a direct comparison between Umlaut and other cases of mutation. Umlaut differs from the central cases of mutation in section 2.1 in that it involves mutation of a vowel rather than a consonant and in that the mutation-tier feature is not predictable in all environments. From this latter fact it follows that each stem vowel must be lexically specified for the feature [back] and that a Delinking Rule will be necessary. But Umlaut is like the mutations in Fula, Nuer, and Chemehuevi in other significant ways: it requires us to project an independent mutation tier and to postulate a floating autosegment, normally a part of a suffix, which associates with a neighboring morpheme. Umlaut, rather than being a peculiar and isolated process among the languages of the world, fits in squarely with a class of "triggered" morphological rules.

The analysis is attractive not only because it shows Umlaut to be much like other mutation phenomena. More important, it also eliminates the need which existed in the previous segmental analysis for an arbitrary diacritic to trigger Umlaut. In Lieber (1980) I proposed an analysis of Umlaut which required only one segmental Umlaut rule: $[+syl] \rightarrow [-bk]/ \underline{\quad} C_0[+U]$. Affixes which regularly triggered Umlaut (that is, those in [37a]) were given the diacritic $[+U]$. Umlaut variable suffixes (37b) each had two allomorphs, one marked $[+U]$ and the other $[-U]$. If a stem was followed by any morpheme bearing the $[+U]$ marker, the Umlaut rule was triggered. The diacritic $[\pm U]$, of course, was an arbitrary and ad hoc device to get the Umlaut rule to operate. It had no function beyond its use in the Umlaut rule. No such arbitrary device is needed here, however. "Triggering" is a much more general phenomenon in the present framework; that is, it is a function of floating autosegments which undergo association to neighboring morphemes.

There in fact appears to be an additional bit of empirical evidence in favor of the floating autosegment analysis of Umlaut. The evidence concerns the appearance of the voiceless palatal fricative [ç], the so-called "ich-laut." Kloeke (1982, and references cited therein) argues that [ç] is not an underlying segment in German, but rather is derived from the voiceless velar fricative [x], the "ach-laut," when preceded by a front vowel. A possible statement of this rule is as follows:[29]

(49) $\begin{bmatrix} -son \\ -ant \\ +cont \end{bmatrix} \rightarrow \begin{bmatrix} -back \\ -cor \end{bmatrix} / \quad [-bk](C)\underline{\quad}$

However, works on German phonetics and pronunciation like Wängler (1967) and *Siebs Deutsche Aussprache* (de Boor 1969) always mention another environment in which [ç] appears, namely, in the diminutive -**chen**. At first glance, the [ç] in -**chen** appears unproblematic. Assuming a rule like (49) and **any** analysis of Umlaut, -**chen** would have an underlying form with [x], would trigger umlaut on the stem it attaches to, and then rule (49) would operate in the environment of the newly fronted stem vowel to change [x] to [ç]. Still, there are problems that arise if we assume that it is the fronted stem vowel which causes rule (49) to apply: (i) there is at least one word in German, **Frauchen**, where Umlaut idiosyncratically fails to occur, yet the diminutive suffix is still pronounced with [ç], and (ii) -**chen** is pronounced with [ç] even in isolation.

These facts receive an immediate explanation if we assume the floating autosegment analysis of Umlaut. If the diminutive morpheme is represented as in (39b), the underlying [x] will **always** be preceded by a [−bk] feature which will condition the operation of rule (49). The floating autosegment will be there, even when the morpheme occurs in isolation, to trigger the change of [x] to [ç]. Thus, within this theory -**chen** does not have to be treated exceptionally.[30] In contrast, in a theory which uses an arbitrary diacritic like [+U] to trigger Umlaut, -**chen** does have to be treated as an exception. If -**chen** appears in isolation, or if it fails to trigger Umlaut in the exceptional **Frauchen**, there is no [−bk] feature to trigger the application of rule (49). We would be forced to resort to yet another diacritic within the segmental analysis to explain the shape of -**chen**. Thus, the floating autosegment analysis appears to be superior to the segmental one on both theoretical and empirical grounds.

Another reason for preferring the autosegmental analysis of Umlaut to the segmental one is that it leads us to expect the locality of the Umlaut process. In my earlier segmental analysis, I pointed out that Umlaut seemed to be a local process, but that this observation did not follow from any one principle or combination of principles in the theory. Instead, the locality of Umlaut was stipulated in the environment of the Umlaut rule, since no vowels could intervene between the trigger and the segment to be umlauted. We have seen above, however, that autosegmental mutations are local processes (with the exception of the case discussed in section 2.2). If Umlaut is treated autosegmentally, it would follow from the theory that it ought to be local.

The present analysis, then, is superior to a segmental one, assuming that Umlaut **is** local. If it is, then we should not expect to find cases where an umlauting affix affects the first vowel in a disyllabic stem, rather than the vowel closest to it. We must, in fact, look carefully at this prediction for German, since there appear to be at least prima facie cases of nonlocal mutation. Consider examples such as those in (50):

(**50**) mütterlich
Bäuerlein

jämmerlich
Trömmelchen
säuberlich

The words in (50) suggest that an initial stem vowel **can** umlaut if the vowel that intervenes between it and the autosegmental trigger is a schwa.

But schwa is a vowel with a special status in German. In fact, as Wurzel (1970) has argued, the distribution of schwa in native stems is largely predictable, which suggests that schwa is inserted into stems by a rule of Epenthesis, rather than being present underlyingly. Wurzel (1970, p. 170) provides the following examples, which illustrate the distribution of schwa in monomorphemic stems:

(51) Schwa occurs between:

[l] and [r]	Keller
[m] and [r]	Eimer
[m] and [l]	Hammel
[n] and [r]	Donner
[n] and [l]	Tunnel
Obstruent and [r]	Vater
Obstruent and [l]	Segel
Obstruent and [m]	Atem
Obstruent and [n]	Segen

Schwa does not occur between:

[r] and [l]	Kerl
[r] and [m]	Wurm
[r] and [n]	Horn
[r] and obstruent	Ort
[l] and [m]	Halm
[l] and [n]	Köln
[l] and obstruent	Zelt
[m] and obstruent	Samt
[n] and obstruent	Front
Obstruent and obstruent	Kraft

Identical sonorants never occur, either together or separated by schwa, nor do nasals co-occur in either way. It seems that schwa occurs (i) between any consonant and **r**, (ii) between nasals or obstruents and **l**, or (iii) between obstruents and nasals. As the examples in (52) also suggest, schwa intervenes between a glide and **r**:

(52) Feier [fayər]
Feuer [fɔyər]
Bauer [bawər]

I do not intend to give an exhaustive analysis of schwa in German, since this discussion would inevitably lead to the question of whether schwa is present or absent underlyingly in inflectional and derivational affixes, a question which is well beyond the scope of the discussion here.[31] I refer the reader to Wurzel (1970) and Kloeke (1982) for thorough accounts of German schwa (although segmental rather than autosegmental). However, the tentative rule of schwa insertion in (53) does seem to account adequately for schwa in native stems:[32]

(53) Epenthesis

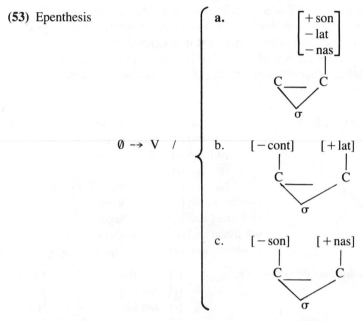

(53a) inserts an epenthetic vowel in environment (i) above, (53b) in environment (ii), and (53c) in environment (iii). The rule has two features which require some explanation. First, it is stated to insert a V slot rather than a complete schwa. I am assuming that the remaining (melody) features of schwa can be inserted by the default mechanism, since other vowels in German will always be fully specified.[33] Second, (53) inserts this vowel slot only between tautosyllabic segments of the sort indicated. This restriction on Epenthesis is justified on the following grounds. Whereas Epenthesis occurs in the (a) forms in (54) where the final segment has no choice but to be syllabified with the preceding segment, no Epenthesis takes place in the (b) forms. In the latter cases, the final sonorant appears to have been syllabified with the following syllable, which is provided by the inflectional or derivational morpheme.

(54) a. Feuer   **b.** fëurig
      Bauer   bäurisch
      Segel ⎫   Segler
      segeln ⎭
      Atem   ⎧ atmet
                 ⎩ Atmung

Note that these examples suggest that Epenthesis is a rather late rule; it occurs after both inflectional and derivational affixes have been added and the resulting word syllabified.

But if the latter is true, then examples such as those in (50) no longer challenge the locality of Umlaut. At the stage of derivation at which Umlaut occurs (presumably wherever a relevant stem and suffix are attached), no schwa intervenes between the first stem vowel and the umlaut trigger:

(55)

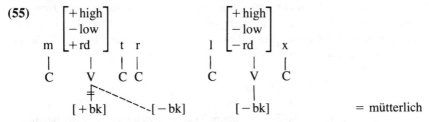

In this case, the stem-final r cannot be syllabified with the following syllable, so Epenthesis operates, inserting a V slot. It thus seems that Umlaut can be added to our other examples of mutation; like the classic cases in Fula, Nuer, and Chemehuevi, it turns out to be local.[34]

I will end this section by recapitulating the two reasons why the autosegmental analysis sketched here is preferable to the segmental analysis given in Lieber (1980). First, where the latter analysis was forced to make use of the arbitrary diacritic [± U] to trigger umlaut, the present analysis requires no diacritics, and in fact makes use only of a triggering device—the floating autosegment—which is well motivated elsewhere in autosegmental theory. Second, whereas it was noted in Lieber (1980) that Umlaut was a local process, it was admitted there that the locality of the process did not follow from anything in that theory. However, we have seen that locality is a property predicted by my theory for mutation processes in general. Thus, what might otherwise be seen as a puzzling property of Umlaut receives a good explanation here.

2.4 PHONETICALLY QUIRKY MUTATIONS

So far the mutations we have considered make good phonetic sense. In Fula, initial consonants showed up as continuants in some environments, as stops in others, and as prenasalized stops in still other environments. The mutation autosegments could easily be represented as combinations of the features [continuant] and [nasal], one set of values for each environment. Similarly, in Nuer final consonants appeared regularly as voiced stops in some environments, as voiceless stops in others, and as voiceless continuants in a third set of environments; the mutation autosegments were combinations of [voice] and [continuant], again one set of values for each environment. And finally, in Chemehuevi, where consonants appeared as voiceless stops, as corresponding voiced continuants, or as prenasalized consonants, depending upon environment, the features [voice], [nasal], and [continuant] combined to produce the regular and reasonably uniform mutations.

Not all mutations are as well behaved as the ones in Fula, Nuer, and Chemehuevi, however. Some languages exhibit alternations of initial or final consonants that clearly should be termed "mutations," but these alternations do not divide up neatly like the ones above, where one class of consonants (such as stop or fricative) appeared in each morphological environment. Rather, in a single morphological environment, these other cases will show some forms as stops, others as fricatives, or some as voiceless, others as voiced, and so on. Let us consider first the sort of initial mutations that appear in Mende (all Mende data are from Rice and Cowper 1984):

(56)   Env. 1   Env. 2

a.	f	v	fà	'for'	gbé và	'what for'
	s	j	séléí	'the banana'	nya jèlèí	'my banana'
b.	p	w	pómà	'behind'	ndòpóì wómà	'behind the child'
	t	l	téí	'the chicken'	nyá lèí	'my chicken'
c.	k	g	kùlɔ́	'in front of'	bí gùlɔ́	'in front of you-sg.'
	kp	gb	kpèkɛ̀ì	'the razor'	nyá gbèkɛ̀í	'my razor'
d.	mb	b	mbètɛ̀í	'the platform'	nyá bètɛ̀í	'my platform'
	nd	l	ndèndèí	'the boat'	nyá lèndèí	'my boat'
	nj	y	njéí	'the goat'	nyá yèí	'my goat'
	ng	y	ngílèí	'the dog'	nyá yìlèí	'my dog'
		w	ngólíí	'the ear, tail'	nyá wòlìí	'my ear, tail'
e.	v	v	vɔvɔí	'the lungs'	nyá vɔvɔí	'my lungs'
	j	j	jɔwéí	'the chain'	nyá jɔwèí	'my chain'
	b	b	bèlèí	'the trousers'	nyá bèlèí	'my trousers'
	d	d	dɔ́wìí	'the duck'	nyá dɔwìí	'my duck'
	g	g	gìlíí	'the kidney'	nyá gìlíí	'my kidney'
	gb	gb	gbàtòí	'the whip'	nyá gbàtòí	'my whip'
	m	m	mèmɛ̀ɛ́	'the mirror'	nyá mèmɛ̀ɛ́	'my mirror'
	n	n	nɛ̀ɛ́sìí	'the pine-apple'	nyá nɛ̀ɛ̀sìí	'my pine-apple'
	ny	ny	nyàhɛ́ì	'the woman'	nyá nyàhɛ̀í	'my woman'
	ŋ	ŋ	ŋɔ̀nìí	'the bird'	nyá ŋɔ̀nìi	'my bird'
	l	l	lómbòí	'the patch'	nyá lòmbòí	'my patch'
	h	h	hàkáà	'the calf of the leg'	nyá hàkáà	'my calf'
	w	w	wàlèí	'the slate'	nyá wàlèí	'my slate'
	y	y	yî	'things, stuff'	nyá yìí	'my stuff'

Leaving aside the identification of environment 1 and environment 2 until section 2.5, let us concentrate on the actual initial mutations exhibited in (56). First of all, it is evident that many segments in Mende never take part in consonant mutations at all; those segments that are voiced but not prenasalized in environment 1 appear unchanged in environment 2. And of the other segments, the continuants in environment 1 appear voiced in environment 2, and most noncontinuants in environment 1 (but not **k** and **mb**) appear as voiced continuants in environment 2. At first glance, at least, it is not so easy to see what sorts of floating autosegments could ever produce these effects.

Quirky mutations like the one in Mende are by no means isolated occurrences. Another representative example is the Lenition mutation in Welsh (Aubery 1976, Jones and Thomas 1977, Rhys-Jones 1977):

(57) Welsh	Env. 1	Env. 2 (Lenition)
a.	p	b
	t	d
	c [k]	g
b.	b	f [v]
	d	dd [ð]
	g	Ø
c.	m	f [v]
	ll [ɫ]	l
	rh [r̥]	r

Unless otherwise noted, the symbols in (57) represent both the symbols used in Welsh orthography and the phonetic value of these symbols. Once again, it is not important at this point to go into the environments in which mutation takes place, that is, whether the features are prefixes, suffixes, or clitics. What **is** important, however, is the nature of the Lenition mutation itself. It opposes voiced stops to the voiceless ones in the environment 1 series of consonants, and voiced continuants to the environment 1 voiced stops. Again, it is not easy to see how a simple floating autosegment could produce this array of segments.

It has been suggested that cases like Mende and Welsh present a real challenge to the autosegmental theory, since it is difficult to see how a single floating autosegment could characterize each morphological environment. However, I will argue that these quirky mutations in fact present no problem at all for a framework which includes a theory of prespecification, and indeed that this theory alone makes interesting and correct predictions about possible quirky mutations.

I will show first how we would account for Welsh using prespecification. Let us say that the mutation features for environment 1 are [− voice, − cont] and that those for environment 2 (Lenition) are [+ voice, + cont]. Initial consonants of stems in Welsh will be underspecified, as they were in Fula, Nuer, and Chemehuevi—but the amount of prespecification of the features [voice] and [continuant] will be much higher than in the other languages. Specifically, we will have to say that stems beginning with the initial consonants in (57a) will always be prespecified [−cont] and that those beginning with the initial consonants in (57b) will always be [+voice]. (58) illustrates what the result will be when the mutation features are added:[35]

(58) a.

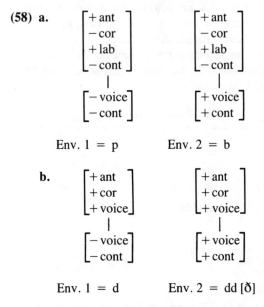

$$
\begin{bmatrix} +\text{ant} \\ -\text{cor} \\ +\text{lab} \\ -\text{cont} \end{bmatrix}
\qquad
\begin{bmatrix} +\text{ant} \\ -\text{cor} \\ +\text{lab} \\ -\text{cont} \end{bmatrix}
$$

$$
\begin{bmatrix} -\text{voice} \\ -\text{cont} \end{bmatrix}
\qquad
\begin{bmatrix} +\text{voice} \\ +\text{cont} \end{bmatrix}
$$

Env. 1 = p   Env. 2 = b

b.

$$
\begin{bmatrix} +\text{ant} \\ +\text{cor} \\ +\text{voice} \end{bmatrix}
\qquad
\begin{bmatrix} +\text{ant} \\ +\text{cor} \\ +\text{voice} \end{bmatrix}
$$

$$
\begin{bmatrix} -\text{voice} \\ -\text{cont} \end{bmatrix}
\qquad
\begin{bmatrix} +\text{voice} \\ +\text{cont} \end{bmatrix}
$$

Env. 1 = d   Env. 2 = dd [ð]

In (58a) the stem melody is already specified for continuancy, so the mutation feature for continuancy is overridden. The floating autosegment provides only the feature for voicing. In (58b), the opposite is true. The stem melody provides the feature for voicing, so this feature is not supplied by the mutation autosegment. But the autosegment does determine continuancy.[36]

For the consonants in (57c) similar treatments are possible. If we assume that **m** is prespecified [+voice] and also has the feature [+nasal],[37] then we will end up with the configuration in (59) after the mutation features are attached:

(59)

$$
\begin{bmatrix} +\text{ant} \\ -\text{cor} \\ +\text{lab} \\ +\text{nas} \\ +\text{voice} \end{bmatrix}
\qquad
\begin{bmatrix} +\text{ant} \\ -\text{cor} \\ +\text{lab} \\ +\text{nas} \\ +\text{voice} \end{bmatrix}
$$

$$
\begin{bmatrix} -\text{voice} \\ -\text{cont} \end{bmatrix}
\qquad
\begin{bmatrix} +\text{voice} \\ +\text{cont} \end{bmatrix}
$$

Env. 1 = m   Env. 2 (+ (60)) = f [v]

The representation in environment 1 is straightforward. The [+ voice] feature will override the [− voice] feature on the autosegment. For environment 2 we must make one additional assumption, however: that is, we must assume, since there are no nasal continuants in Welsh, that the feature combination [+ continuant, + nasal] is ruled out. If we assume that there is some sort of low-level phonetic rule in Welsh like the one in (60), then the second representation in (59) will be adjusted to give the correct output [v].

(60) [+ cont]   →   [− nasal]

The rest of the consonants in (57c) pose no additional problems; **rh** and **r** must be prespecified [+ cont], as must **ll** and **l**. Thus it appears that there are no mechanical obstacles in the way of treating Welsh Lenition with floating autosegments. It is true that the use of prespecification adds some complexity to the grammar of Welsh and therefore comes at some cost, but presumably there is no more cost involved in using prespecification than there would be if we used segmental rules to create initial mutations in Welsh, as we will see shortly.[38]

Mende mutations can be treated similarly. Let us say that the mutation features for environment 1 are [− voice, − cont] and those for environment 2 [+ voice, + cont]. Most initial consonants of stems will be underspecified to some extent. However, of all the consonants listed in (56), only stems beginning with those in (56b) will have initial consonants completely unspecified for the features [voice] and [continuant]. The initial consonants in (56b) will have representations like those in (61) after the mutation features have been added:

(61)
$$
\begin{bmatrix} + \text{ant} \\ - \text{cor} \\ - \text{nasal} \\ + \text{lab} \end{bmatrix}
\qquad
\begin{bmatrix} + \text{ant} \\ - \text{cor} \\ - \text{nasal} \\ + \text{lab} \end{bmatrix}
$$

$$
\quad \begin{bmatrix} - \text{voice} \\ - \text{cont} \end{bmatrix}
\qquad\qquad
\begin{bmatrix} + \text{voice} \\ + \text{cont} \end{bmatrix}
$$

Env. 1 = p   Env. 2 = w

The mutation autosegment supplies both missing features in both environments.

On the other hand, for all of those consonants in (56e) that do not mutate at all, we must assume that initial consonants of stems are not underspecified at all. Stems, for example, which begin with invariant **b** are prespecified [+ voice, − cont], and those that begin with invariant **v** are prespecified [+ voice, + cont]. The mutation autosegments will fail to attach to these segments at all.

The remaining cases in (56) require some degree of prespecification. Stems beginning with the initial consonants in (56a) will be prespecified [+ cont], so that only voicing will be supplied by the mutation autosegments. Stems beginning with the consonants in (56c) will be prespecified [− cont]; again, voicing will be supplied by the mutation autosegment, but the initial consonants in these stems will remain stops in both environments.

Even the facts in (56d) can be accounted for fairly neatly within the auto-segmental framework. Let us say that stems beginning with the consonants in (56d) actually have representations something like that in (62):

(62)   [+ nasal]   [− nasal]

$$
\begin{bmatrix}
\alpha\,\text{ant} \\
\beta\,\text{cor} \\
+\,\text{voice}
\end{bmatrix}
$$

In other words, the class of consonants in (56d) will be inherently prenasalized. When the mutation autosegments are attached, we get (63):

(63)

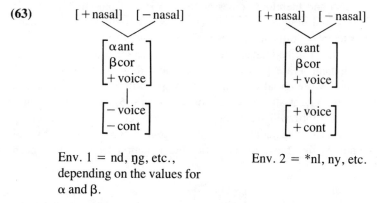

Env. 1 = nd, ŋg, etc.,   Env. 2 = *nl, ny, etc.
depending on the values for
α and β.

In environment 1, the [voice] feature on the stem melody overrides the feature provided by the autosegment. But the representation in environment 2 is obviously inadequate as it now stands, since the output is incorrectly prenasalized. However, we can remedy this problem quite easily. Suppose that the grammar of Mende, like that of Welsh, has the low-level phonetic rule (60). (60) will change the first [+ nasal] to [− nasal] (and then degemination of this feature will occur), and the correct output will be obtained.[39]

It is thus possible to characterize the difficult and phonetically incoherent mutations in Mende and Welsh as the effects of floating autosegments. Admittedly, the analyses proposed here require the use of a fair amount of pre-specification, and perhaps seem unnecessarily convoluted. They bristle with duplicated features. Still, they use only the theoretical devices that are made available by our theory. Moreover, there is at least one good reason to believe that they should be preferred to segmental analyses.

Rice and Cowper (1984) simply list the alternations in Mende as a series of segmental redundancy rules: f -→ v; p -→ w, s -→ j, k -→ g, mb -→ b, etc. Presumably, a number of these alternations could be collapsed if the rules were stated in terms of features. A segmental analysis of Welsh Lenition would also consist of a list of rules, perhaps something like the rules in (64):[40]

(64) Welsh Lenition $[-\text{voice}] \rightarrow [+\text{voice}]$

$[+\text{voice}] \rightarrow \begin{bmatrix} +\text{cont} \\ -\text{nas} \end{bmatrix}$ in Lenition environments

$g \rightarrow \quad \emptyset$

In principle, the more bizarre or phonetically incoherent a mutation, the more segmental rules we would need to account for that mutation. And indeed, in the segmental treatment there is nothing to stop us from adding to the list of mutation rules.

The segmental analyses of the Mende and Welsh mutations in a way look comfortingly simple, but there is a larger theoretical reason why they cannot be correct. In principle, a segmental treatment of mutation would allow us to express any sort of hypothetical mutation at all. It places no restrictions on the sort of phonetically quirky mutations that we should expect to find in languages. Consider, for example, the hypothetical mutation in (65):

(65) Env. 1   Env. 2

b	→	p
d	→	t
g	→	k
f	→	b
θ	→	d
x	→	g

We could easily write the set of segmental rules in (66) to describe this mutation:

(66) $[+\text{voice}] \rightarrow [-\text{voice}]$
$[+\text{cont}] \rightarrow \begin{bmatrix} +\text{voice} \\ -\text{cont} \end{bmatrix}$

But as far as I know, there is no language which has a mutation like this. And significantly, there seems to be no way of using a floating autosegment and the device of prespecification to express this mutation. If, for example, we proposed that the floating autosegment for environment 1 were [−voice, −cont], then we would have to say that **b, d, g** were prespecified [+voice], **f,θ, x,** [+cont]. But then, no matter what we would propose as the floating autosegment for environment 2, **b, d, g** would have to remain voiced, **f, θ, x** as continuants. If we proposed, on the other hand, that the floating autosegment in environment 1 were [+voice, +cont], **b, d, g** would have to be prespecified [−cont], **f, θ, x** [−voice]. Again, regardless of what the floating autosegment is taken to be in environment 2, **f**, θ, **x** could not show up as the voiced sounds **b**, **d**, **g**. I leave it to the reader to confirm that the two other logical possibilities for the environment 1 floating autosegment, [+ voice, − cont] and [− voice, + cont], lead to exactly the same sorts of problems.Thus, the autosegmental theory would predict—correctly as far as I know—that there should be no language with the particular quirky mutation in (65). In other words, the autosegmental treatment of mutations makes predictions as to what a possible mutation might be. Insofar as these predictions are correct, the autosegmental theory is to be preferred over the less restrictive segmental analysis.

2.5 Nonmorphological Mutations

Mende is of some interest to the autosegmental analysis of mutation for another reason. Rice and Cowper (1984) argue that it is not always the case that mutation is a purely morphological phenomenon analyzable as a floating autosegment which either is or is part of a discrete prefix or suffix. They show that mutation occurs in Mende in a particular syntactic configuration, and they conclude that no analysis which makes use of floating autosegments is possible for Mende. I will argue here that they are correct when they say that mutation in Mende is not morphological in the narrow sense, but that it is nevertheless possible, and in fact desirable, to treat it autosegmentally. In fact, I will show that there is at least one other case where mutation is not morphological. The Philippine language Chamorro (Topping 1968) seems to have a process which is very much like Umlaut in German, except that it appears to be purely phonological. But cases like these are exactly what we would expect, given the autosegmental framework we have been developing here. This framework, as we have seen above, is not exclusively a theory of phonology or of morphology, but rather is a theory of distinctive feature representations. What we are calling "mutations" are processes affecting certain configurations of features; we would therefore expect to find some which are morphological and others which are not. Let us look first at Mende and then at Chamorro.

The facts of mutation in Mende are as follows (all data are taken from Rice and Cowper 1984). The series of initial consonants listed in environment 2 in (56) occurs where indicated in (67) (= Rice and Cowper's [3]); Rice and Cowper call these the "mutated forms":

(67) a. [_{VP}NP V]   The initial consonant of the verb mutates.

        ì nyá wókɔ̀ɛlɔ́   'he imitated me'
        he me imitate   (pókɔ̀ɔ 'imitate')

   b. [_{NP}NP N]   The initial consonant of the noun mutates.

        ndòpóí bòwèí   'the child's knife'
        child   knife   (mbówɛ́í 'the knife')

c. [_{NP}N Adj Adj] The initial consonants of the adjectives mutate.

ngílà jèmbè lèlíí ná　　'that big black dog'
dog big　　black that　(sɛ́mbɛ́ 'big',
　　　　　　　　　　　　ʈèlí　'black')

d. [_{pp}NP P] The initial consonant of the postposition mutates.

ndèndéí bù　　　　'in the shade'
shade　under　　(mbù 'under')

e. [_SNP Prt [_{VP}V]] In some intransitive sentences, the initial consonant of the verb mutates.

mú vèmbɛ́ìlɔ́ ngúlíí hỳ　'we swung on the tree'
we swung　　tree　on　(mú vèmbɛ́ìlɔ́ 'we
　　　　　　　　　　　　swung'
　　　　　　　　　　　　fèmbɛ́í　'the swing')

f. [_NN N] fèfè léndèí　　'sailboat'
wind boat　　(ndèndèí 'boat')

(68) a. [_{VP}e V] If the object of a transitive verb is phonologically null, mutation fails to occur.

ndòpóì ＿＿ fèmbɛ́ngà　'the child swung it'
child　　swing
ndòpóì mbòmèí　　　'the child swung the
vèmbɛ́ngà　　　　　hammock'

b. [_{pp}e P] If the object of a postposition is phonologically null, mutation fails to occur.

＿＿ mbù　　　'under it'
ndèndèí bù　　'under the boat'

c. [_{VP}t V] If the object of a transitive verb is extracted leaving a trace, mutation fails to occur.

gbɛ́mìá ndòpóì ＿ kpàndìá 'What has the child heated?'
ngúlɛ́í mìa ndòpóì ＿＿ kpàndìá 'It's the oil that
　　　　　　　　　　　　the child has heated'
ndòpóì ngúlɛ́í gbàndìá　　'The child heated the oil'

d. [_SNP Prt [V…]] In some intransitive sentences, the initial consonant of the verb fails to mutate.

tí kàkpángà ngì má　'they surrounded him'
*tí gàkpángà ngì má
*tí kàkpángà

Rice and Cowper (1984) summarize the syntactic environments in which mutations occur as follows (= their [5]):

(69) If a lexical item of a major category c-commands and is immediately to the right of any phonological material then the initial consonant of that item mutates.

In other words, what I have arbitrarily designated as environment 2 in (56) is the general syntactic position designated by the arrows in (70):

(70)

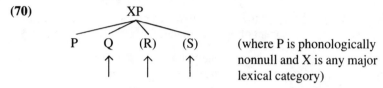

(where P is phonologically nonnull and X is any major lexical category)

It is easy to see how most of the environments in (67) fit into configuration (70). The only one that needs some clarification is (67e). According to Rice and Cowper, sentences like the one in (67e) have the structure (71):

(71)

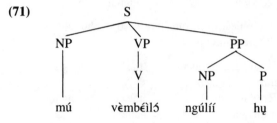

The PP in this sentence is in S, rather than in VP. Since VP does not branch in this structure, V c-commands the subject NP and mutation occurs. In contrast, in the sort of sentence illustrated in (68d), mutation cannot occur. The PP here is within the VP, the VP is therefore branching, and the V does not c-command the phonological material which precedes it:

(72)

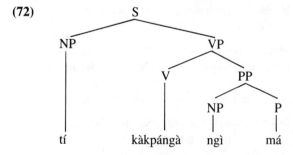

As Rice and Cowper (1984) correctly point out, mutation in Mende is probably not triggered on an initial consonant by the morpheme to its left. Such an analysis would be cumbersome in that every Mende noun and adjective (and also particles) would have to end in a floating autosegment [+ cont, + voice].

In addition, it would have to be stipulated that this autosegment attaches just in case the item to its right c-commands it. And mutation in Mende does not appear to be a morpheme in its own right. It is not a noun class morpheme as in Fula, or a verb tense morpheme as in Nuer; that much is clear.

Rather, as Rice and Cowper seem to suggest, it is the effect of a syntactic rule of some sort, a rule which inserts [+voice, +cont] as a kind of clitic to the left of any lexical item in the environment described in (69). The clitic then attaches to the initial consonant of the stem in the usual way, as illustrated in (73):

(73)

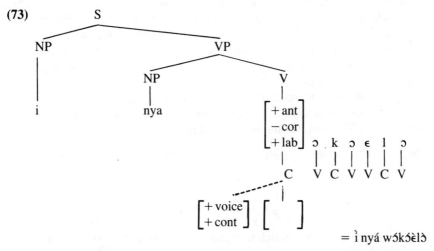

= ì nyá wɔ́kɔ́èlɔ̀

We will assume that the features [−voice, −cont] are added as default features if an initial consonant remains underspecified at the end of a derivation. Note that these are exactly the same default features as those we postulated for Chemehuevi. This fact suggests that [−voice] and [−continuant] are the unmarked features for consonants and should be the universal default features (see Chomsky and Halle 1968).

Although this analysis of Mende forces us to say that not all cases of mutation are morphological in precisely the same way that mutations in Fula, Nuer, Chemehuevi, and German are, I would like to suggest that it is completely unproblematic when viewed in light of other autosegmental analyses. This analysis suggests that autosegmental representations are assembled as an ongoing process throughout the derivation of a sentence. While the phonological content of most words in most sentences in most languages is already fully assembled by the time words are inserted into sentences, in some cases bits of phonological content in the form of floating autosegments can be provided as part of the syntactic derivation. But this in fact is nothing unusual. A similar thing seems to happen in some tonal systems. For example, in Etsako, an associative construction is marked by a floating H tone between the two nouns (data from Elimelich 1976, as cited in Schuh 1978):

(74) /àmὲ ´ èθà/ → ámêθà 'water of father'
/únò ´ òké/ → únôké 'mouth of a ram'
/ódzí ´ ɔ́mɔ̀/ → ójɔ́mɔ̀ 'crab of a child'
/ɔ̀té ´ èθà/ → ɔ̀têθà 'cricket of a father'

(Additional tonal rules raise to H all Ls preceding the floating H.) It appears that this floating H is inserted into a tree in a syntactic configuration not unlike (although clearly more limited than) the one described for Mende. According to Tadadjeu (1974), as cited in Schuh (1978), a similar situation obtains in Dschang Bamileke, where the associative marker is either H or L, depending on the class of the first noun in the associative construction. It is thus possible that the floating autosegment [+ voice, + continuant] in Mende is simply an associative marker, a kind of morpheme perhaps, but one which appears only in certain syntactic configurations. This sort of mutation, then, is no problem in principle for the present theory.

Nor is the sort of mutation process found in Chamorro a problem for the present theory, even though it again is not morphological. According to Topping (1968), Chamorro has the vowels in (75):

(75)

	Front	Back
High	i	u
Mid	e	o
Low	æ	a

When preceded by the particles, prefixes, or infixes in (76), an initial stem vowel is always fronted:

(76) Topping (1968, 69)

i	definite, focus-marking common article
si	definite, focus-marking personal article
ni	non-focus-marking common article
gi	'to, at'
in	'we (excl.)'
en	'you (pl.)'
-in-	goal focus infix
sæn-	directional prefix
mi-	'lots of'

(77)

guma'	'house'	i gíma'	'the house'
nána	'mother'	si nǽna	'Mother'
fógon	'stove'	ni fégon	'the stove'
ókso'	'hill'	gi ékso'	'at the hill'
tuŋo'	'to know'	in tíŋo'	'we (excl.) know'
tuŋo'	'to know'	en tíŋo'	'you (pl.) know'

góde	'to tie'	g-in-éde	'thing tied'
húlo'	'up'	sæn-hílo'	'in the direction up'
lágu	'north'	sæn-lǽgu	'towards north '
ótdot	'ant'	mi-étdot	'lots of ants'

As the examples in (77) show, all prefixes, particles, and infixes with front vowels condition the change on the stem vowel, and only the first vowel of the stem is fronted. We can account for these facts autosegmentally in much the same way that we did for Umlaut.[41]

Let us assume first that in Chamorro the feature [back] is projected on a separate autosegmental tier. Since the frontness or backness of vowels in either stems or affixes is not predictable, we will have to assume that morphemes are underlyingly specified for this feature. The first pair of forms will therefore have lexical representations like those in (78):

(78) a. $[+\mathrm{bk}]$ $[+\mathrm{bk}]$ **b.** $[-\mathrm{bk}]$ $[+\mathrm{bk}]$ $[+\mathrm{bk}]$

$$\mathrm{g}\ \begin{bmatrix}+\mathrm{hi}\\-\mathrm{lo}\end{bmatrix}\ \mathrm{m}\ \begin{bmatrix}-\mathrm{hi}\\+\mathrm{lo}\end{bmatrix}\ '\qquad \begin{bmatrix}+\mathrm{hi}\\-\mathrm{lo}\end{bmatrix}\ \mathrm{g}\ \begin{bmatrix}+\mathrm{hi}\\-\mathrm{lo}\end{bmatrix}\ \mathrm{m}\ \begin{bmatrix}-\mathrm{hi}\\+\mathrm{lo}\end{bmatrix}\ '$$

$$\mathrm{C}\quad \mathrm{V}\quad \mathrm{C}\quad \mathrm{V}\quad \mathrm{C}\qquad\quad \mathrm{V}\quad \mathrm{C}\quad \mathrm{V}\quad \mathrm{C}\quad \mathrm{V}\quad \mathrm{C}$$

Let us assume as well that Chamorro also has a Delinking rule which breaks the first [back] association in the stem and a Spreading rule which allows [−bk] to reassociate rightwards.[42] We will then get the derivation in (79):

(79) $[-\mathrm{bk}]$ $[+\mathrm{bk}]$ $[+\mathrm{bk}]$

$$\begin{bmatrix}+\mathrm{hi}\\-\mathrm{lo}\end{bmatrix}\ \mathrm{g}\ \begin{bmatrix}+\mathrm{hi}\\-\mathrm{lo}\end{bmatrix}\ \mathrm{m}\ \begin{bmatrix}-\mathrm{hi}\\+\mathrm{lo}\end{bmatrix}\ '$$

$$\mathrm{V}\quad \mathrm{C}\quad \mathrm{V}\quad \mathrm{C}\quad \mathrm{V}\quad \mathrm{C}\quad =\ \mathrm{i\ gima'}$$

The [−bk] feature of the particle fills in the feature that has been lost through delinking.

This process is like German Umlaut in that it involves fronting of stem vowels that are already specified for the feature [back]. But it is also unlike German Umlaut in one significant way: it is phonological rather than morphological. Topping's description suggests that **any** particle, prefix, or infix containing a [−bk] vowel will have this effect. This process in Chamorro deviates from the central cases of mutation in a number of ways; it involves lexical specification of the [back] feature, delinking, and in this case a limited spreading. It is perhaps on the periphery of what we might call "mutation." Still, it involves projection of an independent tier and bears enough resemblance to these cases to be included in this chapter.

2.6 MUTATION SUMMARY

Having looked at a good sampling of mutation processes from a number of unrelated languages, we can now begin to draw some conclusions. First, we can conclude that the present autosegmental framework can not only account for all of the mutation processes we have seen here—those which involve simple phonetic alternations and those, like Mende and Welsh, which involve complex alternations, those which are morphological and those which are not —but can also make interesting and correct predictions about the range of possible mutation processes and the locality of mutation processes. Such predictions, we saw, are not available within a segmental analysis. Indeed, the first prediction is available only within the present framework, since it derives from the theory of precedence of features developed in chapter 1. Thus, in the analysis of mutation the present framework proves extremely fruitful.

Moreover, what has developed here is the same sort of picture we saw developing with infixation in chapter 1, only on a somewhat larger scale. There we began to see that what was called "infixation" in one language did not turn out to be formally identical to phenomena that were called "infixation" in other languages. While all infixation processes had a common element in the autosegmental analysis—prespecification of features on one or more skeleton slots— they differed in other elements. The same is obviously true of mutations. While some mutations involve underspecification of lexical stems (Fula, Chemehuevi, Nuer, Welsh), others work on fully specified stems (German, Chamorro). (We will see in the next chapter that harmony processes can also be distinguished in this respect.) While most involve floating autosegments, one (Chamorro) did not. And while most are morphological, a few (Mende, Chamorro) are not. In fact, when we carefully examine all these mutation processes, it appears that there are only two elements in the autosegmental analysis that all cases of mutatation have in common. First, all involve the projection of an independent mutation tier. And second, such processes appear never to involve unbounded spreading of the mutation features. Rather, in all cases mutation features affect a single neighboring segment. We will see in the next chapter that harmonies differ from mutations in this last respect alone.

NOTES: CHAPTER 2

1. Rice and Cowper (1984) make this claim about Mende alone.

2. A few notes on Fula phonology might be useful at the outset. First, **sh** [š] is a palatal fricative in the Gombe dialect described by Arnott (1970). In other dialects the expected dental stop or a palatalized dental stop appears in alternation with **s**. Second, **w** alternates with both labials and velars. I will assume here the analysis of Anderson (1976), in which some **w**'s are basically labial and others basically velar. Finally, **y** also appears in two series—the palatal one before back vowels and the velar one before front vowels. Note also that the consonants **m, n, ny, ŋ, l, t** and the glottalized consonants **ɓ, ɗ, 'y** and **'** do not participate in the gradation system.

3. The analysis given there differs in details from the one given here, but it could easily be translated into the present framework.

4. The class numbering system is taken from Arnott (1970).

5. The reader might wonder why I am calling the features in (4) "prefixes," since in the final phonological representation they do not strictly **precede** the initial segment of the stem. We might, for example, conceive of an analysis in which the mutation features are inserted by some sort of morphological process which would fill in missing features on the initial consonant of the stem in the environment of certain class-marking suffixes. In such an analysis, the mutation features would not have to be called "prefixes."

My reason for rejecting this alternative lies in the conception of morphology offered by Lieber (1980, 1983a) and Marantz (1982) and defended explicitly in Lieber (1986). In these works, it is suggested that the simplest and best constrained conception of morphology is one which is entirely **configurational**. In a strictly configurational theory, all morphemes are listed in the lexicon with morphological subcategorizations, that is, indications of what sort of morphological constituent they attach to. The only "processes" allowed in word formation in such a theory are (1) a process of lexical insertion in which morphemes are inserted into binary-branching trees such that their subcategorizations are satisfied, and (2) a process of feature percolation whereby features of the outermost morpheme, including its category, percolate to the top of the morphological tree (see Lieber [1980, 1983a] for a detailed statement of feature percolation). For example, the morphemes **happy** and **-ness** would have the lexical representations in (i). The suffix **-ness** has a subcategorization which indicates that it attaches to an adjective and produces a noun. (ii) illustrates the word tree that would result after lexical insertion and feature percolation:

(i)   happy   [hæpi]   [__]_A

       -ness   [nɛs]   [[X]_A——]_N   'the abstract quality of X'

(ii)

Such a configurational theory of word formation is highly restrictive. It claims that all morphemes —that is, all meaningful units—are "things" listed in the lexicon and that morphological "processes" are highly limited. No morphological processes other than lexical insertion and feature percolation are sanctioned within such a theory.

Now, to the extent that such a restrictive theory is highly valued, we would want to treat consonant mutation within this theory: that is, although it may be possible to postulate the morphological process described above for inserting the mutation features in Fula, such a move introduces a new process into the theory and is therefore undesirable. On the other hand, we will see that if the mutation features in Fula are treated as prefixes, Fula and the other mutation languages can be fitted into a configurational theory of morphology without complicating it.

There is a further reason for treating the mutation features in Fula as prefixes. We will see shortly that in other languages with mutation, the mutation features actually appear as part of overt prefixes (if the mutation is initial—see Chemehuevi, below) or suffixes (if the mutation is final— see Nuer)—that is, as part of morphemes which have complete segments in addition to the floating autosegment.

6. Noun class membership is not predictable on any grounds—semantic, phonological, or otherwise. Although class 1 is generally the singular class for humans and class 2 the corresponding plural class, the other classes are not correlated with any coherently defined semantic fields.

7. I have illustrated an invariant noun paradigm with a stop-initial noun **beebe**. There are also invariant continuant-initial nouns (**sooro** 'flat roofed building') and invariant prenasalized stop-initial nouns (**mbosam** 'bone marrow').

8. See Lieber (1984) for a comparison of the autosegmental account with previous segmental ones (Anderson 1976, Skousen 1972) and for arguments that the autosegmental account is to be preferred.

9. All Nuer data are from Crazzolara (1933).

10. Crazzolara assumes a phonological rule h → Ø / __ k operating on the underlying form **jah + ko** and others like it.

11. This is true of all the "irregular" forms Crazzolara cites except for one form ending in an invariant **dh** (1933, 159) and two forms ending in alveolars where three different allomorphs appear, but not in the expected environments.

12. All data in this section are from Press (1979).

13. Since the nasalizing prefixes actually produce prenasalized stops, I have chosen to represent them as a sequence of [nasal] features attached to a single autosegment.

14. So far I have suppressed the mutation tier for all but the marginal (initial or final) consonant which mutates. This has merely been a way of making the representations easier to read, and has no theoretical significance.

   Note also that in (26) the melody and the mutation tier are both independently attached to the skeleton. This appears to be the simplest assumption, but see McCarthy (1983) for an argument that in the Semitic language Chaha the mutation tier attaches to melody segments and melody segments to skeleton slots.

15. We must assume that if stems like the one in (28b) appear in isolation, or with suffixes other than the lexically marked one, the final floating C is deleted or left phonetically unrealized.

16. The same argument—that we do not have to stipulate that the initial (or final) consonants of stems are underspecified, hence that fully specified initial (final) segments are ruled out on independent grounds—can be made for Nuer and Chemehuevi, although different mutation features are involved in each case. In Nuer the mutation features are various values of the features [continuant, voice]. Nuer does not allow either voicing or continuancy "contours," so regardless of the features a Nuer stem might bear on its final segment, once a mutation suffix is attached, an inadmissible contour will result and the representation will be ruled out. In Chemehuevi the mutation tier consists of the features [voice, continuant, nasal]. The only sorts of "contours" Chemehuevi permits are [+ nas][− nas] (prenasalization) and [− cont][+ cont] for an affricate (although apparently the only affricate that occurs is the voiceless [c]). But it is easy to show that neither of these contours will arise if the Chemehuevi prefixes are attached to stems with already specified initial segments (the prefixes are repeated below):

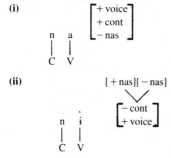

(i)

(ii)

If (ii) were attached to an already specified initial segment, the representation would immediately be ruled out; three [nasal] features would be attached to the same C. And if (i) were attached to an already specified initial consonant, that representation would also be ruled out. No matter what values of [voice, nasal, continuant] were chosen, the result would be an inadmissible contour, since (i) contains the minus value for [nasal] and the plus value for [continuant]; that is, neither the prenasalized contour nor the affricate contour could ever result.

17. Partially variable stems will never give rise to the sort of representation given in (34). Since the initial consonant in these cases is prespecified for only one of the mutation features, the prefix will anchor to that consonant and fill in what is missing.

18. Briefly, I argue there that the autosegmental analysis, because it assumes that underlying forms of noun stems are underspecified for the mutation features, allows us to make more accurate predictions as to the range of possible noun paradigms that should occur in Fula. The segmental analyses, Anderson (1976) and Skousen (1972), each of which must choose one member of the noun paradigm as underlying (that is, the stop-initial stem, the continuant-initial stem, or prenasalized stop-initial stem), make less accurate predictions. For example, if stop-initial stems are taken as underlying, as is done in Skousen (1972), all continuant- and prenasalized stop-initial stems must be derived by regular phonological rules. This then predicts that there should be no noun paradigms in Fula in which stop-initial stems are invariant. Yet there are such paradigms, as shown in section 2.1.1. Similar false predictions are made if either of the two other possible stems is taken as underlying. As shown above, however, the autosegmental analysis of mutation in Fula makes more accurate predictions.

19. Roughly, we will assume that words like **bartig** or **ämtlich**, which can be generated by the grammar alongside **bärtig** and **amtlich**, are possible words, although nonoccuring, except possibly dialectally. Facts like the following argue for this analysis. First, there are some forms with Umlaut variable suffixes where both possible derivatives exist, some with slightly different meanings, others varying according to ideolect (for example, **förmlich** and **formlich**; **Schläger** and **Schlager**, etc.). Second, there are forms like **tonig, tieftonig,** and **hochtonig** alongside **eintönig, vieltönig, hochtönig**, and **misstönig**; it seems that even if the form **tönig** is not an actually occurring word, it must be generated alongside **tonig** and available for further derivation. Such facts, among others (see Lieber 1980), argue for the "overgenerating" analysis of umlaut assumed here.

20. We do not in fact have to use lexical linking here. The feature [back] could be unlinked in the lexical entry and a rule of association linking [back] to [+ syl] would create the initial linkings. The direction of linking would be right to left, since in the suffixes we want the leftmost [back] feature to be left floating.

21. We will see below that there are harmonies as well as mutations which require underlying representations to be fully specified for the harmonizing feature.

22. Actually, we must assume that the feature [back] is projected only for vowels, that is, that [back] attaches only to [+ syl]. For consonants it is safe to assume that there is no [back] specification and that [back] is filled in by default near the end of the derivation but before the operation of rule (49).

23. Another affix which regularly conditions Umlaut is one that we might write **Ge . . . e**. This affix makes abstract nouns from verb stems (**bauen** ~ **Gebäude**). Exactly how this is represented autosegmentally depends upon how we choose to treat affixes which appear to be discontinuous. Since I have nothing to say about this issue here, I will leave the representation of this affix open.

24. Note that since the value of the feature [back] for stem vowels is unpredictable in German, these vowels will always be specified for backness by the time that rule (40) operates. Thus, there will never be anywhere for the back feature delinked by (40) to reattach. Note also that Pulleyblank (1983, 135) suggests that features dissociated by delinking rules cannot reattach in any case.

25. We must assume for these two affixes that either **both** umlauted forms (that is, with -**er** and -**st**) are lexicalized or neither umlauted form is. Perhaps this effect could be made to follow within some well-articulated theory of the paradigm.

26. Another derivation is possible here, of course, depending upon how the rules are ordered:

Plural stem	Affen
Dative plural	Affen + n
e-Epenthesis	Affen + en
e-Deletion	Affen + n
Degemination	Affen

In other words, if Degemination were ordered before e-Epenthesis and e-Deletion, then the two (seemingly superfluous) steps shown above would not take place.

27. **Bäch** is the plural stem without any case endings.

28. I have shown elsewhere (Lieber 1980, 1982) that both allomorphs must be listed since both can be the input to rules of derivation and compounding, which are clearly part of the morphological component.

29. This statement of the rule accounts only for the distribution of [ç] in native words in German. See Kloeke (1982) and references cited therein for ways of extending the rule to foreign words in German. Note also that although the rule in (49) is stated as a segmental rule, it could be recast as an autosegmental rule. Nothing hinges on this statement here.

30. The derivation of the word **Frauchen** does have to be treated as exceptional within anyone's analysis of Umlaut, since -**chen** is a suffix which normally does trigger Umlaut. Here we might assume that the word **Frau** is simply lexically specified not to allow attachment of the [− bk] floating autosegment with -**chen**. The segmental analysis would probably have to resort to lexical specification of this stem also, perhaps by diacritic.

31. Above, of course, I assumed Wurzel's (1970) analysis, in which even inflectional schwa is inserted by rule.

32. An alternative to rule (53) would be to assume that Epenthesis works in conjunction with syllabification in German. When a final nasal or liquid is left unsyllabified by rules creating syllables, schwa is inserted to permit syllabification.

33. Nothing crucial hinges on this decision: that is, rule (53) could be written so as to insert both the V slot and the melody features for schwa simultaneously.

34. Note that although cases like **mütterlich** in German conceivably might have been analyzed as having [+ back] prespecified on the second stem vowel (the schwa), there is good evidence that the schwa is not in fact there underlyingly and therefore that we need not resort to prespecification. In other words, because prespecification is highly marked within this theory, the theory forces us to choose the other possible analysis for German. For Chaha, however, prespecification appears to be the **only** option.

35. Here and in the other representations in this section, I am representing only the floating autosegments (such as [− voice, − cont]) and the underspecified initial segment of a stem. In a full analysis of of Welsh, the mutation features would, of course, be prefixes or be part of prefixes or other morphemes like prepositions and clitics. The melody features would be part of a complete stem. See Lieber (1983b) for a discussion of some of the environments in which mutation occurs in Welsh. See section 2.5 for a fuller discussion of Mende. Note again (note 30, chapter 1) that the DFF can "jettison" one feature of the mutation tier if only one of the mutation features is prespecified in the core.

36. The segment [g] must be treated as utterly exceptional in any framework. Here we might assume a special rule which deletes the [ɣ] that has been created in environment 2.

37. Since Nasalization is also a mutation, we might assume that initial consonants are in general not specified for the feature [nasal] either. The environment 1 features would actually be [− voice, − continuant, − nasal], and the environment 2 features [+ voice, + continuant, − nasal].

38. The other mutations in Welsh, Nasalization and Frication, are phonetically quite regular:

Env. 1		Nasalization		Frication	
p		mh	[m̥]	ph	[f]
t		nh	[n̥]	th	[θ]
c	[k]	ngh	[ŋ̥]	ch	[x]
b		m			
d		n			
g		ŋ			

We might assume that initial consonants in Welsh are also underspecified for the feature [nasal]. In environment 1, consonants receive the [− nasal] feature and in the Nasalization environments the feature [+ nasal].

The Frication case is somewhat more difficult, but not impossible to work out in the autosegmental framework. In this case, only the first three consonants in the above list undergo a mutation, and these are the ones which we have given a prespecified [− continuant] feature. Yet in the Frication environment, they show up as [+ continuant]. Since the [− continuant] inherent specification would override any [+ continuant] floating autosegment, it seems that Frication cannot be handled in this way. There is, however, another possibility in this case. Traditional grammars of Welsh refer to the Frication mutation as **Aspiration**. Suppose that the consonants that show up as **p, t, c** in environment 1 are underlyingly unspecified for the feature [aspirated]. The Lenition and Nasalization mutations will supply the feature [− aspirated], and the Frication/Aspiration mutation will supply the feature [+ aspirated], in a floating autosegment. We will then assume that a low-level and perhaps historically late rule changes [− voice, + aspirated] segments to [+ continuant].

39. Actually, the appearance of **b** as the reflex of **mb** in environment 2 requires more comment. Let us assume that after the nasal features have been degeminated in the environment 2 form in (63), the result for the [+ ant, − cor] segment is [β]. But this is not a segment of Mende. Let us then assume that a low-level phonetic rule changes the [β] to [b], so that the alternation that appears on the surface is **mb ~ b**. Larry Hyman (personal communication) informs me that in Kpelle the expected bilabial continuant appears, although it is implosive.

40. For another segmental approach to Welsh mutations, see Sproat (1982-ms).

41. In fact, it is likely that German Umlaut was once phonologically conditioned too. If so, it would have worked much like the process in Chamorro does, except that the triggers would have been suffixes rather than prefixes and initial particles.

42. Note that we must assume once again that a delinked feature cannot be relinked (see Pulleyblank 1983, 135).

Chapter 3

HARMONY

Harmony processes have received a great deal more attention in the generative literature than mutation processes have, and there has been widespread agreement that some harmony processes at least are best treated autosegmentally (Clements 1980a, Halle and Vergnaud 1981, Poser 1982). But there are still several sorts of harmony that have been difficult to treat within previous autosegmental frameworks—harmonies with neutral segments, harmonies which require directional linking or spreading, harmonies which seem to change features rather than adding features, harmonies which seem to be sensitive to vowel length, and harmonies which contain "blockers," that is, segments which prevent the spread of harmony but do not start a new harmony domain. Some of the above problem cases, it has been claimed, are better treated within a metrical framework than within an autosegmental one. But this bifurcation of harmony processes into those which are autosegmental and those which are metrical is problematic for at least two reasons. Foremost is the problem of language acquisition; if two analyses are potentially possible for any given harmony process, then how is the child (or the linguist) to decide between them?[1] Second, harmonies that are analyzed within the metrical framework in principle cannot be compared to autosegmental harmonies; in bifurcating harmony processes into two sorts, we lose the ability to gauge relative formal complexity, relative markedness, and so on, and thereby the ability to predict the probability of occurrence of any given type of harmony. Having available only a single framework in which to analyze harmonies would therefore be preferable.

In this chapter I will attempt to defend the claim that **all** harmonies should be treated autosegmentally. We will see that the autosegmental framework we have been developing here provides everything necessary to do so. We will also see that harmony processes, like mutation and infixation, are not all formally identical to one another. Some require underspecification of stems, others not. Some require Delinking rules, others not. Some require prespecification, and others do not. Still, there will be one common formal element that underlies all harmonies, namely, that all require the unbounded spreading of the harmonizing feature, and this element will provide us with an interesting basis for comparing harmony and mutation in section 3.4.

Since harmony has already been treated quite extensively in other autosegmental frameworks (Clements 1980a, Halle and Vergnaud 1981), it might be useful from the outset to highlight those points on which my analysis will differ from others that have been proposed. With this in mind, I will first briefly sketch the major features of harmony processes within the present framework, as well as the parameters along which these processes will differ. The taxonomy of harmony processes which will emerge will provide a framework for the harmony analyses to be given below.

First, as in all other autosegmental frameworks, harmony here will involve the projection of a feature or features ([nasal], [back], [round], [ATR]—henceforth the **harmonizing features**) on a separate autosegmental tier. In previous autosegmental analyses (Clements 1980a, Halle and Vergnaud 1981, Poser 1982), the core to which the harmonizing feature attaches is largely underspecified for that feature. One exception has previously been sanctioned. As noted in section 1.6.3, opaque segments, those which do not themselves undergo harmony but which trigger harmony on succeeding segments, have been analyzed in the past as features on the harmony tier which are lexically linked to segments in the core (Clements 1980a, p. 24). For example, we saw in Turkish that nonhigh vowels did not undergo rounding harmony, but triggered rounding harmony on succeeding vowels; this fact was represented by linking the feature [round] to every nonhigh vowel in the lexicon:

(1) (= (chapter 1–93))   g   i   d   +   I   y   o   r   +   I   m
                                                                 |
         [− rd]   [+ rd]

We saw in section 1.6.3, however, that the present framework, unlike previous ones, also had a convenient way of dealing with so-called neutral segments. These were the segments that neither underwent harmony nor triggered harmony; as far as the harmony process was concerned, these segments were simply invisible. In the present framework, it was proposed in section 1.6.3 that neutral segments were those which were prespecified for the harmonizing feature in the core. Thus, when the harmonizing feature was linked to the core, the prespecified value would always override the value provided by the harmony tier, given the DFF. Neutral segments, in other words, were simply one manifestation of prespecification.

The present framework also differs from earlier proposals in another way. At least two previous autosegmental frameworks (Halle and Vergnaud 1981, Poser 1982) have assumed that autosegmental harmony invariably has the following two characteristics. First, the rules associating harmony feature to core are always bidirectional, and second, the morphemes to which the harmonizing feature attaches are always underspecified for that feature. But there is nothing in the present framework which forces us to make these assumptions.

Indeed, I will assume the opposite here, namely, that association can be directional and that all morphemes in a particular language can be underlyingly fully specified for the harmonizing feature. I have shown above (section 1.4) that there is a reason to believe that Association and/or Spreading are sometimes directional in tone systems, in the linking of melody to skeleton, and in mutation processes. If directional Association and Spreading are needed for these other cases, then I see no reason why we should not also make use of them for harmony processes. In fact, it would seem odd if we could not find harmony processes which required directional rules of Association and Spreading. I will also try to suggest that it is arbitrary to require underspecification of the core in all cases of autosegmental harmony. Specifically, there is a class of harmonies that have been referred to in the literature (Poser 1982) as "feature-changing" harmonies; these are cases in which all morphemes seem to have inherent values for all features, and yet in certain contexts they still seem to harmonize. I will argue that since the devices of lexical linking and Delinking are independently needed in autosegmental theory, there is no reason why they should not also be put to use in the analysis of feature-changing harmonies. We have, in fact, already used these devices in analyzing Umlaut in German and mutation in Chamorro. The payoff here will be as follows. By using directional Association and Spreading, lexical linking and Delinking rules in the analysis of harmony systems, I will be adding nothing to autosegmental theory, but I will be eliminating from linguistic theory the need for the metrical formalism and for the bifurcation of harmony processes into autosegmental versus metrical.

The elimination of metrical analyses for harmony systems will be a positive result for other reasons as well. First, at their best, metrical analyses are based on natural prosodic divisions like **moras**, **syllables**, or **feet**. In contrast, for harmony analyses within the metrical framework, it was often the case that the domain of harmony corresponded to no standard hierarchical unit. In the languages in question (see below for examples), harmony units were entirely independent of all other sorts of linguistic units. Second, it has never been proven that for metrical harmony systems the binary-branching of metrical trees does any work. Attempts to show that the relative depth of embedding of a particular segment corresponds to the degree of nasalization, rounding, or whatever (that is, that the distance from the harmony trigger determines the amount of nasalization, roundness, etc.) seem to have failed (Poser 1982). And finally, for independent reasons, the need to use metrical theory to analyze other phonological phenomena such as stress systems has been questioned (Prince 1983).This fact calls into question the usefulness of any metrical analysis. Eliminating metrical harmonies therefore seems desirable on a number of grounds.

The harmony analyses given within the present framework will involve setting the following four parameters: (i) what the harmonizing features are and whether both or only one of the values of those features is projected, (ii) whether all segments are already lexically specified for the harmonizing feature or not, (iii) whether there is any lexical linking (that is, opaque segments) or prespecification (that is, neutral segments), and (iv) what the direction of association and spreading is. Fixing the first two parameters will be the most important in determining the major characteristics of each harmony system. To begin with the second parameter, if core segments are largely underspecified in the lexicon for the harmonizing feature, then we will have what might be called a "feature-adding" harmony. If, however, morphemes are already specified for the harmonizing feature, then we will have a feature-changing harmony: that is, we will see that harmony processes are distinguished from one another in exactly the same way that mutation analyses were.

How the first parameter is set also has an important role in distinguishing harmony systems. It has been shown (Halle and Vergnaud 1981) that for some harmony systems only one value of the harmonizing feature triggers or induces harmony (for example, only [+ ATR] in Kalenjin; see below), whereas in others both the plus and minus values do. Halle and Vergnaud have called the former sort of harmony "dominant" harmony. For lack of a better term, let us call the latter sort "ordinary" harmony.

Now since these parameters are in principle independent of one another, we ought to find four different kinds of harmony systems. These are mapped out in (2):

(2)

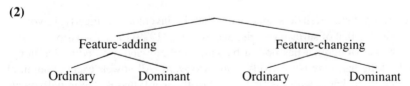

In the sections that follow, I will show that three of the four sorts of system do, in fact, exist, and will suggest that the absence of the fourth sort of system follows from the present autosegmental framework as well. In section 3.1 I will give examples of feature-adding harmonies, both ordinary (Khalka Mongolian) and dominant (Kalenjin). Section 3.2 will cover the one sort of feature-changing harmony that seems to exist—the ordinary feature-changing harmony of Chumash. Out of the Chumash analysis will emerge one possible reason for the absence of dominant feature-changing harmonies. In section 3.2 I will also attempt to redeem a promissory note made back in section 1.4.3. There I suggested that the framework being developed predicted that there should be no harmony or mutation process based on the feature [anterior]. Since Chumash has been cited in the literature (Poser 1982) as an example of [anterior] harmony, I will look at it in detail here, and argue that it is not in fact a counterexample to this prediction. Finally, in section 3.3 I will look at a case of harmony in Andalusian Spanish that seems to provide a strong case for metrical harmony, and argue that it too is just as well treated autosegmentally.

3.1 FEATURE-ADDING HARMONIES

3.1.1 Feature-Adding, Ordinary

Ordinary feature-adding harmonies are perhaps the most widespread and best studied of all harmony systems. Among them can be included harmony in Turkish, Finnish, Hungarian, Akan, and Guarani, and also the backness harmony of Classical Mongolian that I discussed in section 1.6.3. Recall that in the Classical Mongolian example all vowels in the core (except for [i], which was neutral) were underspecified for the feature [back]; stems could be either [+ back] or [− back], indicating that either value of the harmonizing feature could appear on the harmony tier. The [back] feature was linked to [+ syl] and [− ant, − cor] segments and spread left to right.

In this section I will discuss the case of Khalka Mongolian, which is both more challenging and more theoretically interesting than most cases of ordinary feature-adding harmony—more challenging because of the complexity of the data, and more interesting theoretically because it has previously been analyzed as metrical (Steriade 1979).[2]

The surface vowels of Khalka are set out in (3):

(3) i   ü   u
    e   ö   a   o

I will accept here Steriade's conclusion that the inventory of underlying vowels is identical to that of surface vowels. See Steriade (1979) for a discussion.

Khalka Mongolian has both a backing harmony and a rounding harmony. The backing harmony is relatively straightforward. All vowels except noninitial [i] agree in backness with the first vowel of the word: that is, the initial vowels of words, including [i], trigger backing harmony. Noninitial [i], however, is neutral with respect to both backing harmony and rounding harmony; it does not undergo either, but it also does not block either. Initial vowels—but not all of them—also trigger rounding harmony. All initial nonhigh vowels will trigger rounding, but of the high vowels, only [i] will. In fact, [u] and [ü] in any position will not undergo rounding harmony, they will not trigger it, and they will not permit its spread: that is, they are not **neutral** to rounding harmony since neutral segments typically permit harmony to spread past them. Rather, these two segments block harmony. Rounding in Khalka thus spreads from an initial vowel other than [u] or [ü] to succeeding vowels until a [u] or [ü] is reached, and there the spread of rounding stops. (4) contains some of the relevant data:

(4) a.

Infinitives	Distributives	Optatives	Passive + infinitive
ot-ox 'to keep a watch on'	xoš-ood 'by twos'	bol-oosoi 'become-OPT'	sons-ogd-ox 'to be heard'
örg-öx 'to raise'	dörb-ööd 'by fours'	örg-öösei[3] 'raise-OPT'	örg-ögd-öx 'to be raised'
avr-ax 'to save'	tab-aad 'by fives'	avr-assai 'save-OPT'	al-agd-ax 'to be saved'
nem-ex 'to add'	nej-eed 'by ones'	nem-eesei 'add-OPT'	nee-gd-ex 'to be opened'

b.

oril-ox 'to weep'	xorin-ood 'by twenties'	oril-oosoi 'weep-OPT'	oril-ogd-ox 'to be wept'

c. ir-ex
'to come'

d. Stems:

ünee	sudar
'cow'	'chronicle'

e.

Causative +	infinitive	Plurals	
boogd-uul-ax 'to hinder'	nül-üül-ex 'to write'	ger-üüd 'yurts'	nom-uud 'books'

As the examples in (4a) show, if a Khalka word contains only nonhigh vowels, all vowels agree in backness and roundness. (4b) illustrates the role of noninitial [i]; if the initial vowel is nonhigh, both backness and roundness harmonies spread over [i]. (4c) shows that if [i] is initial, however, a succeeding nonhigh vowel will agree with it in both roundness and backness. But if the initial vowel is [u] or [ü], as (4d) shows, the succeeding nonhigh vowel will agree only in backness. Finally, (4e) illustrates the behavior of noninitial [u] and [ü]; these vowels undergo the backing harmony, but they block the spread of rounding.

We can analyze Khalka as follows within our autosegmental framework. First, we will say that the initial vowels of all stems are opaque for both harmonizing features, [back] and [round]. Noninitial [i]s will be completely neutral; that is, they will have both [− back] and [− round] prespecified in the phonological core. All other noninitial high vowels (those that will surface as [u] and [ü]) will be opaque for the feature [+ round]; in other words, they will have a lexically attached [+ round] feature on the harmony tier. This will leave all nonhigh vowels underspecified for both [back] and [round] and high vowels except [i] underspecified for [back]. The words **sons-ogd-ox**, **oril-ogd-ox**, **ir-ex**, **ünee**, and **boogd-uul-ax** will have the lexical representations in (5):

(5) a. $[+\mathrm{rd}]$ (sons-ogd-ox)

b. $[+\mathrm{rd}]$ (oril-ogd-ox)

c. $[-\mathrm{rd}]$ (ir-ex)

d. $[+\mathrm{rd}]$ (ünee)

e. $[+\mathrm{rd}]$ $[+\mathrm{rd}]$ (boogd-uul-ax)

The reasons for projecting [back] and [round] on two separate autosegmental tiers will become apparent shortly. Let us assume now that Khalka has Spread-

ing rules which spread [back] and [round] rightwards, attaching them to [+ syl].
After Spreading we will have the representations in (6):

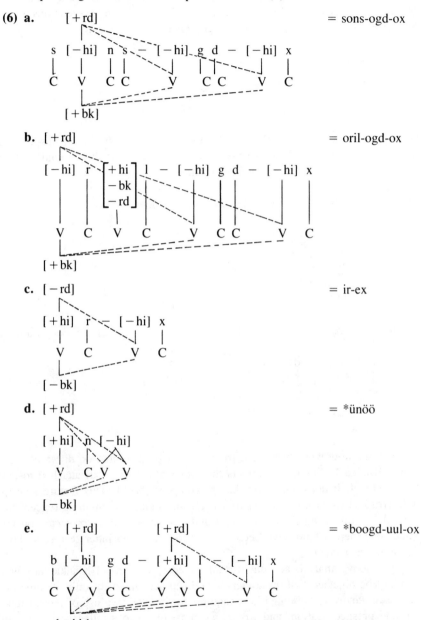

(6) a. = sons-ogd-ox

b. = oril-ogd-ox

c. = ir-ex

d. = *ünöö

e. = *boogd-uul-ox

As (6) illustrates, the backing and rounding harmonies spread properly in (a)–
(c), where there are no high round vowels; in (6b) the core specifications for
[back] and [round] override the features from the harmony tiers. However, we

get incorrect results for (6d) and (6e) because the [+rd] feature from the [+high] vowel has in each case spread to following vowels. What seems to be needed in our account is a special rule for Khalka which delinks any associations which have been spread from a [+round, +high] vowel:

(7) Khalka Delinking

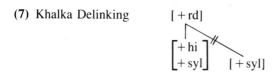

Once this delinking occurs, the vowels following [u] and [ü] will be unspecified for the feature [round]. We need only assume then that a default [−round] feature is supplied to such vowels late in the derivation:[4]

(8) a.

[+rd]   [−rd]   = ünee

   [+hi] n [−hi]

    V C V V

   [−bk]

b.

   [+rd]   [+rd]   [−rd] = boogd-uul-ax

  b [−hi] g d − [+hi] l [−hi] x

  C V V C C V V C V C

  [+bk]

We can see now why [back] and [round] must be projected on different tiers. While Khalka Delinking (7) affects the propagation of [+rd] attached to any [+hi] vowel, it does not affect the spreading of [back]. This feature spreads uninterrupted to [+high, +round] vowels and indeed to anything (except the neutral [i]) following them. If [back] and [round] had been projected on the same tier, there would have been no way to delink the latter feature without delinking the former.

The above analysis accounts for all the complex facts of Khalka harmony. It might be objected that these facts have been accounted for only at some expense; the analysis presented here requires fairly extensive use of lexical linking and prespecification, and worse, we must resort to a rather costly rule of Delinking to account for the blocking effect of [+high, +round] vowels. I would like to argue, however, that such an analysis is still to be preferred to a metrical one. Let me therefore give a brief sketch of Steriade's analysis.

Steriade (1979) argues first that each metrical harmony rule needs to stipulate two sets of elements: a first set A, which is the set of opaque elements, and a second set B, which is the projection (that is, the elements on which the metrical trees are constructed). She then stipulates the following convention (1979, 32):

(9) a. The intersection of A and B defines the set of triggering elements.
  b. The members of A not contained in B are the segments blocking the rule.
  c. The members of B not contained in A are the segments undergoing the rule.

Given these additions to metrical theory, Steriade states the backing harmony (her FH) as in (10a) and the rounding harmony (her RH) as in (10b) (1979, p 33):

(10) a. Front harmony (FH) **b.** Round harmony (RH)

A: $\begin{bmatrix} + \text{syl} \\ - \text{bk} \end{bmatrix}$ A: $\begin{bmatrix} + \text{syl} \\ + \text{rd} \end{bmatrix}$

B: $[+ \text{syl}]$ B: $\begin{bmatrix} + \text{syl} \\ - \text{hi} \end{bmatrix}$

Direction: Left to right Left to right

Harmonizing feature: $[- \text{bk}]$ $[+ \text{rd}]$

In other words, for backing harmony all vowels are projected, [−back] vowels are triggers, and there are no blockers. For rounding harmony, nonhigh vowels are projected, nonhigh round vowels are triggers, and high round vowels are blockers. Steriade argues that all vowels except the initial ones are unspecified for [back] and that noninitial nonhigh vowels are unspecified for [round]. To ensure this pattern, she states the condition in (11) (1979, 34):

(11) $[+ \text{syllabic}]$ is $\left\{ \begin{matrix} \begin{bmatrix} \pm \text{round} \\ - \text{high} \end{bmatrix} \\ [\pm \text{back}] \end{matrix} \right\}$ in all and only the environments $\#C_0$ ____.

Finally, since FH spreads only [−back] and RH only [+round], Steriade must assume that the features [+back] and [−round] are default features to be filled in on stems whose triggers (that is, initial vowels) are [+back] and/or [−round]. Presumably, FH will work as follows:

(12) nül-üül-ex

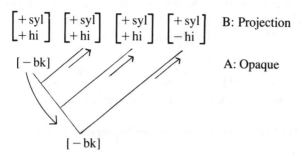

boogd-uul-ax

$$\begin{bmatrix} +\text{syl} \\ -\text{hi} \end{bmatrix} \quad \begin{bmatrix} +\text{syl} \\ -\text{hi} \end{bmatrix} \quad \begin{bmatrix} +\text{syl} \\ +\text{hi} \end{bmatrix} \quad \begin{bmatrix} +\text{syl} \\ +\text{hi} \end{bmatrix} \quad \begin{bmatrix} +\text{syl} \\ -\text{hi} \end{bmatrix} \quad \text{B: Projection}$$

None   A: Opaque

For the first example in (12) there is a trigger, namely, the first vowel. A left-branching tree is built starting at this segment, and the harmonizing feature percolates down to the other projected vowels. In the second example, however, there is no trigger, since the first vowel is inherently [+back]; the remaining vowels must get their [back] feature by default.

With FH we come to the first difficulty of the metrical analysis. Since the projection is [+syl], the vowel [i] will be projected along with all other vowels. Given the condition in (11), we must assume that noninitial [i] will be underspecified for the feature [back], although (11) would allow the underlying specification [−round]. Noninitial [i], for example in a word like **oril-ox**, would regularly undergo FH (or in this case, receive the default [+back]) and end up as [ɨ]. [ɨ] would then have to undergo a rule of absolute neutralization, which would return it to the surface vowel [i]. One major disadvantage of the metrical treatment, then, is that it requires a rule of absolute neutralization in addition to the other metrical machinery.

A second disadvantage appears when we look at RH. Here it is hard to see at all how the metrical machinery is meant to operate. Consider the derivation in (13):

(13) boogd-uul-ax

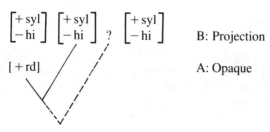

The projection omits the [+ high, + round] vowels, which presumably are un-derlyingly specified as [+ round]. (11) will permit this. The opaque element is the first [+ round]. The problem arises when tree construction begins. A left-branching tree begins at the first vowel, and clearly it must end before the [+ high, + round] vowels. But these are not projected. How then can the tree "see" them? In other words, it seems that the device that Steriade has added to metrical theory to account for blocking segments, namely, the condition in (9), will not work unless the operation of tree construction is redefined. We saw above that the blocking effects of [+ high, + round] vowels could be handled within an autosegmental framework by adding a rule of Delinking. Now, while this rule might come at some cost, its operation is at least clear and well de-fined, and it is not unlike other Delinking rules independently needed within autosegmental theory. The autosegmental treatment of blocking segments there-fore seems preferable at this point.

Added to this are the general objections to metrical harmony analyses which I mentioned above. First, the metrical trees constructed in the analysis of Khalka do not correspond to any independently needed prosodic unit; they pro-ceed from the first vowel and stop at any [+ high, + round] vowel for RH, a span which does not correspond to a mora, a syllable, a foot, or any other prosodic unit. Second, the binary-branching trees again do no real work. The depth of embedding of a particular vowel does not correlate with degree of backness or degree of roundness or anything else. Once again, the nonhier-archical structures of the autosegmental analysis, since they make no special claims in these respects, seem better suited to the data at hand.

Khalka Mongolian, then, complex as it is, can be treated as an ordinary feature-adding harmony within the present framework.

3.1.2 Feature-Adding, Dominant

Dominant feature-adding harmonies occur less frequently than ordinary ones, but they do exist. One example that has appeared recently in the generative literature is that of Kalenjin. Halle and Vergnaud (1981) discuss the East Afri-can language briefly and propose an autosegmental analysis within a slightly different framework than the one here; their analysis differs in several ways. I will point out below where it differs and why the analysis to be presented here is to be preferred (data are from Halle and Vergnaud 1981, unless otherwise specified):

Kalenjin has two sets of vowels:

(14) **a.** i   u   **b.** I   U

       e   o   ɛ   ɔ

              á   a

Dominant: [+ ATR]   Recessive: [− ATR]

The former set, called the "dominant" set, are all [+ATR], and the latter recessive set are [−ATR]. It appears from the description of Kalenjin that some morphemes always have [+ATR] vowels. Let us call them "dominant" morphemes. Other morphemes, perhaps the majority, can appear with vowels of either set. They have [+ATR] vowels if they appear in a word with a dominant morpheme. Otherwise they appear with [−ATR] vowels. This pattern is illustrated in (15):

(15) **a.** kI − a − gɛr   'I shut it'
      kI − a − bar − In   'I killed you (sg.)'

   b. ki − á − **ge:r** − in   'I see you (sg.)'
      ki − á − **ger** − e   'I was shutting it'

In addition to the dominant morphemes and the morphemes which harmonize, Kalenjin also has three morphemes which remain [−ATR] in all contexts, and which prevent the spread of [ATR] harmony past them. These morphemes— **ka-** 'perfectivizer', **ma-** 'negative', and −**kɛ** ~ **gɛ** 'reflexive'—have been called "opaque" affixes. Their behavior is illustrated in (16):

(16) ki − á − un − gɛ   'I washed myself'
    ma − ti − un − gɛ   'Don't wash yourself'
    ka − **ma** − á − ge:r − ák   'I didn't see you (pl.)'

As these examples show, the [+ATR] features of the stems 'wash' and 'see' propagate as far as the opaque affixes and no farther (apparently the **ka-** in the third example is **not** the perfectivizer).

These facts can be dealt with easily within the present framework. First, it is obvious that the feature [ATR] will be projected on its own tier in Kalenjin. Harmonizing morphemes will be unspecified for this feature, but dominant morphemes will have the [+ATR] feature as part of the lexical representation. In addition, Kalenjin will have the Initial Association rule in (17a) and the Spreading rule in (17b):

(17) **a.** Attach [+ATR] to [+syl] left to right.
   b. Spread [+ATR] to [+syl] bidirectionally.

Finally, let us say that the default value of [ATR] is [−ATR]; if a vowel fails to be specified in the course of an autosegmental derivation, then [−ATR] is filled in. Given these assumptions, the examples in (15) will be derived as follows:[5]

(18) **a.** k $\begin{bmatrix} +\text{hi} \\ -\text{bk} \end{bmatrix}$ − $\begin{bmatrix} -\text{hi} \\ +\text{lo} \\ +\text{bk} \end{bmatrix}$ − g $\begin{bmatrix} -\text{hi} \\ -\text{lo} \\ -\text{bk} \end{bmatrix}$ r   → Spreading (n.a.)

$\rightarrow$ Default

$$k \begin{bmatrix} +\text{hi} \\ -\text{bk} \end{bmatrix} - \begin{bmatrix} -\text{hi} \\ +\text{lo} \\ +\text{bk} \end{bmatrix} - g \begin{bmatrix} -\text{hi} \\ -\text{lo} \\ -\text{bk} \end{bmatrix} r$$

$$[-\text{ATR}] \quad [-\text{ATR}] \quad [-\text{ATR}]$$

b.

$$[+\text{ATR}]$$

$$k \begin{bmatrix} +\text{hi} \\ -\text{bk} \end{bmatrix} - \begin{bmatrix} +\text{lo} \\ +\text{bk} \end{bmatrix} - g \begin{bmatrix} -\text{hi} \\ -\text{lo} \\ -\text{bk} \end{bmatrix} r - \begin{bmatrix} +\text{hi} \\ -\text{bk} \end{bmatrix} n \qquad \rightarrow \text{Spreading}$$

$$[+\text{ATR}]$$

$$k \begin{bmatrix} +\text{hi} \\ -\text{bk} \end{bmatrix} - \begin{bmatrix} +\text{lo} \\ +\text{bk} \end{bmatrix} - g \begin{bmatrix} -\text{hi} \\ -\text{lo} \\ -\text{bk} \end{bmatrix} r - \begin{bmatrix} +\text{hi} \\ -\text{bk} \end{bmatrix} n$$

In (18a), since there is no specification of [ATR] to spread, all vowels get
[−ATR] by default. However, in (18b), Spreading occurs in both directions from
the stem.

To account for the sort of example in (16), we need only make one more
assumption, namely, that the three opaque morphemes, **ka-**, **ma-**, and **kɛ ~
gɛ**, are lexically linked to a [−ATR] feature. The last example in (16) will then
be derived as illustrated in (19):

(19)

$$[-\text{ATR}] \qquad\qquad [+\text{ATR}]$$

$$k \begin{bmatrix} +\text{lo} \\ +\text{bk} \end{bmatrix} - m \begin{bmatrix} +\text{lo} \\ +\text{bk} \end{bmatrix} - \begin{bmatrix} +\text{lo} \\ +\text{bk} \end{bmatrix} - g \begin{bmatrix} -\text{hi} \\ -\text{lo} \\ -\text{bk} \end{bmatrix} r - \begin{bmatrix} +\text{lo} \\ +\text{bk} \end{bmatrix} k$$

$$\Downarrow \text{ Spreading}$$

$$[-\text{ATR}] \qquad\qquad [+\text{ATR}]$$

$$k \begin{bmatrix} +\text{lo} \\ +\text{bk} \end{bmatrix} - m \begin{bmatrix} +\text{lo} \\ +\text{bk} \end{bmatrix} - \begin{bmatrix} +\text{lo} \\ +\text{bk} \end{bmatrix} - g \begin{bmatrix} -\text{hi} \\ -\text{lo} \\ -\text{bk} \end{bmatrix} r - \begin{bmatrix} +\text{lo} \\ +\text{bk} \end{bmatrix} k$$

$$\Downarrow \text{ Default}$$

$$[-\text{ATR}] \qquad [-\text{ATR}] \qquad\qquad [+\text{ATR}]$$

$$k \begin{bmatrix} +\text{lo} \\ +\text{bk} \end{bmatrix} - m \begin{bmatrix} +\text{lo} \\ +\text{bk} \end{bmatrix} - \begin{bmatrix} +\text{lo} \\ +\text{bk} \end{bmatrix} - g \begin{bmatrix} -\text{hi} \\ -\text{lo} \\ -\text{bk} \end{bmatrix} r - \begin{bmatrix} +\text{lo} \\ +\text{bk} \end{bmatrix} k$$

According to (17), only the [+ATR] feature spreads. The [−ATR] of the opaque prefix does not. Instead the first vowel receives its [−ATR] by default. Note that in Kalenjin both values of the feature [ATR] appear on the harmonizing tier, but only one value, [+ATR], actually harmonizes, given the Spreading rule in (17). A **dominant** harmony might therefore be more carefully defined in the present framework as one in which only one value of the harmonizing feature **spreads**.

It is interesting to note also that some dialects of Kalenjin also have a sort of morphological harmony based on the feature [ATR] (Clements 1980a, citing Tucker 1964). In one case, it appears that harmony is a way of deriving singulars from plurals. In the first (singular) set of nouns in (20), the recessive vowels occur, and in the second (plural) set, the corresponding dominant vowels occur (Clements 1980a, 35):

(20)   Singular   Plural

      tàrÍ:t   tằrí:t   'bird'
      nyÌ:rI:t   nyì:rì:t   'chameleon'
      ŋélyέp   ŋélyèp   'tongue'

We can account for such cases as follows. Suppose that Kalenjin also has a plural morpheme which consists solely of the floating autosegment [+ATR] and which is marked to attach to a certain class of nouns.[6] These nouns would in underlying form be unspecified for the feature [ATR]. If they appear in the plural, all vowels will receive the [+ATR] feature from the plural morpheme. In the singular the noun stems will be supplied with [−ATR] by default.

As mentioned above, Halle and Vergnaud (1981) have also analyzed Kalenjin within an autosegmental framework. My analysis follows theirs in projecting [ATR] on an autosegmental tier, in giving dominant morphemes a lexically specified [+ATR] feature, and in giving opaque morphemes a lexically specified [−ATR] feature.[7] It differs in two major respects. Halle and Vergnaud assume, first of all, that all vowels in all morphemes are redundantly specified in the core as [−ATR]. Second, they assume that features from an autosegmental tier always override the same feature specified in the core. Together these two provisions give the effect of our default provision; if a [+ATR] feature spreads to a given vowel in Halle and Vergnaud's analysis, this feature overrides the core [−ATR] feature. Otherwise the vowel surfaces with its underlying [−ATR].

There are two reasons to prefer this analysis to that given in Halle and Vergnaud (1981). First, their analysis requires quite a bit more prespecification than this one does—every vowel in their analysis starts out [−ATR], and often this feature is obliterated by the harmony. Second, and much more important, Halle and Vergnaud's provision for which feature takes precedence cannot be correct. We have seen in analyses of Fula, Nuer, Akan, and elsewhere that lexically prespecified features (usually in the core) always take precedence over the same feature appearing on its normal projection (usually on an autosegmental harmony or mutation tier). To maintain Halle and Vergnaud's analysis of Kalenjin would force us to add to the grammar of Kalenjin a rather ad hoc and certainly language-particular rule governing precedence and in fact reversing the usual precedence of duplicated features. Since the present analysis does not need such a rule, it is clearly to be preferred.

3.2 FEATURE-CHANGING HARMONY

Feature-changing harmony is far more rare than feature-adding harmony. While there are a substantial number of good examples of the latter (ordinary: Mongolian, Turkish, Finnish, Hungarian, Akan, Guarani, Igbo; Dominant: Kalenjin, Hindi/Urdu, Andalusian Spanish), I know of only one clear example of ordinary feature-changing harmony, and no examples of dominant feature-changing harmony. The former example is that of sibilant harmony in Chumash, a native American language of southern California. In this section I will first present an autosegmental analysis of Chumash, and then address the obvious question of why feature-changing harmony is so much rarer than feature-adding harmony. The Chumash example will suggest an answer to this question; because feature-changing harmony requires a rather powerful sort of Delinking rule, it is surely a highly marked sort of process.

Chumash sibilant harmony will turn out to be of interest for at least two other reasons as well. Poser (1982) has analyzed it as an [anterior] harmony, a sort of harmony which is predicted by this theory not to exist, and second, has claimed that Chumash sibilant harmony is a metrical process. I will try to show here that the first claim is false and that the second has little or no support.

The facts of Chumash are as follows. The segments [s], [c'] and [š], [č'] appear to be mutually exclusive in Chumash.[8] According to Beeler (1970), [s] and [š] are alveolar sibilants, and [c'] and [č'] are aspirated velar sibilants. The exact difference between [s] and [š] and between [c'] and [č'] will be discussed immediately below. Stems containing sibilants contain members of either one pair or the other, but not both. (21) illustrates the citation forms of several stems:

(21) osos   'heel'
    pšoš   'gopher snake'
    ac'is   'beard'
    č'umaš   'the islanders'

In addition, many prefixes and suffixes of Chumash contain sibilants (chart from Beeler 1970):

(22) Prefixes

    s –   3rd person subject, possessor
    – iš –   dual

− su −	causative
− sa? −	future
− sili −	desiderative
− ič −	associative
− uš −	'with the hand'

Suffixes

− Vč	'having been affected by'
− š	intensive, repetitive
− Vš	resultative
− us	3rd person object (with certain verbs)
− waš	perfective
− šiš, − šaš	reciprocal object

When a word is formed by concatenating several morphemes, all sibilants in the resulting word come to agree with the word-final sibilant:

(23)
kiškín	'I save it'
kiskinus	'I saved it for him'
pušpel	'You hold something' (Ventureño)
puspelus	'You hold it for him' "
ts − 'owow	'It is white' (Ventureño—Poser 1982)
ts − eqel	'He makes' "
tš − iqipš	'It is closed' "
tš − keweyeš	'It is notched' "

The examples in (23) show clearly that sibilant harmony is triggered by the word-final sibilant whether it is in the stem or in an affix. The examples in (24)⁹ suggest further that this sibilant harmony is unbounded. If several sibilants occur in a word, all harmonize with the final one:

(24) šapitš^{h}olit   'I have a stroke of good luck'
                    /s + api + tš^{h}o + it/
                    3 quick   good 1obj

    sapits^{h}olus   'He has a stroke of good luck'
                    /s + api + tš^{h}o + us/
                            3obj

    šapitš^{h}olušwaš   'He has had a stroke of good luck'
                    /s + api + tš^{h}o + us + waš/
                                    past

The first step in analyzing this harmony is to determine what the harmonizing feature is. Poser (1982) suggests that the relevant feature is [anterior], although he does note that this position is arguable. If this were the case, then Chumash would stand as a counterexample to our claim that [anterior] harmonies are impossible. Recall that this was a crucial prediction of the present framework; since the melody-skeleton linking rule was stated so as to attach segments containing [anterior] to slots containing [+cons], it was necessary that [anterior] always be present on the melody tier, and never be autosegmentalized on its own tier. However, a look at some original sources for the Chumash data (Beeler 1970, Harrington 1974) indicates that Chumash is not, in fact, a counterexample to the present theory. Beeler and Harrington claim that the distinction between [s], [c'], on the one hand, and [š], [č'], on the other is a distinction between apical and blade sibilants. As mentioned above, both [s] and [š] are in fact described as alveolar in Beeler (1970), and [c'] and [č'] as velar. If so, we almost certainly do not have an example of [anterior] harmony here. Instead, since the distinction between apical and blade consonants is usually captured by the feature [distributed], we have a harmony based on the feature [distributed].

If the harmonizing feature is [distributed], we can then analyze Chumash in the following way. First, it is clear from the examples in (21)–(24) that segments in Chumash cannot be left underlyingly unspecified for the feature [distributed]. Chumash harmony, in fact, seems to be similar to German Umlaut and to Chamorro mutation in this respect. In citation form, and in forms with no other sibilants, each morpheme in Chumash has a distinct identity; there are morphemes in which all sibilants are [+distributed] (**pšoš**, −**waš**−, −**š**) and others in which all sibilants are [−distributed] (**osos, s**−, −**us**). It is not at all predictable which value will occur in the citation form of a morpheme. In its lexical entry, then, each morpheme must be specified for a particular value of [distributed]. After initial association, the representations in (25) would result:

(25) a.   [−distr]   (−us   3obj)
  |
−u $\begin{bmatrix} +\text{strid} \\ +\text{ant} \\ +\text{cor} \end{bmatrix}$

  V   C

  b.   [+distr]   (−waš past)
  |
w   a $\begin{bmatrix} +\text{strid} \\ +\text{ant} \\ +\text{cor} \end{bmatrix}$

  C   V   C

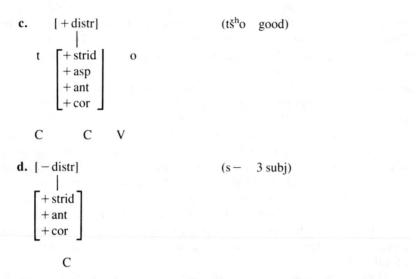

When morphemes like those in (25) are built into words, we will then have representations like those in (26):

(26) a.

| [−distr] | | | [+distr] | | [−distr] |

$$\begin{bmatrix} +\text{strid} \\ +\text{ant} \\ +\text{cor} \end{bmatrix} + \text{a p i} + \text{t} \begin{bmatrix} +\text{strid} \\ +\text{asp} \\ +\text{ant} \\ +\text{cor} \end{bmatrix} \text{o} + \text{u} \begin{bmatrix} +\text{strid} \\ +\text{ant} \\ +\text{cor} \end{bmatrix}$$

C V C V C C V V C

b.

$$\begin{bmatrix} +\text{strid} \\ +\text{ant} \\ +\text{cor} \end{bmatrix} + \text{a p i} + \text{t} \begin{bmatrix} +\text{strid} \\ +\text{asp} \\ +\text{ant} \\ +\text{cor} \end{bmatrix} \text{o} + \text{u} \begin{bmatrix} +\text{strid} \\ +\text{ant} \\ +\text{cor} \end{bmatrix} + \text{w a} \begin{bmatrix} +\text{strid} \\ +\text{ant} \\ +\text{cor} \end{bmatrix}$$

C V C V C C V V C C V C

We must now add to the grammar of Chumash the language-particular Delinking rule in (27):

(27) Chumash Delinking

$$\left(\begin{array}{c} [\text{distr}] \\ \neq \\ [+\text{strid}] \end{array} \right) \quad \begin{array}{c} [\text{distr}] \\ \neq \\ [+\text{strid}] \end{array} \quad \begin{array}{c} [\text{distr}] \\ | \\ [+\text{strid}] \end{array}$$

The Chumash Delinking rule is meant to disassociate any [distributed] feature which is to the left of any other [distributed]. If Chumash then has a Spreading rule which allows the feature [distributed] to spread leftward to [+strident] segments, then we will obtain the correct results. The lexical forms in (26) will have the derivations in (28):[10]

(28) a.

$$
\begin{array}{llll}
[-\text{distr}] & [+\text{distr}] & [-\text{distr}] \\
\not\mid & \not\mid & \mid \\
\begin{bmatrix} +\text{strid} \\ +\text{ant} \\ +\text{cor} \end{bmatrix} + \text{a p i} + \text{t} \begin{bmatrix} +\text{strid} \\ +\text{asp} \\ +\text{ant} \\ +\text{cor} \end{bmatrix} \text{o} + \text{u} \begin{bmatrix} +\text{strid} \\ +\text{ant} \\ +\text{cor} \end{bmatrix}
\end{array}
$$

$\Downarrow$

$$
\begin{bmatrix} +\text{strid} \\ +\text{ant} \\ +\text{cor} \end{bmatrix} + \text{a p i} + \text{t} \begin{bmatrix} +\text{strid} \\ +\text{asp} \\ +\text{ant} \\ +\text{cor} \end{bmatrix} \text{o} + \quad \text{u} \begin{bmatrix} +\text{strid} \\ +\text{ant} \\ +\text{cor} \end{bmatrix} \quad [-\text{distr}]
$$

= sapits^holus

b.

$$
\begin{array}{llll}
[-\text{distr}] & [+\text{distr}] & [\text{distr}] & [+\text{distr}] \\
\not\mid & \not\mid & \not\mid & \mid \\
\begin{bmatrix} +\text{strid} \\ +\text{ant} \\ +\text{cor} \end{bmatrix} + \text{a p i} + \text{t} \begin{bmatrix} +\text{strid} \\ +\text{asp} \\ +\text{ant} \\ +\text{cor} \end{bmatrix} \text{o} + \text{u} \begin{bmatrix} +\text{strid} \\ +\text{ant} \\ +\text{cor} \end{bmatrix} + \text{w a} \begin{bmatrix} +\text{strid} \\ +\text{ant} \\ +\text{cor} \end{bmatrix}
\end{array}
$$

$\Downarrow$

$$
\begin{bmatrix} +\text{strid} \\ +\text{ant} \\ +\text{cor} \end{bmatrix} + \text{a p i} + \text{t} \begin{bmatrix} +\text{strid} \\ +\text{asp} \\ +\text{ant} \\ +\text{cor} \end{bmatrix} \text{o} + \text{u} \begin{bmatrix} +\text{strid} \\ +\text{ant} \\ +\text{cor} \end{bmatrix} + \text{w a} \begin{bmatrix} +\text{strid} \\ +\text{ant} \\ +\text{cor} \end{bmatrix} \quad [+\text{distr}]
$$

= šapitš^hološwaš

The autosegmental analysis of Chumash thus depends upon having a rather powerful sort of rule, a Delinking rule which may iterate in unbounded fashion across a word. But while this is not in and of itself a particularly attractive rule, it does have a positive consequence. I mentioned above that feature-changing harmonies were very rare. In fact, Chumash is the only example with which I am familiar. If, however, feature-changing harmonies require unbounded Delinking rules like the one in (27), and if this sort of rule is highly marked and therefore very costly to a grammar, then we would expect feature-changing harmonies to be rare, perhaps virtually nonexistent.[11]

Poser (1982) chooses to treat Chumash sibilant harmony as a metrical harmony,[12] so it might be worthwhile at this point to examine his analysis and see whether it possesses any advantages over the one presented here. Poser assumes that the harmony projection consists of all sibilants, that is, consonants which are [+strident], that the opaque or triggering element is the last sibilant, and that a tree is built upon the projection as shown in (29):

(29)

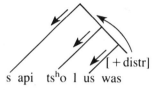

s api tsʰo l us was

(I have changed Poser's analysis here only in that I will continue to use the feature [distributed] rather than the incorrect [anterior].) The feature [+distributed] percolates from the most deeply embedded element to the top of the tree, from whence it percolates down each branch and changes the value of this feature on the other terminal elements.

As Poser himself points out, however, the ability of the metrical tree to **change** features must be stipulated within his version of metrical theory. Other versions of metrical theory (see Steriade's [1979] analysis of Khalka) assume that all terminal elements but the triggering elements are underspecified for the harmonizing feature and that the metrical machinery simply fills in missing features. In fact, it appears that Poser's only reason for counting Chumash harmony as a metrical process is that the autosegmental theory of harmony available to him at the time required all harmonies to be feature-adding. In other words, Poser chose to complicate the metrical theory rather than violate the then-current restriction on autosegmental rules. But we have seen here that this restriction— that all autosegmental processes require some degree of underspecification and that there is no delinking—cannot be maintained, independent of harmony systems. So Poser's main justification for the metrical analysis vanishes.

In other respects the metrical analysis of Chumash harmony has no apparent advantages. In this case, as in others, the binary-branching tree structure does not explain anything; the "distributedness" of the sibilants does not decrease with distance away from the harmony trigger. Nor does Poser's metrical analysis explain why feature-changing harmonies are much rarer than feature-adding ones. Since the two are consigned to entirely different theoretical frameworks, there is no way to compare their relative complexities, and therefore no way to show that the latter is more marked than the former. Since this observation does seem to follow within the present autosegmental framework, it is to be preferred on those grounds.

3.3 THE METRICAL RESIDUE

We have seen in earlier sections that even such relatively complex and unusual harmonies as those of Khalka and Chumash can be accounted for with our usual menu of autosegmental devices: projection of a feature or features on autosegmental tiers, linking, spreading, lexical linking, prespecification, and delinking. This is a significant result, because both of these cases had previously been treated within a metrical framework. Those analyses alone, however, do not justify the claim made at the beginning of this chapter that the metrical framework can be dispensed with entirely. I will try to defend this claim here.

Metrical formalism has typically been used for harmony processes of four sorts: (i) cases where autosegmental analyses just did not seem to work, (ii) cases of feature-changing harmony, (iii) cases in which harmony appeared to be directional, and (iv) cases in which harmony seemed to correlate or interact with some prosodic unit. Khalka represents the first sort of case and Chumash the second. We have seen that linking and spreading rules frequently need to be directional, so there is no reason why directional harmonies could not be treated autosegmentally rather than metrically. In fact, the nasalization harmony of Coatzospan Mixtec which we looked at in section 1.4.4.1 was treated in exactly this fashion. This leaves the last sort of case to be accounted for autosegmentally, and it proves to be the most difficult.

In fact I know of only one case in which a harmony process seems to interact with or be affected by an independent prosodic unit; this is the case of laxing harmony in Andalusian Spanish that is discussed in Zubizarreta (1979). Briefly, the facts of Andalusian are as follows.[13] First, Andalusian appears to have a rule which laxes a vowel before liquids (**1** or **r**) or **s** in word-final position. Zubizarreta (1979,3) states the rule as in (30):

$$(30) \quad \begin{bmatrix} V \\ -hi \end{bmatrix} \rightarrow [+lax] \; / \; \underline{\hspace{1cm}} \quad \begin{bmatrix} +cont \\ +cor \end{bmatrix} \; \# \#$$

Word-final liquids and **s** may then aspirate (Zubizarreta 1979,1):

$$(31) \quad \begin{bmatrix} +cor \\ +cont \\ (+strid) \end{bmatrix} \rightarrow h \; / \; \underline{\hspace{1cm}} \# \#$$

The final **h** may delete optionally; if it does, the preceding lax vowel lengthens.

The data in (32) illustrate the operation of laxing harmony. Here, as in Zubizarreta (1979), lax vowels are marked with a cedilla.

(32) **a.** Singular	Plural
kápa	kápą̈(h)
trása	trásą̈(h)
b. vandéra	vandę́rą̈(h)
mésa	mę́są̈(h)
kavésa	kavę́są̈(h)
serésa	serę́są̈(h)
c. dǫ ǫ́ídǫ(h)	dǫ kúrą̈(h)
dǫ nííñǫ
prę̨sídyǫ(h)

The examples in (32a) suggest that the vowel [a] is opaque. Although it is affected by rule (30) when it occurs in final position, it does not become [+ lax] in proximity to another lax vowel.[14] (32b and c) show the data which are of most interest to us; laxness proceeds leftward from the final lax vowel, but it proceeds no farther than the stressed vowel, unless the stressed vowel is [+ high]. If the stressed vowel is [+ high], laxing does not affect this vowel; it simply continues over the [+ high] vowels as if they did not exist.

The autosegmental analysis of Andalusian is relatively straightforward. Let us assume that vowels in Andalusian Spanish are generally unspecified for the feature [lax]. The exception to this statement will be the vowel [a], which we will consider to be lexically linked to the feature [− lax]. Rule (30) will fill in or change the last vowel to [+ lax] under the relevant conditions. Let us assume as well the Spreading rule in (33).

(33) Spread [+ lax] to [− high] right to left.

Before we see how the analysis works, we need to add only one thing. Zubizarreta points out in her analysis that stressed vowels are always long. If this is the case, we can represent stressed vowels as sequences of two V slots linked to a single melody. This will give us the representations in (34a) as underlying representations for the forms **kápąh**, **serẹsą̈h**, and **prẹsídyǫh** (after the operation of [30]):

(34) a.   **b.**

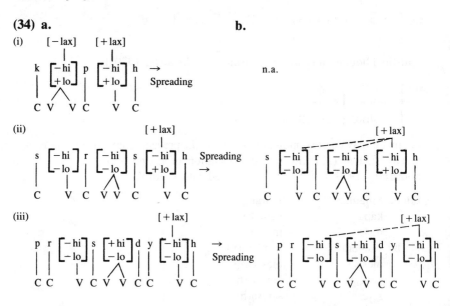

(i) = kapą̈h
(ii) = *sẹrẹsą̈h
(iii) = prẹsidyǫh

If we apply spreading to the representations in (34a), we get those in (34b). So far our harmony works properly in two of the three cases. In the first case, no spreading occurs because the vowel [a] is opaque; its [− lax] specification prevents the propagation of the final [+ lax] feature. In the third case, the spreading goes on in this case to lax the initial vowel. But in the second case the [+ lax] feature has incorrectly spread to the initial vowel. We therefore need to add a Delinking rule to our analysis:

(**35**) Andalusian Delinking   [+ lax]

This rule breaks any link between [+ lax] and a vowel to the left of a stressed (long) vowel. If we assume (as we need to in any case) that the default feature in Andalusian is [− lax],[15] then the derivation of the second example in (34) will proceed as in (36):

(**36**)

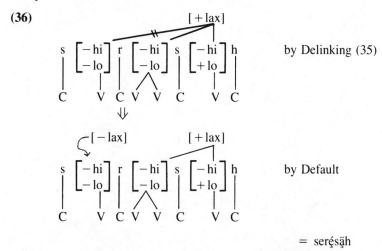

= seré̦ṣä̦h

Thus there is no mechanical problem with treating Andalusian harmony auto-segmentally; the autosegmental analysis requires nothing that is not already needed within autosegmental theory.

The difficulty with the autosegmental analysis is not that it does not account for the data. It is rather that the analysis provides no cogent explanation for the behavior of stressed vowels in Andalusian. Andalusian Delinking (35) merely states the fact that [+ lax] does not spread beyond a long vowel, but it does not explain why this should be the case. Since the metrical analysis of Zubizarreta (1979) purported to give such an explanation, it is necessary to look at this analysis in some detail. Zubizarreta's rule of vowel harmony is stated in (37):

(37) Zubizarreta (1979,9)

Projection: [−hi] peaks
Opaque segment: [+low] vowel
Harmonizing feature: [+lax]
Direction: right to left (left branching)

Zubizarreta counts stressed vowels as long and designates them with the metrical structure of a branching peak (short vowels have a nonbranching peak). A word like **seresah** will therefore start out with the representation in (38):

(38)

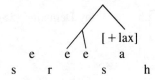

s   r   s   h

High vowels are not projected at all. A tree is then built upon this structure. Zubizarreta makes the direction of the tree-building right to left, but she also stipulates that the tree is constructed as a left-branching tree. Tree construction would produce the structure in (39a):

(39) a.

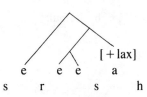

        s   r   s   h

b. *

        s   r   s   h

The tree in (39b) is ruled out on the grounds that it is not uniformly left-branching. Thus the [+lax] feature would percolate to the top of the tree in (39a) and would lax only the vowels up to and including the stressed vowel.

Now this analysis seems to give a nice explanation of the behavior of stressed vowels in Andalusian; their behavior as both undergoers and blockers of laxing harmony seems to follow from the geometry of the metrical representation. I would like to argue, however, that this explanation comes at some cost because it depends upon the ability to stipulate the direction of branching of metrical trees, a power that appears not to be necessary in other metrical analyses.

Under the simplest and most obvious sort of metrical tree-construction algorithm, a R → L (right to left) tree would start at the rightmost opaque element and build a binary-branching tree between this and the next projected element. The process would repeat itself as long as there were adjacent non-opaque projected elements. The result would be a right-branching tree. Similarly, in a L → R rule, the simplest sort of tree to build would be a left-branching one, since it requires the tree-building algorithm to "look" no farther than the projected element immediately to its right. This is illustrated in (40).

(40) a.   **b.**

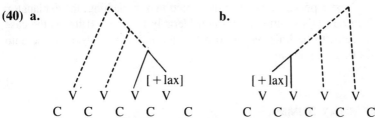

L → R trees which are right branching and R → L trees which are left branching seem to require a much more powerful algorithm. Rather than looking from one immediately adjacent projected element to another, the tree-building algorithm would have to look across a span of projected elements, find the last projected element before an opaque element, and build a binary tree to that. Then branches would have to be built to intervening elements. This is shown schematically in (41):

(41)

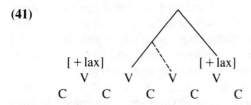

Now although such a tree-building algorithm should perhaps not be ruled out entirely, it should come at some cost to the grammar.

But such an algorithm is crucial for Zubizarreta's solution. A R → L right-branching tree would not give the correct results, as (42) illustrates:

(42) a. *   **b.** *

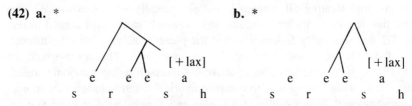

The tree in (42a) would be ruled out just as the one in (39b) was; it is not uniformly right branching. But this time (42b) would also be ruled out because it is left branching rather than right branching. And a L → R left-branching solution would not work either. Since tree construction starts from the leftmost opaque element and proceeds rightward in this case, no tree could be built at all for the above example. So Zubizarreta's explanation of the behavior of stressed vowels follows only within a very powerful version of metrical theory. Although the behavior of stressed vowels follows from the R → L left-branching tree, the latter follows from nothing and must be stipulated. Since no other metrical harmony analysis (see the descriptions of Khalka and Chumash given above) and indeed no stress analyses (Liberman and Prince 1977, Hayes 1980) seems to require the extra power to stipulate the direction of branching, the explanatory value of Zubizarreta's solution seems considerably lessened. If this is the case, then there seems to be little reason to prefer the metrical analysis to the autosegmental one given above.

3.4 HARMONY SUMMARY

I have shown in this section that a variety of different sorts of harmony processes—both ordinary and dominant, feature-adding and feature-changing—can be accounted for within the present autosegmental framework. The major result I have achieved here, in fact, is that the metrical formalism can be dispensed with entirely for harmony. Both Khalka and Andalusian can be treated autosegmentally with no complication to the theory, and in fact it seems that they ought to be treated that way. The metrical analysis of Khalka, we saw, required both an Absolute Neutralization rule and some unspecified but surely complex convention governing the behavior of blocking segments during tree construction. And the metrical analysis of Andalusian, although purporting to explain the behavior of stressed vowels in the Andalusian harmony system, did so only at the expense of permitting a sort of metrical tree building that is very costly.

There are both obvious and subtle advantages to eliminating the metrical formalism from our theoretical arsenal. In an obvious sense, we reduce the complexity of our grammar by doing so and in the process simplify the task of a child in acquiring a first language. To both the child and the linguist, the choice between two distinct formalisms is eliminated. Neither needs to decide which harmony processes are autosegmental and which metrical. The subtle benefit we reap from treating all harmonies autosegmentally is as follows. We saw above that feature-changing harmony was extremely rare, and I argued in section 3.2 that this rarity followed within the present analysis from the markedness of the Delinking rule we needed to account for it. This result would not be available if it were possible to analyze feature-changing harmonies metrically. There would be no way to compare metrical feature-changing harmonies to autosegmental feature-adding harmonies and thereby to determine that the former are formally more complex.

Another thing that has emerged in the course of this chapter is that harmonies, like infixation and mutations, are not always formally identical within the present framework. Some (Khalka, Kalenjin, Andalusian) require underspecification of stems and others (Chumash) do not. Some require language-particular Delinking rules (Chumash, Khalka, Andalusian) and others do not (Classical Mongolian, Kalenjin). Most are phonologically conditioned (Khalka, Chumash, Andalusian), but some are purely morphological (Coatzospan Mixtec) and at least one has both phonological or morphological elements (Kalenjin). Still, in spite of all the formal differences that do occur, all these harmonies have something in common: all involve an unbounded spreading of the harmony feature. In other words, although most languages with harmony have some element that blocks the spread of harmony, if such an element does not occur in a particular word, the harmonizing feature will spread unhindered across the word.

3.5 HARMONY AND MUTATION

One of the chief advantages of treating processes like harmony and mutation within a single integrated autosegmental framework is that we then have a solid basis for comparing what were before essentially incomparable processes. In fact, harmony and mutation make an interesting comparison, since they bear so many similarities. Both involve the projection of a feature or features on an independent tier, and often exactly the same features are involved: we have seen the features [back] and [nasal] as both mutation and harmony features, and although I have not discussed the relevant case here, there is at least one language, Lango (Woock and Noonan 1979), that uses [ATR] as a mutation feature and one, Catalan (Mascaro 1984), in which [continuant] is involved in a harmony process. Both mutation and harmony sometimes require the use of prespecification and Delinking. And both can be divided into feature-adding and feature-changing processes. The Fula, Nuer, Chemehuevi, and Mende mutations and the Khalka, Kalenjin, and Andalusian harmonies are feature-adding. German Umlaut, Chamorro mutation, and Chumash sibilant harmony are all feature-changing processes.

Mutation and harmony are also similar in that neither is a purely morphological or a purely phonological phenemenon. Whereas the harmonizing features in Turkish, Classical and Khalka Mongolian, Chumash, and Andalusian serve no morphological function—they are not themselves morphemes—those in Kalenjin and Coatzospan Mixtec sometimes are. And whereas mutation in Fula, Nuer, and Chemehuevi is purely morphological, in Mende it is more of a syntactic operation and in Chamorro more of a phonological one. This observation in fact allows us to strengthen a conclusion that we reached in chapter 1, namely, that there is no reason to separate autosegmental morphology from autosegmental phonology. The analyses presented in this chapter and in the previous one raise the possibility that there may be no autosegmental processes which are exclusively phonological or exclusively morphological.

NOTES: CHAPTER 3

1. Both Halle and Vergnaud (1981) and Poser (1982) attempt to establish some criteria for making this decision.

2. All Khalka data are from Steriade (1979).

3. Steriade (1979) points out that **örgöösei** appears instead of the expected **örgöösöi**; since there is no surface diphthong **öi** in Khalka, she assumes a Derounding rule **öi** → **ei**. We will assume this rule as well.

4. An anonymous reviewer has suggested that the Delinking rule (7) might be dispensed with if we stipulate that [round] only spreads from [– hi] vowels. The [– rd] of the second vowel in **ir-ex** would be supplied by default. Although there is nothing to directly rule out this analysis, it would force us to assume a sort of spreading rule we have not otherwise needed. The rule assumed here would operate only upon "seeing" the linking of [round] to [– hi]. In other words, this rule would need to see the context of the feature [round]. Rules of this sort do not seem to have been needed very frequently in autosegmental analyses (a rule of spreading for Yawelmani harmony proposed by Archangeli [1984] is the only example I know of), and it is not clear to what extent they are really necessary. Delinking rules seem to be fairly well motivated (see McCarthy 1979, 1981, Pulleyblank 1983), so the analysis proposed here seems preferable.

5. In (18b) I will assume that Initial Association has already taken place.

6. Actually, the situation may be slightly more complicated here. Clements (1980a, 35) describes a class of nouns in Kalenjin where exactly the opposite seems to be the case:

Singular	Plural	
lê:l	lέl-àc	'white'

In this example the [+ ATR] form occurs in the singular, the [– ATR] form in the plural. It is hard to tell, since Clements gives only one relevant example (the other example he gives is apparently from another dialect), but it may be that Kalenjin has a second noun class in which the singular morpheme is [+ ATR]. If so, then Kalenjin nouns would have to be lexically specified for the noun class to which they belong.

7. Halle and Vergnaud (1981) specify that the [+ ATR] feature is a floating autosegment. Their association rules attach and spread floating autosegments in preference to autosegments which are already attached.

8. The data in (21)–(23) are from the Barbareño dialect described in Beeler (1970), except where noted. Beeler does not give enough information to allow a morpheme-by-morpheme gloss for all the examples in (23).

9. These examples are from the Ineseño dialect described by Poser (1982).

10. I have left off the skeleton tier in the following representations because it plays no role here.

11. If we consider the sort of Initial Association and Spreading rules needed for dominant harmonies to be fairly marked as well (that is, they need to specify not only what feature attaches and spreads, but also **what value** of that feature), we might be able to explain the nonexistence of dominant feature-changing harmonies. In other words, dominant feature-adding harmonies are rarer than ordinary ones because they need marked Association and Spreading rules. Ordinary feature-changing harmonies are rare because they need marked Delinking rules. But the dominant feature-changing harmonies would be doubly marked, requiring both the marked Association and Spreading rules and marked Delinking rules—so marked that indeed they might not exist at all.

12. Poser (1982, 151ff) briefly considers an analysis of Chumash sibilant harmony which involves an autosegmental rule of delinking and finds it to be adequate. What is not clear to me from his exposition is whether he means this to supplant or to work in conjunction with the metrical analysis he suggests earlier in his article. In any case, the delinking analysis is adequate by itself and also appears to be superior to the metrical analysis, for the reasons given below.

13. All data in this section are from Zubizarreta (1979). I follow her analysis here in separating the laxing rule in (30), which she calls "High-Level Laxing," from another low-level laxing process which "applies to a vowel when followed by a lax liquid (**l,r**) or a [− cons, − voc] (glides and **h**) in word internal position" (Zubizarreta 1979, 2). See Zubizarreta (1979) for a justification of this separation.

14. In these examples a low-level phonetic rule fronts an **a** which has become lax.

15. If vowels are generally unspecified for the features [lax], then the singular forms in (32) will have to receive the [− lax] feature by default as well.

Chapter *4*

TONE IN AN INTEGRATED THEORY OF AUTOSEGMENTAL PROCESSES

Autosegmental theory began as a theory of tone, and it is perhaps fitting that a reassessment of autosegmental theory should end with a discussion of tone. Here, unlike in the previous chapters, I do not have to make the argument that all tonal processes should be treated autosegmentally; such arguments have been made elsewhere, and to my knowledge no formal system remains in competition to the autosegmental one. Nor will I attempt a broad review of many tonal systems here. Instead I will try to give two specific arguments for the present framework as opposed to other autosegmental ones, based on data from tone languages. The first argument (section 4.1) is that the present framework, with its theory of precedence in duplicated features, allows us to account neatly for an unusual phenomenon that appears in a number of African tone languages, namely, consonantal interference in tone processes. I will show in section 4.1 that only a theory of prespecification like the one developed here can provide a compelling explanation for this phenomenon. The second argument to be given in this chapter (section 4.2) is simply that the analysis of the tonal system of at least one language, Zulu, is substantially simplified by taking advantage of the devices sanctioned by this theory. The analysis to be presented in section 4.2 will do away with the multiple Initial Association rules required in Laughren's (1980) analysis of Zulu,[1] as well as the rule of Tone Metathesis that was needed there. In addition, in the course of my reanalysis of Zulu I will be able to redeem another one of the promissory notes left in chapter 1.

There I suggested that since Initial Association and Spreading were separate rules within this framework, we should expect to see other rules intervening between them; Zulu bears out this prediction.

4.1 PRESPECIFICATION AND TONE

In the last chapter I showed that an integrated autosegmental framework which includes a general theory of the precedence of duplicated features can solve a number of problems in the analysis of mutation and harmony processes. Using prespecification, the associaiton rules developed in chapter 1 and the DFF allowed us to account neatly both for phonetically irregular mutations and for the behavior of neutral segments in harmony systems. The availability of the device of prespecification raises a question for our theory, however. If it is possible to duplicate on different tiers such features as [back], [nasal], [voice], [continuant], and [ATR], is it also possible to duplicate tone features on different tiers? Or to put the question another way, if prespecification is a device made available within our theory, does this device play any role in the analysis of tonal systems? This is a significant question to ask, for two reasons. First, as we saw at the beginning of chapter 1, it seems to be implicit in most tonal analyses to date that tone is projected on a single autosegmental tier; we saw there that Clements's (1984) rule of Kikuyu Tone Shift was based on this assumption. Second, Yip (1982) has argued that there is no evidence available which suggests that tone is ever projected on the segmental tier; all evidence that she is aware of indicates that tone is always autosegmental.

In contrast, our theory would lead us to expect that tone features should be no different than any other features; within this theory we could not permit duplication of some features while prohibiting the duplication of others. In this section I will argue that there is in fact reason to believe that tone features, like other features, are sometimes present on more than one tier. Making use of the device of prespecification in the analysis of tone systems will allow us to solve a problem within current theory—how to explain the influence that certain types of consonants have on tone melodies. In section 4.1.1 I will give a brief overview of this kind of influence, including the behavior of the so-called depressor consonants in some of the southern Bantu languages. I will argue that at bottom all sorts of consonantal interference ought to be explained the same way. Secion 4.2.1 will review the one previous treatment of depressor consonants that has been done within the autosegmental framework, Laughren's (1980) analysis of Zulu, and show that this treatment cannot be extended to some other cases of consonantal interference that have been cited in the literature (Hyman and Schuh 1974). Here I will suggest that if depressor consonants are seen as a case of prespecification of tone features on the melody tier, we will be able to explain not only their behavior in Zulu, but also the behavior of consonantal interference in such languages as Nupe and Ngizim.

4.1.1 Consonantal Interference

It has been noted that consonants in the onset of a syllable often have a predictable phonetic effect on the pitch of the following vowel. Ladefoged (1968, 42) explains this effect and the articulatory reasons for it:

> Many consonant articulations cause a variation in the rate of flow of air through the glottis. This results in a variation in the pitch because the rate of vibration of the vocal cords depends in part on the force with which the cords are blown apart and sucked together by the airstream. Voiced stops and fricatives tend to cause a decrease in the rate of flow through the glottis, and hence a lowering of the pitch, since, in accordance with the principle of economy of effort, all speakers I have observed do not bother to make the delicate adjustments in the tension of the vocal cords which would compensate for the decrease in flow. Conversely, during the first part of a vowel after the release of a voiceless stop or fricative there is a high rate of flow, which results in an increase in pitch as long as there is no countering adjustment in the tension of the vocal cords. It follows that the actual frequency of a given tone as pronounced by a given speaker will vary in accordance with the consonants at the beginning of the syllable.

Voicing in obstruents tends to be correlated with low pitch and voicelessness with high pitch because both voicing and pitch are effects of the manipulation of the same articulatory mechanism.[2] Halle and Stevens (1971), in fact, attempted to capture this correlation by proposing that all laryngeal gestures, including tone on vowels and voicing in obstruents, could be represented by two distinctive features [± stiff vocal cords] and [±slack vocal cords]:

(1) Stiff vocal cords   +   −   −
       Slack vocal cords   −   +   −

H	L	M
voiceless	voiced	sonorants
obstruents	obstruents	

If this system, or one like it, were the proper way of expressing the correlation between voicing and tone, then the phonetic effects described by Ladefoged would be a simple case of the articulation of the consonant spilling over onto the following vowel.

This phonetic "spilling over" appears to have two rather different sorts of phonological effect in languages. In some languages, the spilling over of a consonantal onset onto a following vowel seems to have an indirect phonological effect in that it prevents another preceding tone from spilling over as well. These are the cases that Hyman and Schuh discuss in their (1974) article in which certain consonants act as blockers of tone spreading. For example, in Nupe, when the low-toned prefix è is attached to a high-toned verb stem, the low tone of the prefix spreads to the stem vowel unless the intervening consonant is a voiceless obstruent:

(2) (data from Hyman and Schuh 1974, 106)

pá	'peel'	èpá	'is peeling'
bá	'be sour'	èbǎ	'is sour'
wá	'want'	èwǎ	'wants'

Voiceless obstruents are exactly the ones which seem to share characteristics with high-toned vowels. They are pitch raisers. What seems to be going on, to put it informally, is that spreading of the initial L onto the verb stem cannot take place if there is a pitch-raising consonant simultaneously trying to raise the pitch of the verb stem's vowel. If there is a pitch-lowering consonant (that is, a voiced obstruent) or a pitch-neutral consonant (that is, a sonorant) intervening, spreading of the L tone can take place, since there is no articulatory gesture that would be tugging in the opposite direction.

Hyman and Schuh (1974, 106) describe a similar set of facts from the Chadic language Ngizim. "Synchronically, a high tone syllable is lowered to a low tone when (1) it is preceded by a low tone syllable, (2) it begins with a voiced consonant (obstruent or sonorant), and (3) it is followed by a high tone." Their examples are given in (3):

(3) mùgbá + bái → mùgbà + bái   'it's not a monitor'
    màarə́m + tə́n → màarə̀m + tə́n   'big nose'
    šìitá + bái → šìitá bái   'it's not pepper'

Ngizim also has a process in which a high tone spreads onto a following low-tones syllable unless the intervening consonant is a voiced obstruent (Hyman and Schuh 1974, 107):

(4) ná kàasúw   →   ná káasúw   'I swept'
    á rə̀pcí   →   à rə̀pcí   'open'
    ná bàkə́ tlùwái   →   ná bàkə́ tlù'wái   'I roasted the meat'

In other words, low tones spread over anything except a consonant which is a pitch raiser, and high tones spread over anything which is not a pitch lowerer. Again, to put it informally, spreading of either H or L is impossible if there is an intervening element pulling the pitch of the succeeding vowel in the opposite direction.

With other languages, this "spilling over" of the articulation of a consonant onto a neighboring vowel seems to have a more direct phonological effect. In some of the southern Bantu languages, like Shona, Xhosa, and Zulu, some consonants actually cause the pitch of the neighboring vowel to be lowered. These are the so-called **depressor consonants**. Welmers (1973, 94–95) describes the effect of these consonants in Shona: "Actually, both high and low tone are affected by such consonants: a high tone is realized as a rising glide beginning at a pitch lower than the preceding high, and a low tone is simply lower than it would otherwise be." In Zulu, as we will see below, certain consonants cause the lowering of adjacent low vowels, as well as the shifting of a following high tone to a succeeding syllable.

What is significant about these cases is that all the segments which cause the lowering of neighboring tones are phonetic tone lowerers, that is, voiced segments. But what is even more significant is that **not all** voiced segments have this effect. In Zulu,[3] all of the depressor consonants are described as both voiced and breathy, what Laughren (1980, 264), following Cope (1970), calls "heavy" consonants. Nonbreathy voiced consonants have no phonetic effect on surrounding vowels, just as the regular voiced consonants in Nupe and Ngizim had no overt phonological effect on following vowels (that is, although they blocked the spread of a high tone, they did not lower the following low tone to extra low). But voiced breathy consonants in Zulu do have an overt direct effect in that they cause surrounding low tones to become extra low. Now what would explain this array of observations?

Let us suppose that the depressor consonants of Zulu share some distinctive feature besides [+voice], perhaps [+spread glottis] (Laughren [1984], makes a similar assumption). Let us suppose as well that this particular combination of features stands for an articulatory gesture in which the flow of air through the glottis is decreased even more than it would be for the consonants that are [+voice, −spread glottis]. When the depressor consonants spill over, then, they will substantially lower the pitch of an adjacent low vowel. For regular (nonbreathy) voiced consonants, we might assume that the decreased airflow through the glottis that is associated with the production of the consonants spills over onto a succeeding vowel, just as it does in Zulu, and lowers pitch somewhat, but that the lowering is not enough to be counted as a phonologically distinctive extra-low tone. In languages like Nupe and Ngizim, however, the mere presence of this articulatory gesture is enough to "block" the spread of a preceding high tone.[4] In other words, given this story, the consonantal interference of Nupe, Ngizim, and Zulu is always the result of the articulation of a consonant carrying over onto an adjacent vowel.

The above scenario is obviously speculative, and it is not yet an analysis of consonantal interference. For one thing, it does not yet explain why consonants have no phonological effect on tone melodies in many tone languages. It does, however, give a picture of the phonological effects of consonantal interference that draws together two previously disparate sets of facts. It is meant to suggest that at bottom something similar is going on in all cases of consonantal interference, and that this "something similar" is the effect of a kind of articulatory "spillover." And if I am correct here in classing these phenomena together, then this in turn suggests that there should be some formal similarity in the treatment of these processes, that our theory should provide them with similar analyses. We must therefore go on to consider what the proper analysis of consonantal interference should be.

In the next section I will consider one proposal that has been made for the autosegmental analysis of depressor consonants (Laughren 1980), and show that, in addition to being a questionable analysis of Zulu, it cannot be extended to account for the consonantal influence in a language like Ngizim. I will argue further that there is another analysis possible within the autosegmental framework developed here that will treat all sorts of consonantal influence as formally similar, and will in addition give a coherent account of what I have called here the "spillover" effect.

4.1.2 An Analysis of Consonantal Interference

Laughren (1980) provides a thorough and detailed analysis of the tonal system of Zulu within an autosegmental framework. In section 4.2 I will review much of her analysis of the Zulu data. Here, however, I will briefly sketch her treatment of depressor consonants, and present an alternative.

The first point that is important to note about Laughren's Zulu analysis is that all rules which affect the tonal melodies of words—initial associations, tone shifts, delinkings, spreading—apply before any of the rules associated with the depressor consonants operate. In other words, depressor consonants seem to have a rather low-level effect on already assembled tonal melodies. The core of Laughren's depressor consonant rules is given in (5) (here, as in Laughren [1980], depressor consonants are highlighted—here by boldface):

(5) a. Low Tone Lowering rule   V   C   →   V   C
                                 | |/
                                 L   **L**
                        (mirror image)
                   (**L** = extra-low tone)

   b. Extra-Low Tone Insertion rule   **C**   V   →   **C**   V   /   #____[5]
                                     | | |
                                     H   L H

   c. Extra-Low Tone Spreading rule   **C**   V   →   **C** V
                                  | | |/|
                                  L H   L H

   d. High Tone Rightward Reassociation rule V **C** V → V **C** V / ____$
                                          /| | | /|
                                        L H   L   L H L

Putting aside, for the moment, the derivation of the tonal melodies themselves, let us see how the rules in (5) apply. (5a) will apply in a form like that in (6a) to give (6b):

(6) a. i z i f u u n **d** o → **b.** i z i f u u n **d** o
      | | \ | | | \   \/ |/
      H   L   H   L   H   L   H   **L**

(5a), (5b), and (5c) all operate in (7):

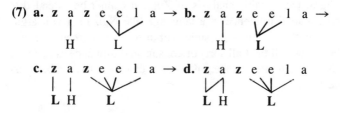

Finally, in (8), rules (5a), (5c), and (5d) operate to give the surface form:

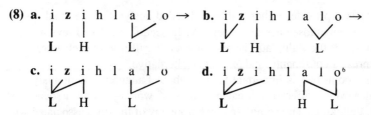

The four rules in (5) have the collective effect of lowering all low-toned vowels adjacent to a depressor consonant to extra low, and deflecting a high tone adjacent to a depressor consonant to the right (unless another depressor consonant intervenes).

Laughren's analysis appears to have a number of attractive consequences. For example, she argues that the failure of the High Tone Rightward Reassociation rule to apply in (7) finds a simple explanation in her analysis; the high tone is blocked from reassociating to the adjacent vowel to its right because for it to do so would result in a crossing of association lines, the intervening depressor consonant having already been linked to the following vowel. Similarly, when a depressor consonant occurs between two vowels linked to the same high tone, it has no effect:

According to Laughren, the depressor consonant in these examples has no effect for a simple reason. If the Extra-Low Tone Insertion Rule (5b) were to operate in these examples, the result would be a crossing of association lines. (5b) therefore fails to operate.[7]

It should be noted that these explanations come at some hidden cost, however. Laughren (1980, 264) states that depressor consonants "insert an extra low tone L into the tonal melody tier." Elsewhere she says that the defining characteristic of depressor consonants is that they become opaque (in the sense of '**opaque**' used in harmony analyses) in the course of the derivation. This statement implies that everywhere they occur, depressor consonants cause the late appearance of a new tone, an extra-low tone, on the tonal tier. But this is not in fact true if we look at Laughren's analysis. As the rules in (5) indicate, an extra-low tone is only **inserted** if the following tone is high. If, however, the following or preceding tone is L, no L is inserted and the depressor consonant simply exerts a direct (albeit unexplained) influence. Nor could Laughren's analysis be modified so that depressor consonants always do insert an **L** tone on the tonal tier. If they did, the analysis would then predict that a depressor consonant occurring between two vowels linked to the same low tone should have no effect on that tone, just as such a consonant between two vowels linked to the same H had no effect; the insertion of the L in both cases would be ruled out since it would result in a crossing of association lines. But in the former case, the depressor consonant **does** cause a lowering of the doubly linked low tone:

(10) o o m p a a n d e → o o m p a a n d e

    | | | ╲╲⌟ | | | ╲╱

    H L   H   L   H L   H   L

In other words, the facts of Zulu force Laughren into the peculiar position of claiming that depressor consonants exert their influence in two different ways, depending upon the context. One conclusion that we could draw is that it is perhaps incorrect to treat depressor consonants as segments which cause the late insertion of a tone into an already assembled tone melody.

This conclusion is strengthened when we attempt to extend this sort of analysis to the consonantal interference found in Ngizim. As we saw above, an initial L tone spreads onto a following H syllable unless that syllable begins with a voiceless obstruent:

(11) (= (3))   mùgbá + bái   →   mùgbà bái

               màarɔ́m + tɔ́n   →   màarɔ̀m tɔ́n

               šìitá + bái   →   šìitá bái

Let us say that voiceless obstruents in Ngizim insert a H tone into an already assembled tonal melody:

(12) **a.** m u g b a b a i **b.** m a a r ə m t ə n

      | | | | | |

      L   H   H   L   H   H

        ⇓   ⇓

    m u g b a b a i   m a a r ə m t ə n

    |---⌐ | |--⌐ |

    L   H   H   L   H   H

c.
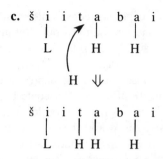

When spreading of the initial L occurs, it will be permitted in the first two cases in (12), but it will be blocked by the inserted H tone in the third case. So far, then, it looks as if the inserted tone analysis of consonantal interference might work. A look at the second spreading process in Ngizim, however, should be enough to prove that this is not the case. Recall that initial H tones in Ngizim also spread to an adjacent syllable, unless the intervening consonant is a voiced obstruent:

(13) (= (4)) ná kàasúw → ná káàsúw
        á rə̀pcí → á rə̀pcí

ná bàkə́ tlùwái → ná bàkə́ tlùwái

In the inserted tone analysis, we would have to say that voiced obstruents in Ngizim insert a L tone into the tonal melody, and that this insertion should block the spread of the H tone:

(14)

n a b a k ə t l u w a i → n a b a k ə t l u w a i →
  H L H   L H   H L L   H   L   H

*
 n a b a k ə ...
  H LL   H

But we have already argued that voiceless obstruents in Ngizim must insert a H tone into the tonal melody to account for the previous case of blocking. This means that H-tone spreading should also be blocked if a **voiceless** obstruent intervenes, which of course does not happen. And if a low tone is inserted in the presence of a voiced obstruent, then this insertion would prevent spreading of the initial L tone. to the adjacent syllable in (12a) as well as in (14), again an incorrect result. In other words, if we simply allow appropriate tones to be attached to appropriate consonants at a late stage in the derivation, then virtually all tone spreading would be blocked.[8]

Of course, it would be possible to state the tone insertion rules in Ngizim in such a way as to obtain the blocking effect only where we want it:

(15) a.

$$
\begin{array}{ccc}
& \left[\begin{array}{c} -\text{son} \\ -\text{voice} \end{array}\right] & \\
\text{V} & & \text{V} \\
| & \nwarrow & | \\
\text{L} & (& \text{H} \\
& \text{H} &
\end{array}
$$

b.

$$
\begin{array}{ccc}
& \left[\begin{array}{c} -\text{son} \\ +\text{voice} \end{array}\right] & \\
\text{V} & & \text{V} \\
| & \nwarrow & | \\
\text{H} & (& \text{L} \\
& \text{L} &
\end{array}
$$

(15a) says that a high tone is attached to a voiceless obstruent only when it is preceded by a low-tone vowel. (15b) says the reverse; a low tone is attached to a voiced obstruent when it is preceded by a high tone. Now although these rules will give correct results, with (15a) operating only in (12a), (15b), in (14), the tone insertion analysis has effectively been drained of any explanatory force it might have had. Tone insertion is no more than a sort of autosegmental diacritic to block spreading exactly where it must be blocked.

In fact, in either of these versions of tone insertion, it does not matter what tone is inserted and attached to a blocking consonant. We could just as easily insert a L in (15a) and a H in (15b) or Hs or Ls in both, and get the same blocking effect. Moreover, with the tone insertion analysis, it would be just as easy to state a rule blocking the spread of a low tone over a voiced obstruent and the spread of a high tone over a voiceless obstruent, a sort of consonantal interference that does not seem to occur. In short, the tone insertion analysis cannot explain why low tone spreading fails to occur **only** across voiceless obstruents and high tone spreading **only** across voiced obstruents. It does not make the obvious connection between the articulatory gestures (and hence the features) of the consonant and the environment in which the blocking occurs; as we saw in section 4.1.1, blocking occurs when the laryngeal gesture of the consonant would pull counter to the gesture of the spreading tone.

I would like to suggest at this point that insertion of a tone at a late stage in the derivation is not the correct way to analyze any of the cases of consonantal interference, and instead that an adequate analysis would have to connect the phonological blocking to the articulation of the intervening consonant. Let us begin first with an analysis of Ngizim that seems better grounded in phonetic fact. We will assume, first of all, that voiceless obstruents always share some feature or features with H tone vowels and that voiced obstruents always share some feature or features with L tone vowels. For our purpose, it does not matter whether the Halle and Stevens (1971) features [stiff vocal cords] and [slack vocal cords] are the proper features or whether some other set of features is to be preferred; any set of features which would class together voiceless obstruents and H, voiced obstruents and L, would be adequate for our purposes.

Let us say as well that these features, whatever they are, are projected on an autosegmental tier for tone-bearing units (usually vowels), but are prespecified in the core for non-tone-bearing units (in Ngizim, consonants).[9] I will represent prespecified consonants schematically as p, t, k or b, d, g, etc. Given
H H H   L L L

these assumptions, Ngizim would have representations like the ones in (16) prior to Spreading:

(16) a.

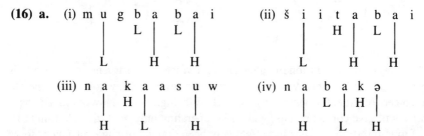

Consonants in Ngizim are therefore to be equated with neutral segments in harmony systems. Let us assume now that Spreading occurs in all cases, since neutral segments should not in general be expected to interfere with autosegmental processes. The result of Spreading is shown in (16b):

(16) b.

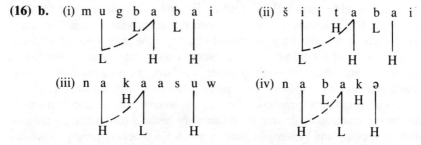

The obvious question now arises as to how the representations in (16b) are to be interpreted. Let us assume that in most languages (that is, those which show no consonantal interference) the prespecified features on the consonants have no effect on the tonal phonology; this would certainly be the unmarked case, given the treatments of neutral segments in this theory. However, let us say that Ngizim and other languages which exhibit consonantal interference have a marked but automatic and rather low-level phonetic rule which could be called **Spillover**:

(17) Spillover
    Prolong tone features of consonantal onset onto following vowel.

Now, it is not completely clear how Spillover should be formalized, or even whether it should be formalized, since it is a low-level phonetic rule—more a last-minute set of instructions to the vocal apparatus than a phonological rule. But its effect in Ngizim is relatively clear. In this language, Spillover has the effect of supplying the beginning of the vowel with another set of tone features regardless of what is already there. Spreading has already resulted in two sequential sets of features on this vowel, and Spillover then superimposes another set of tone features over the first set in the sequence.[10] This is illustrated schematically in (18):

(18) a.   **b.**   **c.**   **d.**

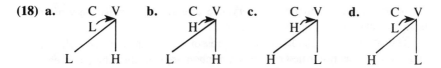

If we assume that the Duplicate Features Filter scans representations such as these and rules out as phonetically uninterpretable those which have simultaneous and conflicting values for duplicated features, then (18b) and (18d) will be ruled out. They correspond, of course, to (16b-ii) and (16b-iv), respectively, just those cases in which Spreading does not occur in Ngizim. In other words, given this story, we arrive at the result that representations with Spreading will not surface if the intervening consonant (that is, the one over which they are spreading) carries a conflicting tone. Low tone does not spread over voiceless (H) obstruents, and high tone does not spread over voiced (L) obstruents.

Moreover, we predict that consonantal interference could not be any different in languages other than Ngizim. There could be no language in which low tone spreads over everything but voiced (L) obstruents and high tone over everything but voiceless (H) obstruents, because these hypothetical cases would create no conflict in features for the DFF to rule out. Treating consonantal influence as another instance of prespecification thus appears to make both phonetic sense and correct predictions.

It also provides us with a reasonable analysis of the Zulu facts. Recall that depressor consonants in Zulu were the voiced, breathy consonants. Let us say that these segments can be represented as z, d, etc., where the boldface L stands

L L

for whatever set of features characterizes voiced, breathy consonants. Let us assume as well that these features, whatever they are, are prespecified in the phonological core of Zulu. Now we saw above that these depressor consonants did two things: they caused adjacent low tones to become extra low and following high tones to shift to a succeeding syllable. These facts can easily be accommodated within the present framework. Let us say that the grammar of Zulu looks something like this:

(19) a. Tone rules (see 4.2)
   b. High Tone Deflection

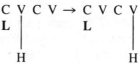

   c. Spreading: Spread T to [+ syl] L to R
   d. Default Tone: L[11]
   e. Spillover: Prolong articulation of **L** (voiced, breathy) consonants onto following L tone.

Zulu phonology will have a number of tone rules which will be worked out in detail in the next section. As in Ngizim, however, the effect of the depressor consonants is an automatic and very late effect, taking place only after tone melodies have been completely assembled.

The analysis in (19) claims that depressor consonants have two effects. The High Tone Deflection rule (19b) is a late phonological rule which causes a high tone following a depressor consonant to move one syllable over (unless the intervening consonant is also a depressor). The lowering of low tones is the effect of a late phonetic Spillover rule (19e) which causes succeeding lows to become extra low. Zulu Spillover is a more specific rule than the Spillover rule of Ngizim, since it refers only to L consonants. However, we must assume that this sort of variation in Spillover rules is possible. As far as I am able to tell, consonants in Zulu other than voiced, breathy ones behave like consonants in most tone languages; they don't spill over, but rather behave like true neutral segments with respect to tonal phonology.

(20) contains derivations illustrating the operation of the rules in (19):

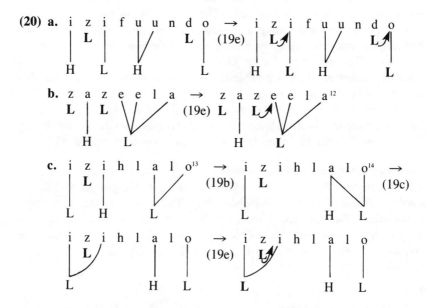

In (20a) and (20b) there is no High Tone Deflection and no Spreading. Late in the derivation, Spillover (19e) occurs, lowering the low tones to extra low.[15] In (20c), the conditions for High Tone Deflection are met. The high tone shifts one syllable to the right. Spreading then fills in a low tone on the toneless second syllable, and finally Spillover lowers the low tones to extra low.

Note that this analysis has no difficulty in accounting for the behavior of depressor consonants sandwiched between either linked low tones or linked high tones (recall that the former were a problem for the tone insertion analysis). (21) gives the relevant derivations:

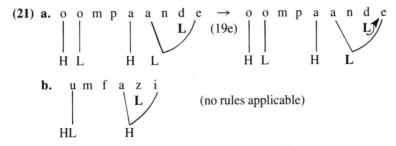

In (21a) only Spillover applies, lowering the final low to extra low, but in (21b) none of the rules in (19) applies. Spillover operates only onto following lows, not onto following highs.

Treating depressor consonants as prespecified segments therefore has a number of positive consequences. First, it allows us to represent all depressor consonants—those followed by high tones and those followed by low tones—in the same fashion. Laughren's (1980) analysis, we saw, was forced to treat them differently. Second, it allows us to simplify the grammar of Zulu. Where Laughren's (1980) analysis needed four rules related to depressor consonants, the present one requires only two.[16] Third, it provides some explanation for the fact that depressor consonants only affect fully assembled tonal melodies; for the most part, the effects of depressor consonants are low-level phonetic effects, the rules I have called "Spillover rules," and low-level phonetic rules are always the last thing to occur in the derivation. Note that the late ordering of all four of the depressor consonant rules in Laughren's analysis remained unexplained. Finally, and most importantly, this analysis ties the effects of the depressor consonants to their articulation and treats depressor consonants in exactly the same way that consonantal interference in other languages was treated.

Moreover, the success of this analysis of consonantal interference leads to an answer to the questions raised at the beginning of this section: are tone features ever projected in the core; is prespecification ever necessary in tonal systems; and are tones always autosegmental? We have seen here that there is good reason to believe that tone features (or laryngeal features) are projected in the core, at least on consonants, and that in most cases these prespecified segments behave in the same way that other neutral segments do.[17] Tones—assuming that tones stand for some set of features—are not always autosegmental, since tone features appear to be necessary in characterizing non-tone-bearing elements.

4.2   THE TONAL SYSTEM OF ZULU

As we have already begun to see in section 4.1, Zulu provides a wonderfully complex tonal system against which we can test the autosegmental theory we have been developing. We have seen that an adequate analysis of the depressor consonants must make use of prespecification. We will see below that the phonology of Zulu also requires lexical linking of tone features, directional spreading, a default low tone, optional delinking rules, and two rules shifting portions of the tonal melody to the right. Except for the last sort of rule, all the devices we need are devices we have already justified and used elsewhere. I will first present an analysis of the Zulu tonal system. My data here are taken from Laughren's (1980) article. I will then briefly sketch Laughren's own analysis and show that the present analysis is to be preferred on the grounds of simplicity.

Zulu stems, both nominal and verbal, and Zulu prefixes have lexically idiosyncratic tonal melodies, whereas suffixes tend to be underlyingly toneless. Stems appear to fall into four classes, examples of which are given in (22):

(22) **a.** L tone class: ntu
                              |
                              L

   b. HL-1 tone class: kole

                              HL

   c. HL-2 tone class: bopho
                              \\/
                              HL

   d. LHL tone class: khathi

                              LHL

Although stems exhibit only three distinct tone melodies, there are four tone classes for stems. (22a) has the melody L, (22d) the melody LHL. (22b) and (22c) have the same HL melody, but they are distinguished by the lexical linking of this melody. In (22b) the HL melody is listed with the stem, but is not linked to it. In (22c), however, the H tone of the melody is linked to the first two stem vowels. Prefixes either have a HL melody or a L melody; which melody appears is predictable from the number of syllables in the prefix.

(23) **a.** isi   ____[stem
         HL
     b. aba   ____[stem
         HL
     c. mu   ____[stem
         L
     d. nga   ____[stem
         L

Let us assume now that Zulu has the Initial Association Rule in (24):

(24) Initial Association
    Associate T to [+ syl], one to one, L to R.

When a HL prefix is concatenated with either a HL-1 or HL-2 class stem, the derivations are perfectly straightforward:

(25) a. i s i [k o l e → i s i [k o l e
                                (24) | | | |
       H L   H L   H L   H L

b. i s i [b o p h o → i s i [b o p h o[18]
                         (24) | |
       H L   H L   H L   H L

In these cases, Initial Association works left to right, linking unassociated tones to vowels. A low tone left unassociated at the end of a tonal melody will receive no phonetic interpretation.

    The first real intricacy of Zulu tonal phonology appears when we concatenate a HL prefix with a stem of either the L class or the LHL class, or, in other words, with any stem whose tone melody begins with L. Here the apparent outcome of this concatenation is a prefix with a LH melody, the reverse of its lexical tone:

(26) a. a b a + n t u → àbántù
                    |
     HL   L

b. i s i + k h a t h i → ìsíkhàthí

       H L   L H L

This final configuration of tones led Laughren to propose a rule of Tone Metathesis which reversed the prefix tone melody when it was followed by a low tone. Here I will show that this sort of rule is unnecessary. Let us say instead that Zulu has the rule in (27), which operates after Initial Association (24) and shifts a prefix tone melody one syllable to the right when it is followed by a low tone (note that Initial Association is always the first tone rule to apply in the derivation; tone shift rules follow Initial Association):[19]

(27) Prefix Tone Shift   V (C) V → V (C) V / ___[$_{stem}$C$_o$V
                       | | | |
                       H   L   HL   L

The forms in (26) will have the derivations in (28):

(28) a. a b a [n t u → a b a [n t u → a b a [n t u
             | (24) | | | (27)   / |
     H L   L   H L   L   HL   L

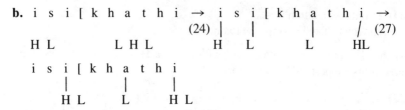

b. i s i [k h a t h i → i s i [k h a t h i →

(24) | | | / (27)

H L   L H L   H   L   L   HL

i s i [k h a t h i

| | |

H L   L   H L

After the operation of (27), the initial vowels in (28) are left toneless. Let us assume that in Zulu, as in other tone languages, the default tone L is attached to a vowel which has otherwise been left toneless at the very end of the derivation. The initial syllable in each word therefore gets the low tone, and the prefix surfaces with the LH melody. On the surface it looks as if the underlying tone melody of the prefix has been reversed, but it has not.[20]

As mentioned earlier, suffixes in Zulu are inherently toneless. They receive their tones from stems:

(29) a. a b a [f o + a n a → a b a [f a n a →

        Vowel   (24)

H L   H L   Deletion   H L   H L

a b a [f a n a

| | | | | |

H   L   H   L

b. a b a [n t u + a n a →

              | Glide

H L   L   Formation

a b a [n t w a n a →

              | (24)

H L   L

a b a [n t w a n a →

| | | (27)

H   L   L

a b a [n t w a n a →

    | | (30)

    H L   L

a b a [n t w a n a →

    | V   Default

    H L   L

a b a [n t w a n a

| | V

L   H L   L

In (29a), after an early rule of Vowel Deletion has eliminated the stem vowel, the stem tone melody simply associates with the suffix vowels. For (29b), we must assume in addition a rule of Spreading:

(30) Zulu Spreading:
Spread T to [+ syl] L to R.

Note that Zulu Spreading is exclusively a left-to-right rule, since the H tone on the second vowel of the prefix in (28a,b) and (29b) does not spread leftward. Spreading will, however, operate on the final L in (29b), associating it with both suffix vowels.

If, however, a number of suffixes are concatenated with a stem in Zulu and the result is more than four syllables long, another rule operates. Like (27), it is a tone shift rule; it relocates the last HL tone melody to the antepenultimate syllable:[21]

(31) Final High Tone Shift V (X) V C V C V → V (X) V C V C V / ___#

$$
\begin{array}{cc}
\text{HL} & \text{H}\quad\text{L}
\end{array}
$$

The operation of (31) is illustrated in (32):

(32)

a b a [n t u + a n y + a n y + a n a →   Glide Formation
H L   L

a b a [n t w a n y a n y a n a   → (24)
H L   L

a b a [n t w a n y a n y a n a   → (27)
H   L   L

a b a [n t w a n y a n y a n a   → (31)
  H L   L

a b a [n t w a n y a n y a n a   → (30)
              H   L

a b a [n t w a n y a n y a n a   → Default
              H   L

a b a [n t w a n y a n y a n a
  L   H   L

Again, when the syllables before the antepenult are left toneless, the default mechanism fills in a low tone.

Initial Association (24), Prefix Tone Shift (27), Final High Tone Shift (31), Spreading (30), and the default mechanism form the core of the Zulu tone rules.[22] These rules, however, interact with another process, which Laughren (1980, 247–48) describes as follows: "In Nguni languages the main stress falls generally on the penultimate syllable. Prepausally this stress is accompanied by a very noticeable lengthening of the stressed syllable which we will refer to as the Penultimate Syllable Lengthening rule." We will adopt Laughren's Lengthening rule here:

(33) Penultimate Syllable Lengthening rule (Laughren 1980, 248)

$$\begin{matrix} \$ \\ | \\ V \end{matrix} \rightarrow \begin{matrix} \$ \\ \wedge \\ V\ V \end{matrix} \quad / \ \underline{\quad} \ \$ \ / \ /$$

Rule (33) appears to operate after Initial Association (24), but before all of the other tone rules. (34)–(36) contain some relevant derivations for forms that will occur prepausally:[23]

(34)

i s i [h l a l o → i s i [h l a l o →
(24) (33)
V C V   C V C V   V C V   C V C V
H L   L   H L   L

i s i [h l a l o → i s i [h l a l o →
(27) (30)
V C V   C V V C V   V C V   C V   V C V
H   L   L   H L   L

i s i [h l a l o → i s i [h l a l o
Default
V C V   C V V C V   V C V   C V   V C V
H L L   L   H L   L

= ìsíhlààlò

(35)

a b a [f o + a n a → a b a [f a n a →
Vowel (24)
V C V   C V   Deletion   V C V   C V C V
H L   H L   H L   H L

a b a [f a n a → a b a [f a n a →
(33) (30)
V C V   C V C V   V C V   CV   V C V
H L   H L   H L   H   L

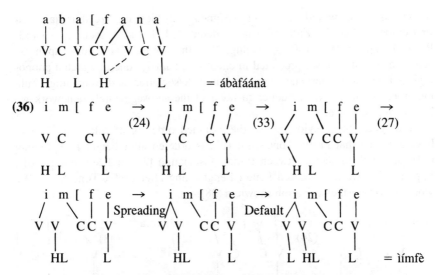

In (34) the first vowel of the stem is lengthened, and after the Prefix Tone Shift rule (27) has operated, Spreading (30) links the final L tone to the final stem vowel and the vowel created by (33).

Now the careful reader will have noticed that I have assumed all along that the tone rules of Zulu are ordered, although I have offered no justification as yet for that ordering. The derivation in (35) provides our first argument for ordering, specifically, for ordering Initial Association (24) before Penult Lengthening (33), and Penult Lengthening before Spreading (30). As we see there, each vowel of the prefix and stem is already associated with a tone when (33) operates. Following the lengthening of the penultimate vowel, Spreading links the second H to the lengthened vowel, giving the correct result **ábàfáánà**. Suppose, however, we had ordered Penult Lengthening before Initial Association. We would then have the derivation in (37):[24]

(37)

```
      a  b  a  [  f  a  n  a   →     a  b  a  [  f  a  n  a   →
                              (33)                            (24)
      V  C  V    C  V  C  V          V  C  V    C  V  V  C  V

      HL         HL                  H  L       H  L
```

```
      a  b  a  [  f  a  n  a   →     a  b  a  [  f  a  n  a
      │  │  │   ╱╱   ╲  ╲   (30)     │  │  │   ╱  ╱╲╲╲
      V  C  VC  V    V  C  V         V  C  V  C  V    V  C  V
      │  │  │  │                     ╱  ╱      │   ╱⸰⸰
      H  L  H  L                     H  L      H  L          = * ábàfáánà
```

In other words, if Penult Lengthening had preceded Initial Association, the Penultimate syllable of **abafaana** would wrongly be given a HL tone sequence. And if Penult Lengthening had followed Spreading, the lengthened vowel would still have ended up with a L tone rather than its correct H tone, since the newly created vowel would have been assigned L by default. We thus have our first evidence that the Zulu rules are ordered: (24) Initial Association → (33) Penult Lengthening → (30) Spreading. Note that we have now come upon exactly the sort of case we predicted in chapter 1, namely, one in which a phonological rule must intervene between Initial Association and Spreading. Zulu therefore provides clear evidence in favor of the autosegmental framework we have developed here.

(36) gives more evidence for the assumed ordering of rules. In (36) we have assumed that Prefix Tone Shift (27) is ordered after Penult Lengthening (33) (and both of them between Initial Association [24] and Spreading [30]). Suppose that we had ordered Penult Lengthening after Prefix Tone Shift. We would then have the derivation shown in (38):

As (38) shows, Prefix Tone Shift fails to apply because its structural description is not met. Penult Lengthening applies to the initial vowel here, and Spreading then links the initial H tone to the lengthened vowel. The result is the incorrect *íímfè. If Prefix Tone Shift (27) follows Penult Lengthening (33), however, and if Spreading (30) follows that, we obtain the correct output. We thus have another rule which must intervene between Initial Association and Spreading.

So far, the only rule for which I have not been able to find a crucial ordering is (31), Final High Tone Shift. Here I will place it after (27), but nothing hinges on this choice. Given this one arbitrary decision, then, Zulu tone rules, including those developed in section 4.1.2 for depressor consonants, will be ordered as follows:

(39) Initial Association   (24)
    Penult Lengthening   (33)
    Prefix Tone Shift   (27)
    Final High Tone Shift   (31)
    High Tone Deflection   (19b)
    Spreading   (30)
    Default
    Spillover

The low-level phonetic rule Spillover is, of course, the last process to affect Zulu tonal melodies.

(40) illustrates the complete derivations of some of the forms with depressor consonants that we encountered in section 4.1.2. Recall (see note 3) that we assumed there Laughren's rule simplifying V X V contours to V X V:

$$
\begin{array}{ccc}
 & \diagup\!\!\!\diagdown & \\
\text{H} & \text{L} &
\end{array}
\qquad
\begin{array}{ccc}
| & & | \\
\text{H} & & \text{L}
\end{array}
$$

(40) a.

```
i  z  i  [ f  u  n  d  o    →        i  z  i  [ f  u  n  d  o    →
   L              L          (24)    | L |    | | | | L |        (33)
V  C  V  C  V  C  C  V                V  C  V  C  V  C  C  V

H     L     H     L                  H     L     H     L
```

```
i  z  i  [ f  u  n  d  o    →        i  z  i  [ f  u  n  d  o    →
| L |    / /   \ L \         (30)    | L |   / /\  \ L \         (19e)
V  C  V  C  V  V  C  C  V             V  C  V  C  V  V  C  C  V
|     |     |      /                  /     /     V      /
H     L     H     L                  H     L     H     L
```

```
i  z  i  [ f  u  n  d  o
| L |   //\  \ L \
V  C  V  C V  V  C  C  V
|     |     V       |
H     L     H       L
```

b.

```
z  a  z  e  l  a    →        z  a  z  e  l  a    →        z  a  z  e  l  a
L        L          (24)     L  | L |  | | /    (33)      L  | L |  /  \  \
C  V  C  V  C  V             C  V  C  V  C  V             C  V  C  V V  C  V

H     L                      H     L                      H     L
```

```
      →        z  a  z  e  l  a       →        z  a  z  e  l  a²⁵
      (30)     L  | L |\  \ \         (19e)     L  | L |\  \ \
               C  V  C  V V  C  V                C  V  C  V V  C  V
               |         V---                    |         V
               H     L                           H     L
```

(40) c.

```
i  z  i  [ h  l  a  l  o    →        i  z  i  [ h  l  a  l  o    →
   L               |        (24)     | L |        |             (27)

H     L      L                       H     L      L
```

```
i  z  i  [ h  l  a  l  o    →        i  z  i  [ h  l  a  l  o    →
   L  |        |            (19b)        L  |        /\          Contour Tone
                                                    /  \        Simplification
   H  L        L                         H  L L
```

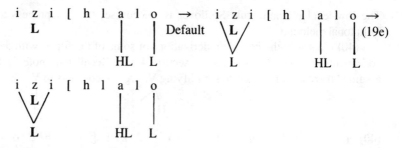

Laughren, in her (1980) analysis of Zulu, also covers a number of dialect rules[26] that I will simply adopt here. These are given in (41):

(41) Laughren (1980, 258–59)

   a. Left Branch Deletion Rule

   b. Right Branch Deletion Rule

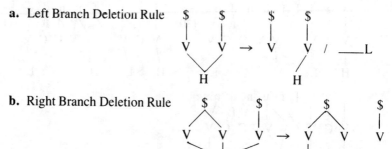

Although Laughren employs a slightly different formalism than the one used here, it can readily be seen that both Left Branch and Right Branch Deletion are Delinking rules. Within the present analysis, these rules will apply after the main tone rules—(24), (33), (27), (31) and (30)—and before the Default convention and Spillover Rule apply. Two derivations involving these rules are given in (42):[27]

(42) a.

```
a m a [ k h o s i   →   a m a [ k h o s i   →
              (24)                        (41a)
HL           H L       H    L       H L
```

```
a m a [ k h o s i   →   a m a [ k h o s i
                Default
H    L          HL      H    L        L  HL
```

b.

```
o o [ m p a n d e   →   o o [ m p a n d e   →
              L   (24)                   L    (33)
V V   C C V C C V       V V   C C V C C V
H L       H   L         H L       H    L
```

```
o o [ m p a n d e    →      o o [ m p a n d e    →
| |     | | | \ L \  (30)   | |    / / / \ | L |   (41b)
V V   C C VV C C V          V V  C C V V C C V
| \         L___/           | |          \_/
H L      H    L             H L      H    L
```

```
o o [ m p a n d e    →      o o [ m p a n d e    →
/ /  / / / \ | L |  Default | |   / / / \ \ L \    (19b)
V V  C C V V C C V          V V  C C V V C C V
| \     /                   | |        |   \_/
H L   H     L               H L      H   L L
```

```
o o [ m p a n d e
/ /  / / / \ | L |
V V  C C V V C C V
| |       \    \_/
H L      H   L
```

The form in (42b) is the one with a depressor consonant that we looked at in section 4.1.2. (42b) shows how the tone contour is assembled start to finish.

This discussion completes my analysis of the Zulu tonal system. It remains only to show that this analysis of Zulu offers substantial improvements over Laughren's analysis. We have already seen that the analysis of depressor consonants within the present framework is both simpler and more explanatory than the tone insertion analysis proposed by Laughren. But I have also implied in the course of this section that my framework allows simplifications over Laughren's with respect to nondepressor-related rules as well. These simplifications occur in two areas of the analysis.

The first, as mentioned above, has to do with the behavior of tone melodies in prefixes. We saw that when a prefix with the underlying melody HL is concatenated with a stem whose tone melody begins with L, the prefix appears to surface with a LH melody. Laughren chose to express this apparent flip-flop in tones directly with a rule of Tone Metathesis:

(**43**) Tone Metathesis rule (Laughren 1980)

    HL → LH / ____ L

       prefix

Now it has generally been assumed in phonological theory that rules of metathesis are powerful rules and that they should not be used unless absolutely necessary. Moreover, to my knowledge, there are almost no tone systems other than that of Zulu that appear to make use of this sort of rule (but see Pulleyblank [1983] for a possible example in Bamileke Dschang and Clark [in preparation] for a reanalysis of this data). And finally, we will see immediately below when we come to the topic of association that the Tone Metathesis analysis of prefixes actually leads to a further complication in Laughren's analysis, one more reason to suspect that it is not the correct rule for Zulu. But we have seen in this section that an autosegmental framework which incorporates a default mechanism has no need for a Tone Metathesis rule. Our analysis shifts the HL melody of the prefix to the second prefix vowel (tone shift rules appear to be needed in any case within tonal systems), and the initial L appears by default. The rule is not particularly powerful, and it causes no complications elsewhere in the grammar.

The other area in which the present analysis leads to simplifications is the area of association rules. Recall that our analysis contained only a single rule of Initial Association (24) and a single rule of Spreading (30). In addition, we assumed at the outset that Zulu stems fell into four classes which were distinguished from one another not only by their tone melodies, but also, in one case, by the way that the melody was lexically linked to the stem. Within this analysis, nothing more needs to be said about association and spreading. The actual rules conform to the schema proposed in chapter 1, and the lexical linking encodes everything that is idiosyncratic about Zulu stems.

Laughren, in contrast, needs a more complex system of association. Working within a framework that allows neither default tones nor lexical linking, a framework whose assumptions about association and spreading are quite different from ours, her analysis requires a number of epicycles that the present analysis does not need.

First, because she does not have the device of lexical linking at her disposal, her analysis requires three different Initial Tone Association rules (ITARs):

(44) Laughren (1980, 296) ITAR-1

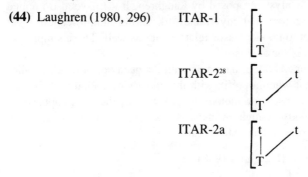

ITAR-2[28]

ITAR-2a

Individual lexical items must be marked for the particular ITAR that applies to them. The stem **kole** is distinguished from the stem **bophe** not in its tone melody (they are both HL stems), but in the initial association rule each is marked for; the former takes ITAR-1, the latter ITAR-2a. In other words, in the present analysis idiosyncrasy is marked directly on lexical entries, whereas in Laughren's analysis it is marked indirectly with stem class diacritics that trigger separate ITARs.

Once these initial linkings are set, a well-formedness condition (WFC) immediately connects succeeding tones, one to one, left to right, and spreads the last tone of the tonal melody to any leftover untoned syllables. Given the way that association and spreading operate in Laughren's framework, we would expect that no rules could apply between ITARs and the operation of the WFC; the latter is simply the automatic concomitant of the former. But it turns out that the ITARs cannot always be allowed to operate blindly, if this is true. Specifically, when prefixes and/or suffixes of certain sorts are concatenated with stems, the lexically marked ITARs must be blocked from applying before they and the WFC produce fully linked forms. In order to do this, Laughren must add two things to her analysis—first, a set of conditions on the operation of the ITARs, and second, a set of rules called "Designated Tone Association rules," which give special instructions for attaching tone melodies to the segmental tier after ITARs have been blocked from operating.

The first condition under which an ITAR must be prevented from operating is when a number of toneless suffixes have been concatenated with a stem, resulting in a derived stem which is quadrisyllabic or longer (for example, [ntu + any + any + ana → [ntwanyanyana). If such a polysyllabic stem is created, Laughren's Constraint 1 (1980, 241) is applicable, and instead of ITAR-1, the special rule in (45b) creates initial linkings:

(45) a. Constraint 1   ITARs cannot apply within a domain where the number of $T = n$ and the number of $t = m$, where $m > n + 1$.

  b. Final High Tone   t   t   t → t   t   t
      Association Rule | / ___#
                  H   L   H   L

Now, Laughren's Final High Tone Association rule (45b) has approximately the same effect as our rule (31), Final High Tone Shift. But because of the assumptions about association and spreading made within her framework, an extra epicycle, the condition in (45a), is needed as well. Because Initial Association and Spreading are rules, however, and because other tone rules can intervene between them in our framework, no such condition is needed here.

A second case in which a special condition on the application of ITARs is needed within Laughren's analysis arises in the derivation of a number of forms with prefixes. Consider, for example, the partial derivation below:

(46) i   m   [f   e

  HL   L

  ⇓   Tone Metathesis

  i   m   [f   e

  LH   L

  ⇓   ITAR-1

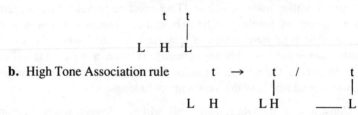

In Laughren's analysis, Tone Metathesis applies in HL prefixes followed by L, regardless of the segmental character of the prefix. If, after Tone Metathesis applies, the usual ITAR for prefixes, ITAR-1, applies, the result is *ìmfè, instead of the correct ímfè. To avoid this incorrect output, Laughren adds to her grammar a second condition, repeated below in (47a), and a second Designated Tone Association rule, repeated as (47b):

(47) a. Constraint 2: ITARs fail to apply in the configuration

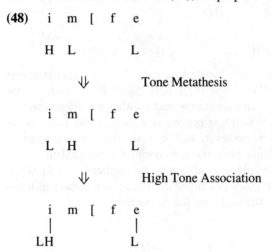

Given the condition and rule in (47), the proper form ímfè can be derived:

(48)   i   m   [f   e

     H   L   L

       ⇓   Tone Metathesis

     i   m   [f   e

     L   H   L

       ⇓   High Tone Association

     i   m   [f   e
     | |
    LH   L

But adding the epicycles in (47) to her analysis in turn requires the addition of further epicycles for Laughren. If Penultimate Syllable Lengthening is applied to the output in (48), an incorrect form is once again generated:

(49)   i   m   [f   e
     | |
    LH   L

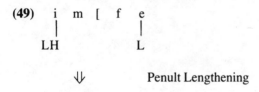

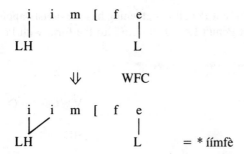

In (49) we can see that the form *íímfè results, rather than the correct ìímfè. Laughren is forced to add another rule to her analysis to block this incorrect result:

(50) Unassociated Tone Docking rule

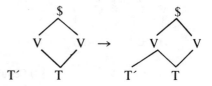

(50) applies to the last representation in (49), and then the initial contour is simplified, as shown in (51):

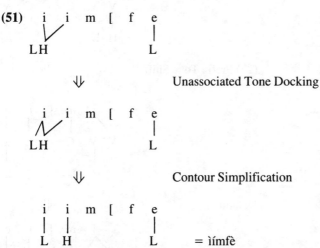

In other words, in the presence of particular prefixes, a condition on the operation of the ITARs and two rules are needed to obtain correct outputs in Laughren's analysis.

In the present analysis, however, none of these epicycles is needed. Prefix Tone Shift, as we saw, applied after our Initial Association and before Spreading to relocate the tone melody of the prefix. But because of the way it is stated, it will only apply in the form **imfe** if Penult Lengthening has previously applied. (52a) derives the form without Penult Lengthening, (52b) the form with Penult Lengthening:

(52) a.

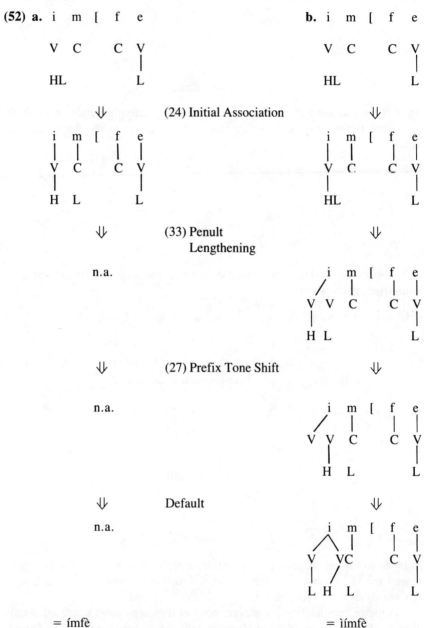

= ímfè   = ìímfè

Since Penult Lengthening does not apply in (52a), Prefix Tone Shift is inapplicable, and no other rules apply. In (52b), Penult Lengthening feeds Prefix

Tone Shift, which in turn creates an untoned vowel that eventually receives L by default. In both cases, to derive these forms we need no more than the rules independently needed for other forms.

If we compare the two analyses as a whole, then, the present one appears to be substantially simpler. In place of the four rules for depressor consonants in Laughren's analysis, we have the single rule of High Tone Deflection (19b), plus a phonetic Spillover rule. In place of a powerful rule of Tone Metathesis, we have a rule of Prefix Tone Shift that appears to give correct results in cases where prefixes contain a single short vowel (that is, cases like [52a]). We have no ITARs, no conditions on ITARs, and only one rule (Final High Tone Shift) relocating tone melodies, in contrast to Laughren's three rules (Final High Tone Association, High Tone Association, and Unassociated Tone Docking). If simplicity is any reason for preferring one autosegmental analysis to another, then the present analysis is obviously to be preferred.

NOTES: CHAPTER 4

1. Here and in what follows I will be referring to Laughren's (1980) analysis of Zulu. In a more recent treatment of the same material, Laughren (1984) presents an analysis which is identical to the (1980) one in most essential ways.

2. See also articles by Hombert (1978), Schuh (1978), Paradis (1984), and Kisseberth (1984) on the relationship between consonant type and tone melody.

3. I will base my argument on the facts of Zulu. From Welmers's (1973) brief anecdote about Shona it is clear that something similar is going on there, but he does not give enough information to tell what class of consonants acts as depressors.

4. Note that in many, perhaps most, languages consonants have no effect at all on the spread of tone.

5. Laughren (1984) no longer lists this Insertion as a separate rule, but it seems clear from derivations (for example, p. 159) that such an insertion is implied by the analysis.

6. A later rule of Contour Simplification eliminates the contour on the penultimate vowel, resulting in the final form:

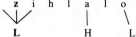

7. In one dialect of Zulu, according to Laughren (1980, 279) a depressor consonant between two H vowels has an effect. First an independently needed rule of Left Branch Deletion delinks the association between the H and the vowel immediately preceding the depressor consonant. This vowel then becomes low, and the L tone spreads onto the following vowel as well. At this point, the depressor consonant lowers the L to extra low.

8. Tones would of course still spread across sonorants.

9. It should be pointed out that this is not at all an unusual assumption. For example, we would have to say the same thing for a language with [back] harmony that affects only vowels. Assuming that such a language also has consonants like [k], [q], [x], [ɣ], [h], [ʔ], etc., that is, consonants for which the feature [back] is also used, a similar story would be necessary. The relevant consonants would be prespecified for the feature [back] and would, of course, be entirely neutral with respect to the harmony process.

10. I am assuming, of course, that Spillover applies automatically and blindly, and that, unlike the association rules, it does not "see" prior specifications of tone features on the vowel, and supplies an extra set of specifications at the beginning.

11. As mentioned before, this is probably not a rule specific to Zulu. L seems to be the default tone in many languages (Japanese, Kalenjin, etc.) and is perhaps the universal default tone. See Pulleyblank (1983) for a discussion.

12. Laughren, quoting Doke (1926), attributes to this form the following melody, where 9 is the lowest pitch and 1 the highest:

8-3 8-9 9

z a z ee l a

In other words, in this form the initial depressor consonant seems to spill over onto a high tone. It is thus possible that Zulu Spillover should be stated to apply to all following tones, but the crucial evidence for this is absent. If, for example, the H tone in a form like (i) were a bit lower than the one in (ii), we could generalize Spillover to apply onto all following tones:

(i) C V C V C   (ii) C V C V C

H   H

Unfortunately, Laughren's article does not give Doke's sort of fine-tuned pitch markings for all forms, so the issue must remain unresolved for the present time.

13. I am starting here from an intermediate representation in Laughren's analysis. In (40c) we will give the full derivation of this form within the present framework, and the representation to which High Tone Deflection applies will be slightly different.

14. We assume a Contour Simplification Rule like Laughren's. See note 3.

15. We must assume that in a case like (20c), Spillover affects not only the tone of the following vowel, but everything linked to that tone as well, even the preceding vowels.

16. We will see below that Spreading and insertion of the Default tone are independently needed for Zulu.

17. This, of course, leads to a further question: if tone features can be projected in the core for consonants, can this ever be the case for vowels? I know of no data which would bear on this issue, and thus must leave this question for future research.

18. In some Zulu dialects, forms like these may undergo a late, optional rule which spreads the initial H tone to the right.

19. Laughren (1984) cites some work by Khumalo (1981) in which a tone shift rule is used instead of Tonal Metathesis. This latter work was not available to me, so I cannot give a comparison with the Prefix Tone Shift rule proposed here.

20. The floating L is not realized phonetically. In Zulu, as in other African languages, a floating L tone between H tones causes the second H to be downstepped, or realized at a pitch slightly lower than the preceding H. The L tone that triggers the downstep is not itself pronounced. When a floating L is followed by a L tone, however, it has no effect at all.

21. The rule is in fact very similar to Laughren's rule of Final High Tone Association, but see below for a comparison.

22. Laughren (1980) also discusses a number of other processes that apply in Zulu, for which we would need to add further rules. Some of these processes appear to vary according to dialect. Of these, we adopt Laughren's statements of Left Branch Deletion and Right Branch Deletion below. Another of these processes, what Laughren calls "High Tone Spreading," appears to be a fast speech rule that also varies from dialect to dialect. I will not attempt to account for it in my analysis, but refer the reader instead to Laughren's thorough discussion of the process.

23. Up to this point I have left the skeleton tier out of representations because it has not been of any consequence in the discussion of tonal processes. Here, however, I will assume that (33) adds a V to the skeleton tier. I will assume, as well, that melody and skeleton are linked by Melody-Skeleton Association (chapter 1–57), and that this linking takes place at the same time that Initial Association (24) applies. I will also assume that there is spreading of associations between the melody and skeleton tiers, and that this spreading occurs at the same time that Tone Spreading does.

24. I will assume that the vowel deletion rule ([fo + ana → [fana) has already applied.

25. See note 7.

26. In other Zulu dialects, Left Branch Deletion occurs only when there is a following syllable. Laughren (1980, 258) states this version as follows:

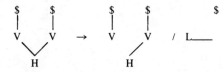

27. In (42a) the Left Branch Deletion rule could actually apply before Spreading, giving the following derivation:

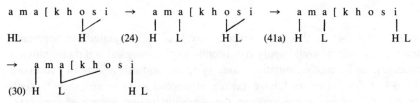

As far as I can tell, there is no way of deciding between the two orderings.

28. This rule is needed only in some Zulu dialects. For the most part, Zulu HL stems choose either ITAR-2 or ITAR-2a. ITAR-2 is, however, the rule which Clements and Ford (1979) argue is needed for Kikuyu.

CONCLUSION
AND
SPECULATION

At the outset of this work I set as my goal an integrated autosegmental theory—one which would apply consistently to phonological and morphological processes, to harmony, mutation, tone systems, and other sorts of processes. In the last four chapters I have mainly attempted to raise and then to settle one major issue of integration: can the same distinctive feature be duplicated on more than one tier, and if a particular feature is allowed to appear on several tiers, how is the precedence of one of these duplicated features to be established? This issue lies at the very heart of autosegmental theory, since it concerns the distribution of distinctive features on autosegmental tiers.

In chapter 1, I proposed that we do allow particular features to be duplicated on more than one tier, but that a filter, the Duplicate Features Filter, should rule out all cases in which a single segment receives two or more simultaneous values for a single feature. In the course of resolving the central issue of chapter 1, we were also led to revise the association rules of autosegmental theory and to state explicitly how they are to operate. This in turn led to a revision of the treatment of so-called preattachment or prespecification. Much of chapters 2 through 4 were then intended to show that the integrative revisions suggested in chapter 1 could have wide ramifications, both empirical and theoretical.

Among the empirical ramifications of this revised autosegmental theory were the following. In chapter 2 we saw that this framework not only provided simple and consistent analyses for central cases of mutation like those found in Fula,

Nuer, and Chemehuevi, but also allowed reasonably simple analyses of the pho-netically bizarre mutations found in Mende and Welsh, and even made correct predictions about the sorts of phonetically bizarre mutations we might expect to find in other languages. We saw that no such predictions were available with a segmental treatment of mutation. Chapter 3 made virtually the same argument with respect to harmony systems: the present autosegmental framework, with the revisions proposed in chapter 1, not only provided simple and consistent analyses of harmonies in Classical and Khalka Mongolian, Kalenjin, Chumash, and Andalusian Spanish, but also obviated the need for metrical treatment of harmony in these and other harmony systems. And this in turn allowed for an explanation of the rarity of certain sorts of harmonies. If all harmonies are treated autosegmentally, it appears that the rarest sort of harmony, feature-changing harmony, requires the most marked sorts of language-particular rules. Again, no similar explanation was available if both autosegmental and metrical analy-ses of harmony were possible. Finally, chapter 4 argued that the revised auto-segmental framework developed in chapter 1 allowed both a cogent explanation for the interference of consonants of various types in tone systems and an analy-sis of the complex tonal system of Zulu that was substantially simpler than one formulated within a different autosegmental framework.

There are also two theoretical points worth noting here that emerge from this integrated framework. The first is that such seemingly disparate phenomena as invariant paradigms in mutation systems, neutral segments in harmony sys-tems, depressor consonants in tone systems, and infixes can turn out to be the same phenomenon when viewed at a higher level of abstraction; we have seen in the preceding chapters that all are cases in which distinctive features that normally are projected on one autosegmental tier in a particular language are prespecified for a particular segment or segments on another tier in that lan-guage. All four of these cases, in other words, involve a similar configuration of features; the actual features in each case might be different, but the overall shape of the representations is the same. And all behave in a similar way; pre-specified features always take precedence over the feature or features provided by the normal autosegmental tier. Thus, one reason for working towards an integrated autosegmental theory is that a truly integrated theory ought to reveal other deep similarities of this sort.

The second theoretical point that we might mention here has to do with the relationship between phonology and morphology. We have seen that a particular tier or n-tuple of tiers in a particular language might be a morpheme. But we have not encountered anywhere in our exploration of mutation, harmony, or tone an autosegmental **rule** or **principle** which is purely morphological. There are mutations and harmonies that are morphological and others that are phono-logical, but the sorts of rules and principles that apply—Association, Spreading, Delinking, the DFF—are the same in either case. To answer a question I raised in the introduction, there indeed appears to be no evidence, at least based on the sort of data we have looked at here, for an autonomous morphological component, where by an "autonomous morphological component," I mean a component of the grammar containing purely morphological rules and principles.

Of course, although we have achieved a somewhat more internally consistent autosegmental theory by resolving the issue of duplicated features, we certainly do not yet have a completely integrated theory. There are still a number of areas where discrepancies or conflicting assumptions have crept into different versions of autosegmental theory. To name just one, there is the problem of what happens to segments that have been left incomplete or underspecified at the end of the derivation. Current theory has at least two different ways of dealing with these segments, and I have in fact used both of them here. Recall that in certain cases incomplete segments fail to receive any phonetic interpretation at all. For example, tone features that are not associated with tone-bearing units at the end of a derivation are not pronounced. Skeleton slots that remain unassociated after a reduplication process has applied also are not pronounced, as the Dakota example in chapter 1 (58) indicated. In other cases, however, incomplete segments receive default values for features missing at the end of the derivation, and in the end they come to be pronounced. As I have mentioned before, it has been argued (Pulleyblank 1983, Clark forthcoming) that tone-bearing units surface with low tone if they are still underspecified at the end of the derivation. Segments in Kalenjin which do not receive [+ ATR] by spreading of the dominant harmony feature surface with the default [− ATR]. And initial segments in Chemehuevi that have failed to receive the features [voice], [continuant], and [nasal] by virtue of association with a prefix bearing floating autosegments surface with the default features [− voice, − cont, − nasal].

Both options appear to be necessary in current autosegmental theory, but present autosegmental frameworks do not offer any way of deciding which option should be used in any given case. Indeed, in present versions of autosegmental theory they are two independent, unconnected options. We do not know if the choice between them is a language-particular matter, nor do we know whether the choice of particular default features is made on a language-particular basis (we would suspect not in the latter case, since the default features we have seen above tended to be the same from language to language) (see Archangeli 1984 on this point). Ideally, in an integrated autosegmental framework we would not treat these two options as independent possibilities, but instead would try to draw them together into a single (sub)theory of underspecified segments. The advantage of integrating different ways of treating underspecified segments in a single internally consistent subtheory is obvious: we would have a much more restrictive theory if we could predict when underspecified segments receive default features and when they fail to get pronounced.

This and other such issues would have to be resolved before we could claim to have a truly integrated theory of autosegmental processes. Still, we have made some progress towards this goal here, and it is relatively clear how we would go about making further progress. It will only be by taking a broad view of phonological and morphological processes, by comparing analyses of tone, harmony, mutation, gemination, reduplication—in short, all sorts of disparate autosegmental processes—that we will succeed in building an internally consistent and truly explanatory theory.

REFERENCES

Abraham, R.C. 1959. *The Language of the Hausa People*, London, University of London Press.

Allen, M. 1978. *Morphological Investigations*, Ph.D. dissertation, University of Connecticut, Storrs.

Anderson, S. 1976. On the Description of Consonant Gradation in Fula, *Studies in African Linguistics*, 7; 93–136.

_____. 1982. Where's Morphology? *Linguistic Inquiry*, 13; 571–612.

_____. 1984. On Representations in Morphology: Case, Agreement and Inversion in Georgian, *Natural Language and Linguistic Theory*, 2; 157–218.

Archangeli, D. 1984. *Underspecification in Yawelmani Phonology and Morphology*, Ph.D. dissertation, MIT, Cambridge, MA.

Arnott, D.W. 1964. Downstep in the Tiv Verbal System, *African Language Studies*, 5; 34–51.

_____. 1970. *The Nominal and Verbal Systems of Fula*, Oxford, Oxford University Press.

Aronoff, M. 1976. *Word Formation in Generative Grammar*, Cambridge, MA, MIT Press.

Awbery, G. 1976. *The Syntax of Welsh*, Cambridge, England, Cambridge University Press.

Beeler, M. 1970. Sibilant Harmony in Chumash, *International Journal of American Linguistics*, 36; 14–17.

Broselow, E. 1983. Salish Double Reduplications: Subjacency in Morphology, *Natural Language and Linguistic Theory*, 1; 317–346.

_____. 1984-ms. Default Consonants in Amharic Morphology, to appear in *MIT Working Papers in Linguistics.*

Chomsky, N. 1970. Remarks on Nominalizations, in N. Chomsky (1972), *Studies on Semantics in Generative Grammar*, The Hague, Mouton.

_____. 1981. *Lectures on Government and Binding*, Dordrecht, Foris Publications.

Chomsky, N., and M. Halle. 1968. *The Sound Pattern of English*, New York, Harper and Row.

Clark, M. 1982-ms. An Accentual Analysis of the Igbo Verb, unpublished ms, University of New Hampshire.

_____. 1983. On the Distribution of Contour Tones, in M. Barlow, D. Flickinger and M. Wescoat, eds., *Proceedings of the West Coast Conference on Formal Linguistics*, Vol. 2, Stanford, Stanford University Linguistics Association.

_____.Forthcoming. Japanese as a Tone Language, to appear in T. Imai and M. Saito, eds., *Issues in Japanese Linguistics*, Dordrecht, Foris Publications.

_____. In preparation. *The Tonal System of Igbo*, Dordrecht, Foris Publications.

Clements, G.N. 1980a. Vowel Harmony in a Nonlinear Generative Phonology: An Autosegmental Model, distributed by the Indiana University Linguistics Club.

_____. 1980b. The Hierarchical Representation of Tone Features, in *Harvard Studies in Phonology*, Vol. 2., distributed by the Indiana University Linguistics Club; 50–107.

_____. 1982. Compensatory Lengthening: An independent mechanism of phonological change, distributed by the Indiana University Linguistics Club.

_____. 1984. Principles of Tone Assignment in Kikuyu, in G.N. Clements and J. Goldsmith, eds., *Autosegmental Studies in Bantu Tone*, Dordrecht, Foris Publications.

_____. 1985. The Geometry of Phonological Features, in C. Ewen and J. Anderson, eds., *Phonology Yearbook*, vol. 2, Cambridge, England, Cambridge University Press.

_____. In press. Compensatory Lengthening and Consonant Gemination in LuGanda, in E. Sezer and L. Wetzels, eds., *Studies in Compensatory Lengthening*, Dordrecht, Foris Publications.

Clements, G. N., and K. Ford. 1979. Kikuyu Tone Shift and Its Synchronic Consequences, *Linguistic Inquiry*, 10: 179–210.

Clements, G.N., and S.J. Keyser. 1983. *C V Phonology: A Generative Theory of the Syllable*, Cambridge, MA, MIT Press.

Clements, G.N., and E. Sezer. 1982. Vowel and Consonant Disharmony in Turkish, in H. van der Hulst and N. Smith, eds., *The Structure of Phonological Representation*, Part II, Dordrecht, Foris Publications.

Cope, A.T. 1970. Zulu Tonal Morphology, *Journal of African Linguistics*, 9; 111–152.

Cowper, E., and K. Rice. 1986. The Phonological Nature of Mende Consonant Mutation, paper delivered at the 17th annual African Linguistics Conference.

Crazzolara, J. 1933. *Outline of a Nuer Grammar*, Vienna, Verlag der Internationalen Zeitschrift 'Anthropos.'

deBoor, H., et al. 1969. *Siebs Deutsche Aussprache*, Berlin, Walter de Gruyter & Co.

DeChene, B., and S. Anderson. 1979. Compensatory Lengthening, *Language*, 55;3; 505–35.

Doke, C.M. 1926. *The Phonetics of the Zulu Language*, Johannesburg, Witwatersrand University Press.

Edmondson, T., and J.T. Bendor-Samuel. 1966. Tone Patterns of Etung, *Journal of African Languages*, 5; 1–6.

Elimelech, B. 1976. A Tonal Grammar of Etsako, *UCLA Working Papers in Phonetics*, 35.

Firth, J.R. 1957. Sounds and Prosodies, in *Papers in Linguistics 1934–1951*, London, Oxford University Press.

Goldsmith, J. 1976. *Autosegmental Phonology*, Ph.D. dissertation, MIT, Cambridge, MA.

———. 1981. Accent in Tonga: An Autosegmental Account, in G.N. Clements, ed., *Harvard Studies in Phonology*, Vol. II., distributed by the Indiana University Linguistics Club; 178–187.

———. 1982. Accent Systems, in H. van der Hulst and N. Smith, eds., *The Structure of Phonological Representations*, Part 1, Dordrecht, Foris Publications.

Gonzalez, J. 1982. The Role of Phonology in Class Distinction in Venezuelan Spanish, unpublished master's paper, University of New Hampshire.

Green, M.M., and G.E. Igwe. 1963. *A Descriptive Grammar of Igbo*, Oxford, Oxford University Press.

Halle, M. 1973. Prolegomena to a Theory of Word Formation, *Linguistic Inquiry*, 4; 3–16.

———. 1986. On Speech Sounds and Their Immanent Structure, unpublished ms, MIT, Cambridge, MA.

Halle, M., and K. Stevens. 1971. A Note on Laryngeal Features, MIT Research Laboratory of Electronics Quarterly Progress Report # 101; 198–213.

Halle, M., and J.-R. Vergnaud. Mss. Three Dimensional Phonology, unpublished manuscripts, MIT, Cambridge, MA.

———. 1981. Harmony Processes, in W. Klein and W. Levelt, eds., *Crossing the Boundaries in Linguistics*, Dordrecht, Reidel, 1–22.

———. 1982. On the Framework of Autosegmental Phonology, in H. van der Hulst and N. Smith, eds., *The Structure of Phonological Representations*, Part 1, Dordrecht, Foris Publications.

Haraguchi, S. 1977. *The Tone Pattern of Japanese*, Tokyo, Kaitakusha.

Harrington, J.P. 1974. Sibilants in Ventureno, *International Journal of American Linguistics*, 40; 1–9.

Harris, J.W. 1983. *Syllable Structure and Stress in Spanish*, Cambridge, MA, MIT Press.

Hart, G. 1981. Nasality and the Organization of Autosegmental Phonology, distributed by the Indiana University Linguistics Club.

Hayes, B. 1980. *A Metrical Theory of Stress Rules*, Ph.D. dissertation, MIT, Cambridge, MA.

Hoenigswald, H.M. 1948. Declension and Nasalization in Hindustani, *Journal of the American Oriental Society*, 68; 139–144.

Hombert, J.-M. 1978. Consonant Types, Vowel Quality and Tone, in V. Fromkin, ed., *Tone: A Linguistic Survey*, New York, Academic Press.

Hulst, H. van der, and N. Smith. 1984. The Framework of Nonlinear Generative Phonology, in H. van der Hulst and N. Smith, eds., *Advances in Nonlinear Phonology*, Dordrecht, Foris Publications.

———. 1985. Vowel Features and Umlaut in Djingili, Nyangumarda and Warlpiri, *Phonology Yearbook*, 2; 277–303.

Hyman, L. 1985. *A Theory of Phonological Weight*, Dordrecht, Foris Publications.

Hyman, L., and R. Schuh. 1974. Universals of Tone Rules: Evidence from West Africa, *Linguistic Inquiry*, 5; 81–115.

Johnson, C.D. 1980. Regular Disharmony in Kirghiz, in R. Vago, ed., *Issues in Vowel Harmony*, Amsterdam, John Benjamins B.V.

Jones, M., and A.R. Thomas. 1977. *The Welsh Language*, Cardiff, The University of Wales Press.

Kaye, J., and J. Lowenstamm. 1984. De la Syllabicité, in F. Dell, D. Hirst, and J.-R. Vergnaud, eds., *Forme Sonore du Langage*, Paris, Hermann.

Khumalo, J.S.M. 1981. Zulu Tonology. Unpublished Master of Arts Dissertation, University of the Witwatersrand, Johannesburg.

Kiparsky, P. 1982. From Cyclic Phonology to Lexical Phonology, in H. van der Hulst and N. Smith, eds., *The Structure of Phonological Representations*, Part 1, Dordrecht, Foris Publications.

Kisseberth, C.W. 1984. Digo Tonology, in G.N. Clements and G. Goldsmith, eds., *Autosegmental Studies in Bantu Tone*, Dordrecht, Foris Publications.

Kloeke, W.U.S. van Lessen. 1982. *Deutsche Phonologie und Morphologie: Merkmale und Markiertheit*, Tubingen, M. Niemeyer.

Ladefoged, P. 1968. *A Phonetic Study of West African Languages*, Cambridge, England, Cambridge University Press.

Laughren, M. 1980. An Autosegmental Account of Tone in Zulu, in G.N. Clements, ed., *Harvard Studies in Phonology*, Vol. 2, distributed by Indiana University Linguistics Club; 218–310.

_____. 1984. Tone in Zulu Nouns, in G.N. Clements and J. Goldsmith, eds., *Autosegmental Studies in Bantu Tone*, Dordrecht, Foris Publications.

Leben, W. 1973. *Suprasegmental Phonology*, Ph.D. dissertation, MIT, Cambridge, MA.

_____. 1978. The Representation of Tone, in V. Fromkin, ed., *Tone: A Linguistic Survey*, New York, Academic Press.

Levin, J. 1982-ms. Reduplication and Prosodic Structures, unpublished ms, MIT, Cambridge, MA.

Liberman, M., and J. Pierrehumbert. 1984. Intonational Invariance under Changes in Pitch Range and Length, in M. Aronoff and R. Oehrle, eds., *Language Sound Structure*, Cambridge, MA, MIT Press.

Liberman, M., and A. Prince. 1977. On Stress and Linguistic Rhythm, *Linguistic Inquiry*, 8; 249–336.

Lieber, R. 1980. *On the Organization of the Lexicon*, Ph.D. dissertation, MIT, Cambridge, MA.

_____. 1982. Allomorphy, *Linguistic Analysis*, 10;1.

_____. 1983a. Argument Linking and Compounds in English, *Linguistic Inquiry*, 14; 251–285.

_____. 1983b. New Developments in Autosegmental Morphology: Consonant Mutation, in M. Barlow, D. Flickinger, and M. Wescoat, eds., *Proceedings of the West Coast Conference on Formal Linguistics*, Vol. 2, Stanford, Stanford University Linguistics Association.

_____. 1984a. Consonant Gradation in Fula: An Autosegmental Approach, in M. Aronoff and R. Oehrle, eds., *Language Sound Structure*, Cambridge, MA, MIT Press.

_____. 1984b. Grammatical Rules and Sublexical Elements, in D. Testen, V. Mishra, and J. Drogo, eds., *Papers from the Parasession on Lexical Semantics*, Chicago, Chicago Linguistics Society.

_____. 1986. Configurational and Nonconfigurational Morphology, paper presented at the Conference on Modularity and Morphology, University of Utrecht.

Lightner, T. 1963. A Note on the Formulation of Phonological Rules, *Quarterly Progress Report of the Research Laboratory of Electronics*, MIT, 68; 187–189.

———. 1967. On the Description of Vowel and Consonant Harmony, *Word*, 21; 244–250.

McCarthy, J.J. 1979. *Formal Problems in Semitic Phonology and Morphology*, Ph.D. dissertation, MIT, Cambridge, MA.

———. 1981. A Prosodic Theory of Nonconcatenative Morphology, *Linguistic Inquiry*, 12; 373–418.

———. 1982. A prosodic account of Arabic broken plurals, in I. Dihoff, ed., *Current Approaches to African Linguistics*, Dordrecht, Foris Publications.

———. 1983. Consonantal Morphology in the Chaha Verb, in M. Barlow et al., eds., *Proceedings of the Second West Coast Conference on Formal Linguistics*, Stanford, Stanford Linguistics Association.

———. 1984. Prosodic Structure in Morphology, in M. Aronoff and R. Oehrle, eds., *Language Sound Structure*, Cambridge, MA, MIT Press.

———. 1986. OCP Effects: Gemination and Antigemination, *Linguistic Inquiry*, 17; 207–264.

———. Forthcoming. *Formal Morphology*, Cambridge, MA, MIT Press.

Marantz, A. 1982. Re:Reduplication, *Linguistic Inquiry*, 13; 435–482.

———. 1984. *On the Nature of Grammatical Relations*, Cambridge, MA, MIT Press.

Mascaro, J. 1984. Continuant Spreading in Basque, Catalan, and Spanish, in M. Aronoff and R. Oehrle, eds., *Language Sound Structure*, Cambridge, MA, MIT Press.

May, R. 1977. *The Grammar of Quantification*, Ph.D. dissertation, MIT, Cambridge, MA.

Paradis, C. 1984. Le Comportement Tonal des Constructions Associatives en Wobe, *Journal of African Languages and Linguistics*, 6; 147–171.

Pesetsky, D. 1985. Morphology and Logical Form, *Linguistic Inquiry*, 16; 193–246.

Poser, W. 1980a-ms. Two Cases of Morphologically Induced Nasal Harmony, unpublished ms, MIT, Cambridge, MA.

———. 1980b-ms. On the Contextual Definition of Opaque Segments, unpublished ms, MIT, Cambridge, MA.

———. 1982. Phonological Representations and Action-at-a-Distance, in H. van der Hulst and N. Smith, eds., *The Structure of Phonological Representations*, Part 2, Dordrecht, Foris Publications.

Press, M. 1979. *Chemehuevi: A Grammar and Lexicon*, University of California Publications in Linguistics, Vol. 92, Berkeley, University of California Press.

Prince, A. 1983. Relating to the Grid, *Linguistic Inquiry*, 14; 19–100.

Pulleyblank, D. 1983. *Tone in Lexical Phonology*, Ph.D. dissertation, MIT, Cambridge, MA.

Rhys-Jones, T.J. 1977. *Living Welsh*, Teach Yourself Books, New York.

Rice, K., and E. Cowper. 1984. Consonant Mutation and Autosegmental Morphology, in J. Drogo, V. Mishra, and D. Testen, eds., *Proceedings of the Chicago Linguistic Society—20*, 309–320.

Schuh, R. 1978. Tone Rules, in V. Fromkin, ed., *Tone: A Linguistic Survey*, New York, Academic Press.

Selkirk, E. 1982. *The Syntax of Words*, Cambridge, MA, MIT Press.

Skousen, R. 1972. Consonant Alternation in Fula, *Studies in African Linguistics*, 3; 77–96.

Sproat, R. 1982-ms, Redundancy Rules and Welsh Mutation, unpublished ms, MIT, Cambridge, MA.
——. 1985. *On Deriving the Lexicon*, Ph.D. dissertation, MIT, Cambridge, MA.
Stanley, R. 1967. Redundancy Rules in Phonology, *Language*, 43; 393–436.
Steriade, D. 1979. Vowel Harmony in Khalka Mongolian, *MIT Working Papers in Linguistics*, 1; 25–50.
——. 1982. *Greek Prosodies and the Nature of Syllabification*, Ph.D. dissertation, MIT, Cambridge, MA.
Stevens, K. 1968. The Quantal Nature of Speech, unpublished ms., MIT, Cambridge, MA.
Strauss, S.L. 1976. The Nature of Umlaut in Modern Standard German, *Cunyforum*, 1; 121–144.
Tadadjeu, M. 1974. Floating Tones, Shifting Rules and Downstep in Dschang-Bamileke, in W.R. Leben, ed., *Papers from the 5th Annual Conference on African Linguistics*, *Studies in African Linguistics*, Supp. 5; 283–290.
Thomas-Flinders, T. 1982. *UCLA Working Papers in Morphology: Inflection*, Linguistics Department, UCLA.
Topping, D.M. 1968. Chamorro Vowel Harmony, *Oceanic Linguistics*, 7; 67–79.
Tucker, A.N., 1964. Kalenjin phonetics, in D. Abercrombie, et al., eds., *In Honor of Daniel Jones*, London, Longmans.
Vago, R. 1980. A Critique of Suprasegmental Theories of Vowel Harmony, in R. Vago, ed., *Issues in Vowel Harmony*, Amsterdam, John Benjamins B.V.
Wängler, H-H. 1967. *Grundriss einer Phonetik des Deutschen*, N.G. Elwert Verlag, Marburg.
Welmers, W. 1973. *African Language Structures*, Berkeley, University of California Press.
Williams, E. 1976. Underlying Tone in Margi and Igbo, *Linguistic Inquiry*, 7; 463–484.
Woock, E., and M. Noonan. 1979. Vowel Harmony in Lango, *Papers from the 15th Regional Meeting of the Chicago Linguistic Society*, 20–29.
Wurzel, W. 1970. *Studien zur deutschen Lautstruktur*, Studia grammatica VIII, Berlin, Akademie-Verlag.
Yip, M. 1980. *The Tonal Phonology of Chinese*, Ph.D. dissertation, MIT, Cambridge, MA.
——. 1982. Against a Segmental Analysis of Zahao and Thai: A Laryngeal Tier Proposal, *Linguistic Analysis*, 9; 79–94.
——. 1983-ms. Redundancy and the C-V Skeleton, unpublished ms, Brandeis University, Waltham, MA.
Zubizarreta, M.-L. 1979. Vowel Harmony in Andalusian Spanish, *MIT Working Papers in Linguistics*, 1; 1–11.

INDEX